The Fame Game

The Fame Game

A Superstar's Guide to
Getting Rich and Famous

SERGEY KNAZEV

SelectBooks, Inc.
New York

This edition published by SelectBooks, Inc.

For information address SelectBooks, Inc., New York, New York.

First Edition

ISBN 978-1-59079-125-7

Library of Congress Cataloging-in-Publication Data

Knazev, Sergey.
The fame game : a superstar's guide to getting rich and famous / Sergey Knazev. -- First edition.
    pages cm.
    Summary: "Founder of entertainment and brand management company who manages careers of the stars tells behind-the-scenes stories of how they reached their fame and offers information and practical advice on how to become a celebrity"-- Provided by publisher.
    ISBN 978-1-59079-125-7 (hardbound : alk. paper)
    1. Fame. 2. Celebrities--Case studies. 3. Publicity. I. Title.
    BJ1470.5.K53 2015
    302.5'4--dc23
                        2014013866

Caricature illustrations by Max Espinoza and Ruben Gerard
Book design by Janice Benight

Manufactured in the United States of America
10 9 8 7 6 5 4 3 2 1

Contents

2.
How to Become and Stay Famous 71

3.
Digital Age: Fame Reloaded 123

4.

How to Play the Fame Game and Win 177

5.
Money, Money, Money: How to Build and Run Fame Business 281

6.

What's Next? 341

Foreword

by Perez Hilton

Fame. It's something many people search for and few find, because—let's be honest—being famous takes hard work! There's still A LOT more to it than that, though!

Sometimes you need money, and sometimes you need luck, but when it comes down to being famous, you always need to be smart and know how to play the game. In Sergey Knazev's book, *The Fame Game*, the rules to becoming one of the Glitteratti are laid out plain and simple, and trust me, there are definitely rules to winning! However, sometimes breaking those rules can be the difference between the big time and fifteen seconds of fame. But you can't break rules the right way until you know what they are!

Over the years, the world of fame has evolved, and so have the people who have attained celeb status. When Elizabeth Taylor became the first nearly fully accessible star in Hollywood, people were obsessed with her life and relationships. Fast forward a few decades later, when Old Hollywood elegance no longer reigned supreme. Instead, scandalous sex tapes like Kim Kardashian's and Paris Hilton's took over, launching entire families to stardom. Even though their rise to fame wasn't so long ago, in the fast moving Internet age, we've already moved on from sex tapes (although obviously we all still love a good sex tape!) to a world where YouTube stars and viral videos sit atop the totem pole. In today's world, fame is a completely different animal, and it's a high-maintenance animal, too!

The Fame Game will give you the recipe to help you find your inner star's spirit animal, using tools like branding, self-promotion, and basically just figuring out why it is that you should be famous. Just having a pretty face or bunz of steel won't get you to the top. You need to learn the art of the publicity stunt, how to get the paparazzi to work for you, the best ways to make social media your bestie, how to establish a fan-base, and of course there's always understanding the business side of things. Will advertisers want to work with you? Why? What can you bring to the table? You'll need a website to promote yourself, a portfolio, and good contacts. Do you have any idea how much all of that will cost? It's a lot to think about, but you'll find all of these answers right inside this info-packed, yet wildly entertaining book by one of today's leading fame and branding experts.

My own journey followed many of these guidelines. I went from blogging daily at a coffee shop, to having one of the largest, most successful entertainment and celeb websites in the world. And I did it by working very hard—not only at creating content people engaged with and promoting work I'm proud of—but also by putting myself out there as a personality and an authority in the world of Hollywood! I befriended the celebs I love, which helped me gain a celebrity following, boosting my fandom even more! And fans are a big key to your success in this game.

If you're reading this, and you want to be as famous as Snooki, you CAN! Take a look at the tools Knazev gives you in this book, put them in your bedazzled toolbox, and get to work making your dreams come true!

And remember, even making the worst dressed list is a good thing, because at least people are talking about you!

—Perez Hilton
Los Angeles, CA
July 2015

Acknowledgments

I would like to dedicate this book to my parents Olga and Boris Knazev and my sister Natalia Knazeva, and thank all my extended family, friends, and colleagues for making this book possible through all their tremendous support and help over the years while this book was in the works.

I would like to thank my extensive Fame Game family. First and foremost, special thanks to Michael East for his boundless trust in me, support, personal inspiration, and encouragement; Zac Albright for being the most loyal, talented, and the hardest working colleague and friend; Igor Glavatskih for being the best web designer and programmer and loyal friend of almost twenty years; Elkhonon Goldberg for being a family in my newly adopted country and for his vote of confidence and encouragement; Richard Flaster for being the best friend and the best business partner one can dream of; Wallace Wang, Sharon Roth, Max Espinoza, Ruben Gerard, and Nancy, Kenzi, and Kenichi Sugihara for sharing with me their friendship, support and talents as editors, illustrators, and publishers to make this book such a fantastic read despite the sometimes puzzling communications that arise from my distinct (but charming) Eastern European dialect; Bill Gladstone and Karen Kinney for their business acumen in publishing—and trust in me as a first-time writer—and Omarosa for her advice and support along the way. I also would like to thank my dear friends and business partners at Perfectomundo Tequila: Richard Cabo, Howard Balaban and Paul Oakenfold for being such great sports, loyal friends, and for making working with them almost criminally fun.

I would also like to thank countless celebrities, lawyers, agents, managers, and other esteemed colleagues that taught me, fought me, inspired me, and gave me the privilege of working with them. The joking about celebrities in this book is all meant to be in fun, and is written with love and respect for these people who have helped to create the Hollywood machine and keep it spinning from both on and behind the stage—many of whom I have been honored to meet, work with, and learn from.

And last, but definitely not least, I would like to thank the illustrious Perez Hilton for writing such a terrific foreword and being such a tremendous encouragement and support.

Introduction

"If cash comes with fame, come fame;
if cash comes without fame, come cash."—Jack London

Everyday in Los Angeles, I see hundreds of aspiring actors climbing out of buses, trains, and airplanes to pursue their dreams of fame and fortune in Hollywood. Many of these fortune seekers are supremely talented, yet the odds are heavily stacked against them.

While we hope for the best, it is a sad fact that most will wind up living in rundown apartments in undesirable (while affordable) neighborhoods working at low wage jobs in dead-end positions as they watch their youth and enthusiasm slowly drain from their once-promising lives. Many will one day pack up and quietly slip back to the familiarity and sanctuary of their hometown where they'll face the remains of their shattered dreams of stardom. (And end as lawyers, accountants, or teachers who reminisce to clients and pupils about their close brush with fame.)

This raises the perplexing question: Why do some people succeed in show business while others fall by the wayside despite their nearly identical or even superior abilities and skills?

The answer is surprisingly simple, but so mundane that it is easy to overlook the obvious. The fact is that people succeed to the extent that they know how to market themselves effectively.

The truth is that almost everyone has a gift—whether it's their appearance or a unique ability in singing, acting, dancing or another craft. This talent is their product, but like any product, **you need to promote that talent to the people who most need what you have to offer.**

Imagine the future of a greatly talented actor arriving in Hollywood. Will he or she succeed or fail? The truth is that it all depends on how this person plays what we will call the "Fame Game." While optimism can be a virtue, the wrong way to play the Fame Game is placing one's bet on chance, hope, and the kindness of fate. Blind optimism in Hollywood is most definitely misplaced.

Instead we should first acknowledge that **everyone is part of the fame game,** a game that plays a critical role in success or failure in virtually all walks of life. For a wannabe actress, fame is the air she breathes. For an existing celebrity, fame is a grave matter of survival and relevance. For a businessman and marketing professional, fame means his or her reputation, which is equal to having money in an account. For a pimply high school kid, having fame is the difference between a depressed outcast and being a popular guy who gets the girl and a long guest list at his birthday party. For most people, fame can mean the difference between a promotion and raise or a "downsizing pink slip."

Fame—when properly channeled—comes with recognition and appreciation by the audience that matters to you and your career. This means that people think you're somebody really special, even if you really aren't. To get people to recognize you, you have to stand out from the crowd.

Some people stand out from the crowd trying to climb on the heads of others, some by adding 12-inch heels, 9-inch nails, or a fresh cut of meat to their wardrobe. Some stand out by following the motto that "sex always sells," while others are noticed for their exceptional talent—although in our media-bombarded society, outrageous displays of sexuality or bizarre styles often win over talent (or at least eclipse it for a little while).

Ultimately, the best way to achieve fame is to take action without waiting for permission from agents, managers, or talent scouts to "discover" you. It doesn't matter if you stand on your head and singlehandedly sing in four-part harmony while doing advanced physics in your head. Nobody **will discover you until you begin to make yourself interesting in the first place.** That's because most agents, managers, and talent scouts are too busy with existing clients already making them money, so they'll only be interested in somebody who is already succeeding. Welcome to the bizarre catch-22 of the Fame Game, but it is what it is and we will work with it. That means *it's up to you* to make yourself famous through your own efforts, either locally through your community newspapers, radio, and TV stations or globally through the Internet.

Whether you're famous locally, regionally, nationally or even internationally, the end result is the same. You have to make people out there know you. Of course once you become famous, you have to know how to use your fame for either good or evil. For example, most people in the government choose evil. (I have a thing about government, as you will see. Feel free to skim those parts if you don't want to hear about it—I won't be offended.)

Fame gives you the power to do what you want. Think of fame as giving you superpowers except you don't have to disguise your identity or wear a costume that involves a cape and tights that look like underwear.

Once you're famous, you can use your fame to do what's most important to you, such as highlighting charitable causes. Angelina Jolie spends her time when she's not making movies helping refugees and adopting children from third world countries. On the other hand, Lindsay Lohan uses her fame to help herself to what she considers "free" jewelry and the latest fashions she believes come as part of the fame package. On perhaps at the more deliberately conniving end of the scale, the Kardashian sisters use their fame to turn their followers into hamsters running the wheel of their money-printing machine.

On a more personal and local level, fame can give you the power (and courage) to change careers or advance further and faster than you might think possible. **Fame is never a goal in itself, but a tool to help you achieve your other goals,** whether that goal is to make more money, help other people, or insult everyone at your high school reunion who treated you poorly when you were classmates. (Won't make you rich but that one can be a cool bonus.)

Now, in a nod to the timeless chicken-and-egg quest, you may be wondering what comes first, the publicity or the fame? In other words, do you need to do something noteworthy in order to become famous, or do you need to acquire fame so you can do something noteworthy?

The answer is simple. Remember, talent has little to do with fame, which is why Kim Kardashian can become famous. **To become famous, you must first become famous.** That means you need to promote and publicize yourself. **If you focus on your talent first and your publicity second, you'll likely never become famous.**

The formula for fame is simple, yet deceptive. The first rule of fame? **Anyone can be famous.** Just look at the long list of singers who can't sing (Britney Spears, who lip-syncs in concert), actors who can't act (Hayden Christensen, whose portrayal of Darth Vader in the *Star Wars* prequels made everyone forget how much they loved the original *Star Wars* films), and reality TV stars—who pretty much have no discernible talent whatsoever (think of everyone on your least favorite reality TV show). If talentless people can get rich after becoming famous, there should be no reason you can't be famous and wealthy, too.

The second rule of fame is that **you can never please everyone**, so just focus on pleasing the ones who will like you and who matter to your career. (That also happens to be the rule of people in general, and knowing this just makes life more relaxing.) After all, your fans are the ones giving you admiration and money while your critics are the ones giving you grief.

Don't worry about your critics because everyone has them. Moreover, playing your cards right will make your critics work for you even better than your fans. But focus on pleasing your fans because they're the ones supporting you. No matter who you are, you will always have both fans and critics, so get used to both praise and criticism coming from people you may consider less intelligent than you are (and sometimes more annoying). Just remember that both your fans and your critics are your Fame Game Family and deserve your attention because they are getting you where you want to go.

So the third rule of fame is to **entertain people in a way that only you can do through your unique talents, personality, and lifestyle.**

Once you identify how to be outrageous and noticed in today's world, the fourth rule of fame is **to publicize yourself to convince others that you are important.** The more people you convince, the more people will want to follow you. The more people you can get to follow you, the more your fame will increase. Really, it's a simple mathematical equation—but getting there requires both creativity and balls.

Fame always starts with getting just one person to recognize you. As soon as you get one person to like you, you can get another person and then another, until your fame gradually expands like the Hindenburg being filled with hydrogen right before it exploded into flames and killed thirty-five people. Ok, that might have been a bit extreme, but we are thinking Hollywood Big now and it's easy to get carried away. Anyway, you get the point: it's an exponential mechanism.

The key is that fame is never bestowed on people like a divine right that royal families get just because their ancestors slept with the right people. Instead, fame is generated, nurtured, and refined—**and it all starts with you.**

The fifth rule of fame is that **nobody will make you famous but you, and you won't get famous until you start taking action, now.** In this book you'll learn how all types of celebrities create, generate, nurture, promote, and monetize their fame so that you can adopt their clever techniques to get rich and get famous too. If you want more control over your life, you need more fame. To get the fame that you deserve, follow the tips in each chapter and apply them in your own life.

Fame awaits you. Now you just have to get ready for the spotlight.

CHAPTER 1

History of the Celebrity Phenomenon

"Obsessed by a fairy tale, we spend our lives searching for a magic door and a lost kingdom of peace."—Eugene O'Neill

Once Upon a Time . . .

Once upon a time, long ago in a land far away from the real world, there was a town called Hollywood. As in most fairy tales, this magic town had trolls that hid under bridges and demanded a passage fee from unsuspecting travelers and wizards that could pull a magical pot of gold out of thin air or turn a frog into beautiful prince. Living among these trolls and wizards were a lucky few chosen to play the roles of princes and princesses while the majority of the people were cast as hapless peasants.

In Hollywood, the trolls were often called "entertainment lawyers" who thrived on problems that they created with amazing skill and ingenuity, only to resolve them later for outrageous fees that can put any mythical creature to shame. The wizards were called "producers" because they could create new stars and magically turn $200 million of profit into a $50 million loss, while adding yet another Malibu palace to their real estate collection. This is the magical place where people flocked to live, lured by the irresistible stardust of tabloids and what used to be a media of journalistic integrity and standards. These aspiring actors and fortune seekers flooded Hollywood every day in search of the fabled keys to stardom.

In Hollywood, everyone was beautiful even if they weren't. In Hollywood, everyone was powerful and famous, even if they had no talent.

In short, it was the ultimate Emerald City. And everyone tried gamely to be the Wizard of Oz, Dorothy, and Toto all rolled into one.

While working menial jobs that often involved serving food to—or perhaps grooming—the very people they wished to become, such fortune seekers dreamt of the day they too would be anointed as the latest Hollywood celebrities.

Yet every night they went to bed feeling older and more defeated, despite the eternal optimism displayed on their carefully styled headshots.

To keep up their spirits, these fortune seekers shared stories with each other. One day they might tell about a waitress who had been discovered by a movie director. The next day they might whisper about a dog walker who had been hired by a famous movie star to walk her Chihuahua, and wound up getting a part in her next movie (although in reality he or she would likely wind up envying the lifestyle of the movie star's Chihuahua).

They shared rumors that reality TV shows weren't based on reality and that lies were accepted as truths. They whispered that the news shows valued ratings over objectivity, and how news anchors were chosen for their appearances rather than for their ability to deliver information. They told how people, starved for actual information, turned away from the news outlets and sought the truth from jokesters, satirists, and comedians shining in the twilight of the late-night shows.

This was the topsy-turvy world that these Hollywood explorers brought back home in their fevered memories. Yet despite such fantastic tales that defied both logic and common sense, their cautionary words failed to discourage the hordes of new fortune seekers. Instead, their stories only fueled their desire to break into show business as quickly as possible by trying to understand the absurd rules of Hollywood.

Relying on the mutterings of these jaded explorers who had actually experienced Hollywood insanity, the new fortune seekers searched for additional clues from celebrity magazines and tabloids. Even though the covers of these magazines offered tantalizing glimpses of perfect faces, they learned the photos had all been airbrushed to make them look more beautiful than they really were.

And despite knowing this, the public still loved them.

To become as beautiful as these perfect Hollywood people, aspiring actors sought the services of the most talented beauticians, stylists, and plastic surgeons. They believed that the secret to achieving stardom was to look just like their Hollywood heroes, the current stars they saw on TV and in the movies.

If a currently popular actress had a big smile, women who could afford it had their lips surgically shaped to physically mimic that same big smile. When a new actress became popular with a distinctly different mouth, the fame seekers rushed back to their plastic surgeons to change their physical appearance to match the lips of the newest actress.

Unfortunately, these misguided women failed to realize that these actors and entertainers had become stars precisely because they didn't imitate existing celebrities. They succeeded because they were something new. That is precisely why Elvis Presley impersonators never made as much money or achieved as much fame as the real Elvis Presley.

While many fortune seekers wasted their time mimicking the latest beautiful people in Hollywood, other confused performers focused on the seemingly logical belief that talent was the deciding factor for gaining admittance to the hallowed gates of Hollywood. Those without talent, they reasoned, would be left to starve. Those with talent would one day be "discovered" and whisked away to the land of milk and honey.

Aspiring stars sought to improve their talent through unending night and weekend classes in acting, improvisation, screenwriting, stand-up comedy, public speaking, dancing, auditioning, voice training, and a myriad of other fields offered by an army of credible experts who thrived off the relentless stream of these desperate fortune seekers. And inexplicably, despite a continual lack of progress, they nurtured their limited resources until they could pay for the next series of classes they felt were certain to at last crack open the doors to Hollywood.

Much like the fame seekers who believed that a physical beauty alone would open the gates to Hollywood, they failed to acknowledge the contradictory evidence. Stars of reality TV shows demonstrated that ordinary people could become rich and famous with no hint of talent whatsoever.

The fortune seekers who believed in physical mimicry were certain that appearances meant everything and talent meant nothing. On the other hand, the talent-obsessed fortune seekers knew that talent made you stand out from the crowd, but failed to realize how little Hollywood values real talent. When it was fresh, it was welcomed, but when it was old, it was easily discarded and flushed away without a second thought.

What both groups failed to see was that **stars are never born; they are manufactured.** And once manufactured, they are further amplified as larger than life by the media. When viewed through the distorted lens of a camera, something called publicity acted like the opposite of funhouse mirrors. Instead of distorting normal images to make them comical, **publicity distorted the ordinary to make them appear extraordinary.** By focusing the public's attention on the images in the mirror and not on the actual person, Hollywood could make even the most despicable scumbag seem like the saintly reincarnation of Mother Teresa.

If word leaked out that the celebrity's perfect show business image didn't quite match a person's actual behavior, this is even better! Hollywood could then nurture the riveting storyline of a good person gone bad. With a tantalizing plethora of photographs, lurid gossip, and tales of impropriety, every star's fall from grace and ultimate redemption could be followed like a religious soap opera, except you didn't have to turn on the TV to see it.

This was the secret all these fortune seekers had been searching for all the time—the only way to get publicity was to be famous, but the only way to be famous was to get publicity. Isn't this is why serial killer psychopaths on death row got marriage proposals after torturing and killing dozens of women? What these hopeful fiancés saw in a psychotic killer wasn't that he would slice their throat open if given half a chance, but that he was famous, and by marrying him, some of his fame might rub off on them. It's a remarkable dynamic. But again, it is what it is. Let's continue.

Fortunately there were a few other ways fortune seekers could become famous. The most unreliable method, which most fortune seekers pursued, was waiting to be "discovered." Every week, this worked for a lucky few, proving this method worked at the same guaranteed rate as waiting to win the lottery. Waiting to be discovered left many aging men and women to totter around Los Angeles, clinging to twenty-year-old headshots of themselves from when they were young and attractive.

Rather than wait to be discovered, a few finally realized the key to stardom was to generate their own fame—then parlay it into something much bigger, much like pushing a snowball downhill. At first, the snowball might be tiny and only seem to grow infinitesimally even after much effort. However, once it reached a certain size, its own bulk would take over. Suddenly its weight would start propelling it downhill, gathering speed and momentum as it rushed down the slope with a life of its own.

That was how the Fame Game worked. This was the secret all those starving fortune seekers in Los Angeles needed to know to pry open the gates to stardom and slip inside before getting crushed by the always fickle swinging doors of Hollywood.

Knowing that you had to generate your own fame and nurture it for years (or even decades) in complete isolation with no guarantee of success would discourage all but the most determined fortune seekers. To make matters even more difficult, most fortune seekers had no clue how to generate their own fame.

That secret, like most secrets, lay in following in the footsteps of those who have gone before you and in gaining a true understanding how Hollywood actually works—for instance, by learning to be as big a publicity maven/virtuoso/whore? (reader's choice here: pick your favorite) as the best of them.

In the early days of Hollywood, the public could only learn about their favorite stars through magazines, TV shows, and movies. When it came to knowing anything about the personal lives of their favorite stars, the public knew almost nothing.

That all changed in 1942 when a new face graced the silver screen, the face of the young girl who was destined to change the fame game of Hollywood forever. Her name was Elizabeth Taylor and she was nine years old when she appeared in her first movie called *There's One Born Every Minute*. This title sounded suspiciously like P. T. Barnum's statement, "There's a sucker born every minute," but in this minute, a star really was born.

Before Elizabeth Taylor, the Fame Game was very different. The lives of Hollywood stars were carefully measured and doled out to the public in small increments while their personal lives remained hidden. But when Elizabeth Taylor became a child star, the world adopted her as its own little girl. As Elizabeth Taylor grew up, so did the public's infatuation with her. For the first time, people clamored for more information about a star that went beyond her public persona.

Suddenly, people were more interested in knowing about her real life, relationships and sexual exploits than her movies. Elizabeth Taylor was no longer just a movie star. She now became a larger-than-life celebrity, famous because she was already famous. Her immense talent aside, Elizabeth Taylor was also in some ways our first "reality star"— and ushered in the beginning of the modern celebrity era.

Elizabeth Taylor: Pioneer of Publicity Manipulation

"I honestly think it is better to be a failure at something you love than to be a success at something you hate."—George Burns

Elizabeth Taylor was born outside of London to parents Francis Taylor and Sara Sothern. Francis worked as an art dealer while Sara was a former actress who retired from the stage in 1926 when she married Francis in New York City. As someone who had already worked in show business, Sara knew what it took to succeed. If she could no longer be a star in the eyes of the public, she knew what it took to put her daughter in the spotlight instead.

Sara soon turned her attention away from her husband, who responded by becoming an alcoholic—a common way people in show business deal with emotional problems, even though it has an unblemished failure rate of 100 percent. While slurring your words and throwing up on your shoes might seem like an odd way to deal with relationship challenges, this type of logic fit perfectly within the realm of Hollywood, and Francis was welcomed as a valid member of the show business world.

Despite the lack of her husband's involvement, Sara devoted herself to turning Elizabeth into a star, enrolling Elizabeth in singing and dance lessons by the age of two. While most two-year-olds could do nothing more impressive than learn to use the toilet, Elizabeth could sing and dance at the same time. Away from formal teachers, Sara coached Elizabeth relentlessly, even when she was exhausted, until she could get Elizabeth to cry on cue.

Today, of course, it's easy to get any intelligent adult to cry on cue just by showing them how much money reality TV stars earn just by eating a salad, shopping, or yelling at people on TV, while most people work hard all year just to make a decent living. Back then, however, getting someone to cry on cue was much harder because it involved actual acting skills.

Whenever Elizabeth appeared in a movie, Sara coached her from the sidelines.

When Elizabeth failed to deliver her lines with conviction, Sara would put her hand on her heart to signal more emotion. When Elizabeth forgot a line, Sara would tap her head. When Elizabeth made a mistake, Sara would give her a stiff glare. When Sara became too overbearing, Elizabeth would give her the finger. (Or so we would like to imagine.)

Elizabeth often chafed at her mother's domineering presence. When she turned sixteen, Elizabeth told her parents that she was sick and tired of making movies and just wanted to be a regular child with an alcoholic father and a domineering stage mother.

Horrified, Sara told her, "But you're not a regular child, and thank God for that." At this point, poor Elizabeth probably realized that she didn't have a regular mother either, but that part of the story often gets lost in the dustbins of history.

By the age of seventeen, Elizabeth had grown up isolated from her peers, and she didn't even need to a Facebook or Twitter addiction to bring this about. Because she worked in show business for much of her childhood, her education suffered to the point where she could only add numbers by counting on her fingers. (Which, truth be told, might have actually placed her math scores above those of her peers who had attended public schools.) Despite these glaring problems, Sara continued to emphasize Elizabeth's physical beauty over her intelligence, blazing a trail for all celebrities to follow in the future.

To improve her already perfect appearance, Sara had Elizabeth's hairline plucked and her eyebrows reshaped. Elizabeth reportedly also had rhinoplasty, otherwise known as a nose job. Even back in those days, Sara knew that nobody would take Elizabeth's beauty seriously unless it had been surgically altered to appear more natural. Ah . . . the beauty of Hollywood irony!

Even though Elizabeth's beauty shone on the silver screen for all to see, Sara knew that nothing made a woman more attractive than if people thought other men were pursuing her. This strategy of following the crowd was known as the "bandwagon effect." This curious desire to conform to popular opinion was responsible for creating popular fads, selling perfumes endorsed by celebrities, pretending to be a fan of sometimes subpar music, etc.

To this end, Sara encouraged MGM Studios to set up "dates" with various leading actors as a way to create the illusion that Elizabeth was popular. A picture of Elizabeth alone might be enough to make her desirable, but a picture of Elizabeth surrounded by several handsome men made her seem more unavailable than before, thereby increasing her appeal. If they couldn't have her, men wanted her even more.

Besides arranging "dates" for Elizabeth and making sure each date received plenty of publicity including photographs, public sightings, and commemorative souvenirs, Sara also arranged for Elizabeth to get engaged to Heisman Trophy-winner Glenn Davis. Sara correctly guessed that instead of worrying about the possibility of world starvation or global thermonuclear holocaust, people would be more concerned about the love life of a football player and a movie star. No stranger to human nature was she.

Only after the engagement ended did Glenn Davis discover that his entire relationship with Elizabeth had been nothing more than a publicity stunt to keep her in the spotlight. After being used by a woman, Glenn Davis reportedly said, "From now on, I'm going to use my status as a professional athlete to take advantage of every loose woman I meet while traveling on the road during my games." Over the next few decades, thousands of professional athletes in the NFL, NBA, NHL, Major League Baseball, the Olympics, and the American Chess Federation followed in Glenn Davis's footsteps, and have Elizabeth Taylor to thank for justifying their actions. Thanks a bunch, Liz!

In 1949, eccentric aviation billionaire Howard Hughes approached Elizabeth Taylor's father as a potential suitor (to Elizabeth Taylor, not the father). This of course was long before Howard Hughes decided that sitting naked in a screening room, urinating in glass jars, and watching the movie *Ice Station Zebra* 150 times in a row was the type of behavior that women might not appreciate in a potential husband.

In his mid-forties at the time he approached Sara and Francis, Hughes had already bedded numerous other famous women including Lana Turner, Ava Gardner, Joan Crawford, Bette Davis, and Katharine Hepburn. Now he told Sara and Francis that if they could persuade Elizabeth to marry him, he would build a movie studio just for her.

Excited by the prospect of being both a matchmaker and a female pimp, Sara urged Elizabeth to marry the eccentric billionaire for both the publicity and the money. (Mostly for the money, but she figured the publicity that a billion dollars could pay for wouldn't hurt either.) To Sara's dismay, Elizabeth refused. "I don't care how much money he has," Elizabeth said. "If I was going to turn myself into a whore just for money, I might as well just change my name to Kim Kardashian." (Ok, so we took a little creative license here. But if KK had been alive at the time, this is what I believe Elizabeth most certainly would have said.)

Rather than have her mother create another phony relationship with another famous celebrity, Elizabeth decided she could live a happier life by creating a real relationship with an abusive, alcoholic gambler instead—which goes to illustrate the surprising fact that the Hollywood woman's intuition may not always hit the bull's eye.

Overlooking his drinking and gambling problems along with his abusive behavior, Elizabeth decided she was in love with Conrad "Nicky" Hilton, the young heir to the Hilton hotel fortune. Conrad Hilton, Jr.'s only redeeming quality was that he wasn't a later family member with the first name "Paris."

As a first marriage, Elizabeth Taylor's wedding brought her a new wave of publicity. MGM Studios pitched in by designing her wedding gown and honeymoon outfits and even offered to hire a stunt double to help consummate her marriage. The publicity Elizabeth Taylor's wedding created brought even more attention to MGM Studios and Elizabeth Taylor's movies. Then, after only nine months, Elizabeth decided on an encore by getting a divorce.

Afterwards, Elizabeth reportedly said, "I guess I didn't know what love was, but I figured that it probably didn't involve a punch to the face by a drunk gambler every Saturday night. I always thought that love was synonymous with marriage. Now I know that it's possible to have love, romance, sex, bitter arguments, angry accusations and emotionally devastating breakups without having to get married at all. And to think gay couples believe they're missing out on life because they're unable to get married. Ha!"

Because the publicity generated by her first marriage proved so successful, Elizabeth Taylor soon caved into the pressure to milk a good thing while it was going, so she agreed to a hastily contrived sequel. Publicized as *Mr. Elizabeth Taylor 2*, her second marriage involved Michael

Wilding, a man twice her age. This age difference proved attractive to both the highly desirable, older male demographics (since they have all the money) while also attracting the younger female demographics that can find romance in anything from dirty old men to teenage vampires and werewolves.

When *Mr. Elizabeth Taylor 2* proved popular, Elizabeth followed up with sequels with rapidly diminishing returns and critical acclaim. *Mr. Elizabeth Taylor 3*, starring Michael Todd, strayed from the formula by ending their relationship through a plane crash rather than a divorce. The critics were not amused and savagely panned the results.

Mr. Elizabeth Taylor 4 found Elizabeth back within the familiar formulaic framework of her first marriage, except this time it was with singer Eddie Fisher, whose big claim to fame would be fathering Princess Leia in a galaxy far, far away.

By this time, the public was beginning to experience what MGM public relations specialists later called "Elizabeth Taylor marriage fatigue." Casting equally famous actor Richard Burton to play the part of the husband in *Mr. Elizabeth Taylor 5* proved a marketing coup and revitalized the Elizabeth Taylor marriage brand while generating additional revenue through the licensing of Elizabeth Taylor and Richard Burton action figures.

To repeat their earlier success, the studios convinced Richard Burton to reprise his role in *Mr. Elizabeth Taylor: Reloaded* (also known under its overseas title of *Mr. Elizabeth Taylor 6*) less than a year later. Despite the same cast and storyline, this marriage failed to generate much enthusiasm with the public.

When the studios were unable to meet the salary demands of Richard Burton to complete an Elizabeth Taylor/Richard Burton trilogy, the studio heads decided to shift the story to a new location and have Elizabeth Taylor marry John Warner, a United States Senator from Virginia for *Mr. Elizabeth Taylor 7*. "The hijinks of having Elizabeth Taylor deal with Washington, DC politics will be hilarious," promised the MGM studio executives. Yet this production proved both a critical and commercial flop.

In desperation, MGM studios considered alternatives to rescue their flailing Elizabeth Taylor marriage franchise. *The Hollywood Reporter* periodically mentioned projects with tentative titles like *Elizabeth Taylor vs. Alien vs. Predator, Die Hard with a Vengeance and Elizabeth Taylor,* and *Harry Potter and the Goblet of Elizabeth Taylor,* but none of them ever reached fruition. (Ok, creative license again. But I do like the sound of these, don't you?)

Finally, MGM studios green-lit *Mr. Elizabeth Taylor 8* and cast an unknown named Larry Fortensky. Yet after eight sequels, MGM studios finally admitted that the Elizabeth Taylor marriage drama franchise had run its course and needed refreshing. That's when they decided to reboot the original *Mr. Elizabeth Taylor* story with a new cast that would appeal to the younger generation.

In a moment where art defines reality, the 2012 Lifetime movie *Liz & Dick* featured Lindsay Lohan in the role of Elizabeth as a young child starlet thrust in the public spotlight, forced to grow up in the public's eye, and doomed to repeat an endless series of failed marriages while churning through multiple husbands faster than the happiest nympho-maniac (non-murderous) black widow spider who ever lived!

Elizabeth Taylor Sparks the "Sexual Revolution of the 1960s"

Besides the ongoing drama and worldwide publicity of her multiple marriages, Elizabeth Taylor broke new publicity-generated ground through her innovative use of blatant sexual innuendo. Up until Elizabeth Taylor, movies and television shows depicted married couples sleeping in separate beds and wearing pajamas that today bring to mind the timeless boudoir stylings of Ernie and Bert from *Sesame Street.*

Even popular magazines like *Life* favored photographs of movie stars living the exotic but sexless life of eunuchs. During the joyful era of McCarthy-inspired communist witch hunts, any published displays of sexuality were considered one step above giving atomic bomb secrets to the Russians. Fortunately, Elizabeth Taylor changed all that.

First, Elizabeth Taylor posed partially nude in *Playboy* magazine, which was unheard of for a movie star of her status at that time. Picture Ronald Reagan posing naked in *Playgirl* magazine as a way to inspire more young people to vote for the Republican Party, and you get the idea how shocking this was for that era.

Elizabeth was also one of the first major movie stars to appear partially naked on-screen, as she did during a love scene for the 1951 film *A Place in the Sun.* In this movie, Elizabeth Taylor played the role of a wealthy socialite. (I guess Elizabeth truly had to stretch her acting muscles to make that portrayal believable.)

Only seventeen years old at the time she appeared in *A Place in the Sun*, Elizabeth exuded such sensuality that many of Hollywood's closet homosexuals were tempted to become straight. By revealing more of her seductive features without showing people what naughty part they really wanted to see, Elizabeth Taylor discovered the oft-repeated advertising maxim that "sex sells, especially when it's linked to prostitution, pornography, and clandestine affairs with any married member of Congress."

By taking away her clothes, Elizabeth discovered that she wielded more power to influence the general public than the president of the United States. Reality TV stars Paris Hilton and Kim Kardashian would later discover the law of diminishing returns when they took off their clothes while capturing their sexual activity on videotape. Only after a time did these two realize what Elizabeth Taylor had known all along: sex is usually more exciting in the imagination than it is in real life. (Calm down—I SAID USUALLY!!)

In lieu of actual talent, stars of the future would strip away more pieces of clothing as a way to further their careers. Once again, Elizabeth Taylor helped usher in a new realm of marketing that Karl Marx proclaimed as "The decline of Western civilization, except for the part with naked women."

Elizabeth Taylor's Passion for Fashion and Jewelry

In the early days, movie stars were known for—what? Appearing in movies. Unfortunately, however, Hollywood could only produce a handful of new movies every year with the notable exception of remakes, sequels and adaptations from graphic novels, comic books and video games.

The result left few opportunities for movie stars to capture public attention on the silver screen. If movie stars relied on their films to generate publicity, they would soon find themselves quickly forgotten after their film premiere by issues deemed more pressing to the American public like "Who shot J. R.?" and "Who's sleeping with Madonna this week?"

Rather than rely on the fickle whims of the public's movie-watching habits to maintain her presence in the spotlight, Elizabeth Taylor once again broke new ground by brilliantly combining her passion for fashion and jewelry into an entirely new industry known as "celebrity-based marketing." The idea was simple. If a celebrity said, endorsed, or sold something, that product must be valuable. You'd have to be a communist or clinically anti-social to think otherwise.

During her lifetime, Elizabeth collected jewelry reportedly worth $150 million (not including the value of the gold-tipped, ballpoint pens she stole from the bank). Some of Elizabeth's collection included a 33.19-carat Krupp Diamond and a 69.42-carat Taylor-Burton Diamond, given to her as a gift from Richard Burton (before he realized that he might have gotten a better return on his investment if he had just picked up a streetwalker on Sunset Boulevard instead.)

Despite winning two Oscars for best actress in long-forgotten movies such as *Butterfield 8* and *Who's Afraid of Virginia Wolf?* (Anyone rent these from Netflix recently?), Elizabeth made sure the world remembered her not as a talented actress (remember, talent means little when trying to stay in the public's eye), but for her fashion sense and jewelry collection.

Elizabeth Taylor created the forerunner of the current celebrity fragrance business in 1987 when she launched her first fragrance called "Elizabeth Taylor's Passion," (which sounded a lot better than the original name of "Elizabeth Taylor's Smell.").

In 1989 Elizabeth launched an accompanying men's fragrance called "Passion for Men." This title was derived from the original name of "The Smell of Money," in honor of the fact that this was the only way most ordinary guys could possibly attract someone as famous as Elizabeth Taylor.

In 1991 Elizabeth introduced her most popular fragrance called "White Diamonds," which sold well over $1 billion in retail sales to women. (I personally don't believe smelling like something associated with a compressed form of carbon make anyone more attractive to men, but what do I know? Anyway, it worked, and we can't argue with success.)

In short, Elizabeth Taylor pioneered the concept of selling anything and everything to people—while simultaneously taking advantage of the additional publicity this generated—slapping her face and name on a box that could contain anything from tap water poured into a perfume bottle to gift-wrapped animal droppings. Whatever the critics might say about the quality of her products, Elizabeth Taylor was a Hollywood marketing trailblazer, turning mass merchandising into yet another

Elizabeth Taylor and Michael Jackson at the 1993
American Music Awards in Los Angeles, CA
(PRN/PR Photos)

publicity coup to further cement her status as a celebrity more perfect than her fans.

Elizabeth Taylor vs. the Paparazzi

In 1960 Elizabeth Taylor became the highest-paid actress of the time when she accepted $1 million to play the title role in Twentieth Century-Fox's *Cleopatra*. During the filming, she and Richard Burton (who played Marc Antony) created an epic scandal that was of no significance to society whatsoever.

Even back then, love affairs between movie stars were nothing new. In fact, affairs were so commonplace in show business, politics, and business (in really any arena that blended money and lots of horny men) that most publications would write about them more out of habit than any intent to provide actual information. Such articles, known as "fillers" in the publication industry, would commonly appear tucked somewhere between the classified ads for used cars and the comic strip for *Garfield*.

However, Elizabeth Taylor put her own unique twist on the topic by having a Hollywood affair with Richard Burton while both of them were married to somebody else. Ordinary love affairs between movie stars were suddenly passé. To truly attract public attention, Elizabeth discovered that you needed a love affair between two people *already married to others*.

Now the media could cover the Elizabeth Taylor/Richard Burton love affair from the delicious new angle of how their on-set romance might be affecting their neglected wife and husband. The media obsessed over their affair on the set of *Cleopatra*, which depicted ancient Egyptians with the historical accuracy of looking no different than white, Protestant Americans in Halloween costumes. A true suspension of disbelief.

Naturally, the public acted outraged (over the Elizabeth Taylor/Richard Burton affair, not over this brand of subtle racism that was occurring in pretty much every movie of this kind at the time). Despite the pretended outcry, most of the public secretly wished they had the balls to pull off a stunt like that without their husband or wife castrating them when they got home that night.

As fury and indignation over the affair grew, the paparazzi took on a new role. In the past, they had often settled for staged shots of movie stars smashing their cars into telephone poles after a drunken spree or getting caught shoplifting from a jewelry store on Rodeo Drive. Under these new circumstances, the paparazzi began the practice of stakeouts, where they hid in places where Elizabeth Taylor and Richard Burton were most likely to appear outside of the MGM studio restrooms.

Each furtively captured photograph fed the insatiable demand for information about Elizabeth Taylor and Richard Burton's affair. No longer satisfied with the information doled out to them by the studio public relations department, the paparazzi now sought their own sources of information, even if they had to lie, bribe, and steal (in an honest fashion, of course) to get the news.

The Vatican, suffering from a publicity crisis of its own, decided to exploit the Burton-Taylor affair to broaden their exposure to both Catholics and non-Catholics alike. Citing the Burton-Taylor affair as "erotic vagrancy," while ignoring real erotic vagrancy involving underage choir boys and oversexed Catholic priests (too big of a topic, we won't even go into THAT here), the Vatican harnessed the tried-and-true technique of latching on to the latest hot topic as a way to stay relevant in the eyes of the public. Years later, Madonna (loosely related to the Vatican by name although not uprightly religious about it), would employ this same method to leech off the publicity of other hot singers to maintain her own face in the spotlight.

During Elizabeth's affair with Richard Burton, the media followed two of the most famous film stars in the world as they committed adultery in the eyes of the Lord for the enjoyment of their fans everywhere. Information and photographs of their over-the-top lifestyle, excessive drinking, and extravagant behavior made the couple perfect role models for trashy TV aspirants who would later gain fame on reality TV shows like *Teen Mom* decades later.

To capitalize on their combined popularity, Elizabeth Taylor and Richard Burton starred in ten films together and even ventured into television. Initially the pair achieved success, but the public began to tire of the lack of drama in their relationship. One critic claimed, "Watching Jessica Simpson's marriage dissolve before my eyes is far more entertaining than watching Elizabeth Taylor and Richard Burton try to live a normal life. C'mon Elizabeth. You defined the rules for reality entertainment, step up your game!"

Max Espinoza/Ruben Gerard

Their marriage got progressively lower Nielsen ratings that only spiked briefly when the pair finally agreed to a divorce. It took decades later for Elizabeth to attract the interest of the paparazzi once more when she announced that her 1991 wedding would take place at Michael Jackson's Neverland ranch.

Correctly sensing that Michael Jackson was just as freakishly eccentric as she was, (and yes, they also shared the bond of childhoods overshadowed by abusive stage parents) she deduced that the paparazzi wouldn't know which way to aim their cameras and might even miss a shot of her completely when confronted with a chance to photograph an overgrown man-child playing with his pet monkey named Bubbles.

With an armada of hot air balloons launched as a shield against prying eyes, Elizabeth Taylor wed a construction worker named Larry Fortensky. To capture the ceremony, a paparazzi parachutist strapped a camera to his helmet and managed to land yards away from the fifty-nine-year-old bride and her thirty-nine-year-old groom. Security guards quickly hustled the parachutist out of sight and proceeded to beat the living daylights out of him just because they could.

Through both accident and later deliberate design, Elizabeth Taylor discovered and defined the role of the paparazzi as the unofficial public relations mouthpiece of the stars. By acting outlandishly, Elizabeth could attract the paparazzi's attention. By "leaking" information, she could make sure they would be where she wanted to be seen so they could capture "candid" photographs of her to further prop up her stardom in the eyes of the public. Let's give credit where credit is due. Elizabeth Taylor was a media marketing genius.

Although celebrities bask in the media spotlight, the paparazzi help put them there. To fully understand the Fame Game, you need to know the crucial role the paparazzi play and why they're willing to risk their lives just to capture a picture of a celebrity caught in a compromising position. At least it's more interesting than working as a portrait photographer in a shopping mall, trying to make crying babies smile and look happy in front of a camera, which is actually the same thing when you think about it.

The Emergence of the Paparazzi

"You can't complain about the pressures, the paparazzi,
the madness. Because that is the job. I've always
understood that's the deal."—Avril Lavigne

On February 2007, pop singer and sex symbol, the mentally-scarred-for-life-from-being-a-child-star Britney Spears, tried to visit her ex-husband, Kevin Federline (nicknamed K-Fed because his only claim to fame was having sex with Britney Spears). At the time, K-Fed was caring for the couple's two children, who very likely will later require decades of intensive therapy due to the psychological damage incurred by growing up with those two. I just hope they will have good health insurance.

Upon arriving at K-Fed's home, Britney Spears knocked on the door several times and shouted in the intercom for K-Fed to open the door. He refused. Enraged, Britney Spears drove away, followed by a convoy of cars filled with freelance photographers known as paparazzi.

When she stopped at a gas station, the paparazzi swarmed her car in an attempt to get her picture. Suddenly, Britney Spears jumped out of the car, whacked the nearest paparazzi with a green umbrella, and then proceeded to bang on the paparazzi's car until her umbrella snapped in half. Despite her efforts to break in the windows and bust in the doors, Britney Spears only managed to make herself look mentally unhinged while making the paparazzi actually look normal.

At this point, you may be wondering, who are these paparazzi? How do they make money by harassing celebrities?

To fully understand who the paparazzi are, you have to go back to 1960, which is an era that many high school students now associate with the Middle Ages, Noah's Ark, or a time when dinosaurs roamed the Earth. In 1960 Federico Fellini directed a popular film called *La Dolce Vita*, which is a phrase that most Americans wouldn't recognize as a foreign language Americans because it's pretty and we have taken it for ourselves. In Italian, "La Dolce Vita" means "The Sweet Life." In English, "La Dolce Vita" means, "How come everybody on the planet can't speak English for my convenience?" In this particular Italian

Max Espinoza/Ruben Gerard

movie, the story revolves around the life of a jaded journalist, Marcello, and his photographer colleague, Paparazzo.

Interestingly, and very poetically, the name Paparazzo bears an onomatopoeic resemblance to the Sicilian word for an oversized mosquito. Fellini even drew an image of the character as a human-like vampire insect, implying that paparazzi, like mosquitoes, are also parasites. Fellini stated that "Paparazzo suggests to me a buzzing insect, hovering, darting, stinging."

Time magazine later introduced the word to the American public in an article titled, "Paparazzi on the Prowl," which might be the last time that *Time* actually contributed anything of importance to American pop culture. In the magazine article, a throng of paparazzi reporters blocked the car of a princess visiting Rome. The article described them as "a ravenous wolf pack of freelance photographers who stalk big names for a living and fire with flash guns at a pointblank."

Soon this term for photographers would spread across the major news and entertainment publications across the globe, as fast as a new strain of syphilis might spread from the loins of a promiscuous professional athlete or conservative congressman. Publications that followed this trend included *Esquire*, *Cosmopolitan*, and *Life* magazines, although *The Weekly World News* preferred to focus on stories about the incredible Bat Boy instead.

Even news-oriented shows like *60 Minutes*—with its primarily senior viewer population—started using the term "paparazzi" to sound modern and up to date along with their other commonly used phrases like "groovy," "23 skidoo," and "That's the cat's pajamas!" No matter how media described these "celebrity bounty hunters," the term "paparazzi" took on a negative and derogatory tone much like the terms "lawyer," "politician," and of course, "president of the United States."

Now many people might wonder why paparazzi devote their lives to photographing celebrities at all hours of the day and night. To test your knowledge about the major motivation behind the behavior of paparazzi (and practically everything that takes place on the planet), ask yourself which of the following questions can be answered by the term "money"?

    A. Why do movie studios make endless sequels of past successful movies instead of trying to come up with original stories in the first place? (Hint: Built-in audience appeal and more predict-able ticket sales.)

B. Why do universities pay football coaches exorbitant salaries rather than invest the money in better classroom supplies and equipment to fulfill their stated goal of improving higher edu-cation? (Hint: National television broadcasting rights.)

C. Why do democracy-loving governments make secret deals to prop up oppressive dictatorships in Third World countries that happen to sell us critical natural resources? (Hint: Saudi Arabia.)

D. Why do young, attractive women have a better chance of being "discovered" by show business than more talented, but plainer looking women? (Hint: How many people look for talent when staring at a *Playboy* centerfold pinned on a wall?)

If you answered "money" to questions A, B, and C, congratulations! You now understand how the world works. If you answered "sex" to question D, give yourself bonus points for understanding the other way the world works.

Despite the obvious answer to a question nobody really needed to ask, *Time* magazine did an in-depth article about the paparazzi and their motivation. Not surprisingly, *Time* discovered that their reason for doing this work was not about snapping photographs and playing with the latest photography equipment. (Unless, of course, there were photography geeks who couldn't get a better job.) Rather, their motives hinged on the great amount of money that entertainment news publica-tions were willing to pay for photos of celebrities in action.

When *Time* published this article in 1961, photographers only made around $500 per photo. Fifty years later the price had jumped to the half a million dollars for a shot that *US Weekly* reportedly paid for an image of Brad Pitt and Angelina Jolie strolling along a beach in Africa.

In comparison, the only guy who paid for a photograph of Presi-dent Obama signing the European Union Emissions Trading Scheme Prohibition Act of 2011 into law was a forty-nine-year-old man named Fred, who still lived at home with his mother. He paid twenty-five cents, which the White House considered a campaign contribution. (Yes, gov-ernment again. It's a compulsion.)

A Day in the Life of the Paparazzi

Now that you understand why the paparazzi do what they do (for money), it's time to learn *how* they do what they do. All types of paparazzi need to create relationships with industry insiders who will tip them off on the whereabouts of a star at any given time or place. However, just as the animals in George Orwell's novel *Animal Farm* discovered that all animals are equal but some are more equal than others, some paparazzi have also discovered that some paparazzi are more equal than others.

At the lowest level are the freelance paparazzi, who create their own assignments and work off tips. Freelance paparazzi work for themselves and sell their photos to the highest bidder. Since they can only rely on themselves, their ability to capture a great shot depends the most on their luck and opportunity along with their latching on to a crowd of better-funded paparazzi.

Higher up on the paparazzi food chain (although in many eyes still lower than a bloodsucking tick. Wait—too harsh?) are those who work for a photo agency. These paparazzi work in teams and coordinate their actions with their fellow photo agency paparazzi through walkie-talkies and cell phones to share information about the latest locations of celebrities. Besides the mutual support of a team, photo agency paparazzi also benefit through the photo agency's contacts.

Photo agencies can send their photographers into red carpet and industry events to capture pictures of celebrities. Such industry events attract large numbers of celebrities who are always interested in meeting other celebrities so they can make the landmark decision about who to have sex with next. Although photographs of celebrities at major industry events may not be "exclusive" or even interesting (would anyone really care to see a picture of Heidi Montag and Spencer Pratt if they hadn't been on a reality TV show?), such pictures can still be sold to tabloid magazines, TV programs, and even celebrity news blogs for a lesser profit.

Whether paparazzi work independently or in a team associated with a photo agency, they follow the same general procedure to hunt, stalk, and track their prey. Since it's still illegal to tranquilize a celebrity and microchip them, or place a tracking collar around their necks, (which may soon be legal in places where laws either don't exist or are routinely broken and ignored, like Washington, DC—oops, I did it again!), paparazzi rely on two methods to find a celebrity.

The first method involves waiting. Lots of waiting. Did we tell you that most of the time paparazzi do nothing but wait? In fact, paparazzi spend more time doing nothing than the vice president of the United States. Paparazzi wait outside the homes of celebrities in case they should emerge from hiding, spot their shadow, and dart back inside to tell their friends that winter may last another six weeks.

The practice of sitting right outside a star's house is known as "door-stepping." Paparazzi can wait twelve to fourteen hours a day, six or seven days a week, just on the off-chance that a celebrity like Katy Perry might one day roll her car into a ditch or at least hit a Jehovah's Witness on the sidewalk.

Other times, paparazzi wait outside "celebrity hot spots" along Rodeo Drive and Robertson Boulevard, haunting popular restaurants, luxury stores, and nightclubs in hopes of capturing a shot of a drunken celebrity looking foolish or doing something idiotic like shoplifting and getting arrested. Of course we don't know any of *those*.

Since many celebrities are shy around the presence of paparazzi, many paparazzi will camouflage themselves to blend in with their surroundings. Some paparazzi might wear military-style camouflage to look like a tree along the street. Others might hide inside special vans with holes cut in the sides to allow them to poke through a camera's telescopic lenses and capture images from a long distance away. Still others will simply blend into the typical surroundings of Los Angeles by pretending to sell crack cocaine on the streets so they look no more suspicious than the other drug dealers peddling their wares to all the people in Hollywood. Wish I was kidding here but I'm not.

Waiting can be tedious and largely unrewarding, so that's why many paparazzi rely on tips. By making friends (translation: paying people off) with Hollywood insiders, paparazzi can receive text messages and phone calls from their informants, letting them know where a celebrity might be heading.

Besides their network of tipsters, paparazzi also rely on a network of spotters. Spotters are people who do nothing but look for celebrities. When they spot one (which is their whole purpose in life; then they can crawl away and disappear like a spent female salmon after laying her

Audrina Patridge with paparazzi in Los Angeles, CA, 2009
(Albert L. Ortega/PR Photos)

eggs), they contact their favorite (translation: the guy who most recently paid them off) paparazzi to alert them to the sighting.

Once they locate a celebrity in public, paparazzi swarm around them like flies. That's how the world of nature works in Hollywood. It's just as shown in National Geographic films when a pride of lions (more like hyenas) are stalking a kill—It's just occurs much less gracefully and with lots of smog.

Roving bands of paparazzi work together to form a triangle around their celebrity targets. If the celebrity turns away from one photographer, the second one will be perfectly positioned to capture the shot. If the celebrity turns away from the second paparazzi, the third one will get a clear shot. With three photographers snapping pictures at all times, at least one camera will always capture a usable picture no matter what happens, even if the celebrity is really ugly.

Many celebrities despise the paparazzi invading their privacy and go to great lengths to avoid being photographed (unless it involves giving up their celebrity status and going back to becoming a nobody like they were before).

When Brad Pitt drives onto the Warner Brothers studio lot, he'll randomly choose one of the many studio exits to leave the paparazzi guessing where he'll appear next. Actor Alec Baldwin once punched a cameraman in the face and broke his nose. Fortunately, the cameraman turned out to be a member of the paparazzi and not part of the production crew filming Alec Baldwin's next movie. Actor Sean Penn reportedly found a photographer in his hotel room in China, and dangled him over the railing of the ninth floor balcony in retaliation. After hearing this, Madonna, who had once been married to Sean Penn, said, "That's the exact same tactic he tried to use on me! Secretly, I think that's just his idea of foreplay."

While some celebrities actively hide or even attack the paparazzi, still others secretly (and not-so-secretly) cooperate with the paparazzi. Known by its sexually suggestive term as "giving it up," such celebrities will pose for the paparazzi so the pictures appear candid as if the celebrity didn't even know they were being taken. With such arrangements, celebrities will have final approval of the shots for sale and even share in the profits.

Actress Gwyneth Paltrow invited New York paparazzo Steve Sands to take the first photographs of her newborn daughter, Apple, who she named after her favorite brand of computer (because naming your daughter Acer or Hewlett-Packard just sounds silly). Sands then sold the photographs to *People* magazine for between $300,000 and $500,000, thereby laying the legal foundation for Apple to sue her mom, Gwyneth Paltrow, years later to gain her share of the cut.

Paris Hilton is the queen of "giving it up," and she cooperates with the paparazzi as well. But in 2007 Britney Spears took this a step further. After inviting paparazzi photographer, Adnan Ghalib, into her house and her bedroom for an "exclusive," they began a romantic relationship that was taken up by the tabloids for many months.

Celebrities who "give it up" for the paparazzi often do so to create some positive publicity, which usually happens after the celebrity has received negative publicity by doing something really dumb.

After attacking paparazzi photographer Jordan Dawes in 2009, actor Sean Penn got thirty-six months of probation and three hundred hours of community service. Following this incident, a more contrite and humble Sean Penn threatened to break another photographer's back after hitting him in the head with a rock. For Sean Penn, that actually represented a huge leap forward in his willingness to work with the paparazzi. You go, Sean!!

Paparazzi Privacy Laws

For every celebrity willing to cooperate with the paparazzi, there are plenty more who try to hide from them or want to attack them. With paparazzi following celebrities like deranged stalkers (but with better suits and more expensive cameras), it's only inevitable that celebrities and paparazzi clash in physical confrontations.

While Sean Penn regularly treats paparazzi like human punching bags, other celebrities have had their share of run-ins as well. Back in 1972, Jacqueline Kennedy Onassis ordered her secret service escort to destroy photographer Ron Galella's camera and film after he took pictures of her in New York City's Central Park. She then sued Galella, claiming harassment. Galella countersued, claiming Jackie O was just a bitch.

The trial lasted three weeks and became a groundbreaking case that resulted in Jacqueline Kennedy getting a restraining order to keep Galella 150 feet away from her and her children. The restriction was later dropped to 25 feet and was ultimately meaningless when Galella simply wore disguises so he could get as close as he wanted. (That just shows you the effectiveness of the American judicial system, so don't ever expect it to rule in your favor either when graft and corruption are much faster ways to get the justice you want in this country.)

In 2008 the actor Keanu Reeves allegedly hit a photographer with his car. Considering the quality of movies Keanu Reeves has appeared in recently, this event might actually be considered a highlight of his acting career.

In the United Kingdom, actress Sienna Miller and singer Amy Winehouse won injunctions to prevent the paparazzi from following them and gathering outside their houses. In the United States, in another twist of Paparazzi stories, the washed up actor/comedian Pauly Shore reportedly tried to win an injunction to force the paparazzi to follow him and gather outside his house to make him feel once again relevant in today's pop culture The paparazzi sued to avoid having their good names tarnished by associating with Pauly Shore, and a sympathetic judge ruled in their favor.

In 2012 the paparazzi captured photographs showing the Duchess of Cambridge sunbathing topless at her cousin's holiday home in France. The royal couple sued the French magazine *Closer*, claiming that the Duchess had a right to privacy. The magazine argued that the public also had a right to drool over pictures of her naked breasts while jerking off with a magazine from the comfort of their home. The court eventually ruled in favor of the royal couple, which meant that the only way the general public would be able to see the Royal Boobs would be if she decided to enter a wet T-shirt contest on a whim.

Perhaps the best-known and most tragic case of the paparazzi invading a celebrity's privacy occurred in 1997. In that year, Princess Diana and her boyfriend, Dodi Fayed, were attempting to flee the paparazzi by riding in a car driven by Henri Paul, who thought it would be a swell idea to engage in a high-speed car chase through a tunnel while intoxicated.

Their car crashed, the pursuing paparazzi sped off, and everyone soon remembered that drinking and driving don't go together. Then someone turned on the TV to watch another major sporting event whose outcome had no direct effect on anyone's personal life whatsoever, and everyone started drinking and driving again.

With everyone from rapper Kayne West grabbing a photographer's camera in Los Angeles airport and smashing it to the ground, to director Quentin Tarantino daring photographers to hit him, confrontations between celebrities and the paparazzi threatened to escalate out of control like your average, run-of-the-mill Middle East peace summit.

In 1999 California passed into law an invasion of privacy statute directed specifically at the paparazzi. The statute prohibits trespass onto another's property "with the intent to capture any type of visual image, sound recording, or other physical impression of the plaintiff engaging in a personal or familial activity." That means if your hot neighbor next door decides to sunbathe in the nude, you can't legally step on her property to get a better look (although don't despair—you *can* peek at her from the safety of your own home).

The law also creates the right to sue for "constructive invasion of privacy" while a plaintiff engages in the same activity described above under the statute, but there is no actual physical trespassing. Constructive invasion of privacy occurs when a defendant uses technology to capture images or sounds that would not have been otherwise accessible to them without trespassing. For example, wiretapping someone's phones without a warrant is wrong, unless you can claim you're looking for terrorists, Muslims, or pretty much any minority citizen who will likely gain much less sympathy from an all-white judge and jury.

One provision under the statute covers committing an assault or false imprisonment to obtain the same images or recordings. Essentially, if you surround a celebrity to prevent the person from moving, you're breaking the new anti-paparazzi law. Of course, if you can induce them to stick around with a baggy full of killer weed, then that's perfectly okay. Kudos to the creative photographer.

In addition, any "person who directs, solicits, actually induces, or actually causes another person" to engage in the activity prohibited by the paparazzi statute can also be held liable. This means that the judges can pretty much decide who might be guilty—including drivers, spotters, magazine publishers, and a general public that places a higher value on celebrity pictures than they do of pictures of their own family.

The new anti-stalking laws were meant to give celebrities the freedom to get drunk, smash their cars into telephone poles, snort cocaine, neglect their children, and punch each other in the face without the embarrassing scrutiny of a paparazzi photographer taking pictures nearby. While legitimate celebrities praised this law as a way to avoid unwanted public exposure (except when it came to making really bad movies; I'm looking at you, Eddie Murphy), there was a way to turn this law into an advantage.

The law specifically protected celebrities from the paparazzi, but what if you weren't a celebrity? If the celebrities didn't want free publicity, then the talentless, wannabe celebrities polluting the nightclubs of Hollywood could take advantage of the paparazzi's sudden desperation for someone to follow. And that was the first time an unknown socialite named Paris Hilton came up with a very good idea.

Paris, Kim, and the New Rules of the Fame Game

"Every woman should have four pets in her life. A mink in her closet, a jaguar in her garage, a tiger in her bed, and a jackass who pays for everything."—Paris Hilton

Paris Hilton was born into the vast Hilton hotel empire founded by Conrad Hilton. She grew up the privileged child of generations of money who had many opportunities handed to her simply because of her last name, but even she could never have dreamed that her stardom would reach the level that it did at its peak (and which she keeps desperately trying to recreate now that her fame has faded like a counterfeit hundred dollar bill left in a washing machine for too long).

At the age of nineteen Paris signed with Donald Trump's modeling agency, despite her misgivings over the furry creature that had somehow latched on to the top of Donald Trump's head. Shortly after that, Paris found herself appearing in numerous advertising campaigns for Iceberg Vodka, GUESS, Tommy Hilfiger, Christian Dior and Marciano, just to name a few. In 2001, at the age of twenty, Hilton began to develop a reputation as a socialite as the tabloids started taking notice of her partying ways because—as we have already established—tracking rich, young, attractive women is always more interesting than covering actual news.

Soon Paris's fame began to "extend beyond the New York tabloids" when several editorial magazines, including *Elle*, the April 2004 issue

Max Espinoza/Ruben Gerard

of *Maxim*, and the October 2005 cover of *Stuff*, asked Hilton to appear in their publication for a spotlight feature about herself.

It didn't take long before Paris began to make cameo appearances in timeless feature films such as *Zoolander* (2001). In 2002 she played one of the leads in the straight-to-video low-budget horror movie *Nine Lives*. Inexplicably, this film was number one on the horror-renting chart for a week before disappearing, but you'd be safe betting the farm it wasn't due to Paris's stellar performance. Beyondhollywood.com felt that "Hilton's presence in the cast is the film's main marketing point," which couldn't have made any of the other cast members happy since they actually took acting lessons and still wound up looking incompetent next to Paris Hilton.

Enter the Sex Tape

In 2004 a homemade sex tape called *1 Night in Paris* featuring Hilton and former boyfriend Rick Soloman was released by Red Light District Video. Soloman sold the film himself, and Paris claimed that the sex tape was leaked without her permission, which led to a defamation lawsuit that was eventually settled out of court.

Shortly after the release of her *1 Night in Paris* sex tape, Paris debuted her reality TV show, *The Simple Life*, on Fox. The timing of her sex tape revelation led many critics to claim that her leaked tape was just a crass ploy to gain publicity to help promote her new TV show. There's no evidence to support that theory but, again, let's just say it worked, so take notes and judge for yourself.

The Simple Life was a huge hit despite its lack of having any redeeming qualities whatsoever. The show centered around Hilton and her BFF Nicole Richie leaving Beverly Hills for a farm, where they'd be given (and ultimately screw up) tasks that they have never been dealt before, such as cleaning, cooking, working, and taking care of themselves in ways that most people learn at a very young age.

At just twenty-two years old, Paris Hilton had finally gained the fame she coveted, making her a frequent fixture of the Hollywood club scene and a feature on front pages of every known magazine and website.

More importantly, Paris parlayed her newfound fame and the media's growing fascination with celebrities to expand her persona and image into a **brand**. She worked tirelessly to turn her brand into one that could be just as powerful and memorable as DDT and Agent Orange. My futile attempt at cutting my sarcasm aside, keep in mind that by allowing herself to be photographed and videotaped everywhere she went, she became a walking endorsement for herself.

Paris hired a publicist to assist in getting her face on the pages of all the prominent newspapers including *The New York Times*, *Time*, and *The Weekly World News*. Interestingly, Paris never really talked about herself because that was one of many topics that she knew nothing about. Instead, she talked about other people. She would mention the designers of her clothes, the name of her favorite nightclub, and most importantly who made the sweater for her dog. Without a guarantee of any return, Paris just threw out free publicity for others.

Fashion designers and nightclub owners soon realized that Paris Hilton was a walking billboard, so they embraced her. She paid attention to them, they paid attention to her, and her endorsements brought crowds through the doors. Crowds through the doors meant money, and money meant a successful business model. The art of convincing gullible people to part with their hard-earned money is what is known in academic circles as "celebrity-based marketing."

The genius of Paris Hilton (which is probably the only time you'll ever see the words "genius" and "Paris Hilton" in the same sentence) emerged when Paris realized that if she were famous, the paparazzi would follow her everywhere she went, and then if she endorsed products, brands, and businesses, the paparazzi would dutifully report her inane recommendations across the globe. For Paris, the paparazzi became her version of Twitter except she could use more than 140 characters to deliver her message.

One of Paris's first ventures was her endorsement of the Parlux Fragrance, Inc. company's perfume called "Paris Hilton," a line of fragrances for both women and men with the tagline "Find out what it smells like to be a Star." Originally set to be a small release in 2004, the high demand led to a much wider launch that generated a 47 percent increase in sales of Parlux products that now include seventeen fragrances endorsed by Paris Hilton.

Enter & Exit the Music

In August 22, 2006, Hilton released her self-titled debut album, aptly named Paris. Given Paris's notoriety, the album reached number six on the Billboard 200 for a week, sold over 600,000 copies worldwide, and the first single, "Stars Are Blind," actually became a massive success around the globe. Unfortunately for Paris, it was her only hit single. Had she not been a global celebrity already, she'd be known simply as a one-hit wonder.

A month later on September 7—in what many think was the beginning of the end predicted by notable religious scholars as one of the signs of an upcoming Parisian Apocalypse—Paris was spotted by LAPD "driving erratically" and arrested for suspicion of driving under the influence. Her blood tests revealed a blood alcohol content of 0.08 percent. After pleading no contest to a reckless driving charge, the heiress was given thirty-six months of probation and fines totaling about $1,500, and her license was suspended in November.

Then in February 2007, police caught Paris driving 70 mph in a 35 mph zone with a suspended license. As part of her probation, the courts ordered Paris to enroll in an alcohol education program, preferably one that didn't have a cover charge and a two-drink minimum.

On May 4, 2007, Judge Michael T. Sauer sentenced Paris to forty-five days in jail for violating her probation. An appeal to the sentence was unsuccessful, and Paris began her jail term on June 5 of that year at the Century Regional Detention Facility, an all-female jail located in Lynwood, California.

Paris tried to appeal the sentence and even went so far as to ask the (then) California governor, Arnold Schwarzenegger, for a pardon. Arnold refused because he said he was too busy fathering a child with his housekeeper. What can I say? Arnold was master of the moral high ground, and Paris was out of luck.

After being released early from jail after three days because of an undisclosed medical condition, Paris thought she was free to go home with her ankle bracelet to serve the rest of her sentence under house arrest. That's when Judge Michael Sauer summoned her to reappear in court and sent her back to jail to serve out her original forty-five-day sentence.

Upon hearing the sentence, Hilton shouted, "It's not right!" and started screaming, which the paparazzi dutifully recorded to show everybody how upset celebrities can get when they can't use their fortune to circumvent justice like any law-abiding billionaire banking executive could do. We get it, this is truly a staggering injustice. While in jail, Paris met clergyman minister Marty Angelo, who taught her that ordinary people actually don't recognize Gucci as a disciple mentioned in the Bible.

Afterwards, Paris claimed a "new beginning" in her life, in which she hoped to live like any ordinary person who just happened to be worth millions of dollars and could reveal her wish to be normal during an interview with talk show host Larry King. Just like the rest of us ordinary folk.

Shortly afterwards, Paris's grandfather, Barron Hilton, pledged 97 percent of his estate (the Hilton family fortune was $1.2 billion) to a charitable organization founded by their great-grandfather, Conrad N. Hilton. Barron apparently did this to prevent spoiling his grandchildren, although it was probably too late anyway.

On July 2, 2010, authorities accused Paris of smoking marijuana at the 2010 FIFA World Cup game between Brazil and the Netherlands. Local police escorted her from the Nelson Mandela Bay Stadium. Paris's publicist, Dawn Miller, stated "I can confirm that the incident was a complete misunderstanding and it was actually another person in the group who did it." The case was dropped shortly after Paris's story checked out. Miller added, "The case has been dropped against Paris and no charges will be made. The authorities have apologized for wrongfully accusing her since she had nothing to do with the incident. Paris is having an incredible time at the World Cup." Clearly. Two weeks later, police detained Paris after catching her in possession of cannabis at Figari airport, Corsica, releasing her soon after, again without charge.

The suspicion of her fading star power came back in June 2011, when her reality show, *The World According to Paris* failed to get high ratings. When asked if her moment of fame had passed, Paris walked out of an interview with *Good Morning America*. Was this really the end of Paris Hilton, thereby proving the existence and benevolence of a higher being? Was she being outshined by other stars?

According to a 2011 poll conducted by Ipsos, 60 percent of the responders voted Paris Hilton as the most unpopular celebrity in America right above O. J. Simpson, Michael Vick and Wily E. Coyote. That being said, Paris Hilton reportedly earns ten million a year in sales of her various products that consumers are still buying-up off the shelves. Experts estimate her net worth to be over $100 million.

The paparazzi helped build Paris Hilton up, but it was her own behavior that helped to bring her down. The same paparazzi cameras that helped turn her into a celebrity also documented her long fall from grace.

The camera never lies—and the paparazzi gave no favors as she fell. While Paris struggled to remake herself with increasing diminishing returns, a protégé and former friend of Paris Hilton studied her methods, befriended the paparazzi, and managed to surpass her in worldwide popularity. The name of this new star, who has just as little talent as Paris Hilton, is Kim Kardashian.

Enter Kim Kardashian

"I couldn't sacrifice my heart for a publicity stunt."

—Kim Kardashian
Interview with Oprah in June 2012

Kim Kardashian's rise to fame looks strikingly similar to that of Paris Hilton. She too came from a respected and well-known Hollywood family that included her father, Robert Kardashian—a part of the team who helped clear O. J. Simpson of the murder of Ron Goldman and Nicole Simpson—and her stepfather Bruce Jenner, a 1976 Summer Olympic gold medalist who may have been one of the few athletes to succeed without the use of drug doping.

Despite her proximity to famous people, Kim Kardashian was a "no name" to the general public. It wasn't until Kim studied (and mastered) Paris Hilton's path to success and applied it effectively to her own life that people started to notice "Paris Hilton's brunette friend."

Kim started her career as a stylist, who helped friends rearrange their closets and sell their old clothes on eBay. She worked for celebrities including Hilton, Nicole Richie, and Lindsay Lohan, but it would be her friendship with Hilton that would allow Kim Kardashian to become what she has today, a rather pointless celebrity who makes responsible mothers of young KK fans across America want to cry—and throw out the TV.

Eventually people started asking who the attractive brunette at Paris's side was. Kim's face (and eventually her behind!) would start showing up in the magazines and on the blogs with Paris, though she had yet to do anything to really make a name for herself. It was from these inane beginnings that Kim Kardashian became a household name.

Enter . . . the Sex Tape

Looking for that "event" to cement her arrival, Kim Kardashian looked no further than her best friend Paris. A sex tape starring Kim Kardashian and Brandy's little brother Ray J was "leaked." Anything you can do I can do better, right? What can we say. It's the sincerest form of flattery. And lucrative too.

Adult film company Vivid Entertainment bought the rights to the video for $1 million and released the film as Kim Kardashian: Superstar. Like her fame mentor, Kim sued Vivid for ownership of the tape, but later dropped the suit when Vivid Entertainment gave her $5 million, which tells you how much she really objected to the sex tape after all.

Though Paris Hilton's tape just created a buzz for her soon-to-premiere reality show, Kim Kardashian's sex tape (which was better, by the way—at least in my humble opinion) is what earned her a reality TV show. Called *Keeping Up with the Kardashians*, the Ryan Seacrest-produced show followed the Kardashian family as they lived their everyday life running their store "Dash" in Calabasas, California. Seacrest described the series: "At the heart of the series, despite the catfights and endless sarcasm, is a family that truly loves and supports one another."

Her presence was becoming as large as her backside, providing plenty of fodder for the celebrity tabloids. What she was wearing, who she was dating, and where she was going became the subject of every blog, magazine, and entertainment news program out there. Kim even posed nude in the December 2007 issue of *Playboy* for a cool $1 million dollar paycheck. Whether she kept her clothes on or tore them off, Kim kept the world wanting to see more.

Since the tape with Ray J came out, Kim's relationships have been front-page news. She dated NFL star Reggie Bush and Dallas Cowboy wide-receiver Miles Austin. In 2010, Kim started dating NBA player Kris Humphries of the New Jersey Nets. They became engaged in May 2011

(Max Espinoza/Ruben Gerard

and married on August 20, 2011, during a heavily promoted, two-part TV special showing the preparations leading up to the ceremony followed by the wedding itself. Kim and Kris made a reported $17 million from the wedding. After just seventy-two days of marriage, Kim filed for divorce from Humphries, citing irreconcilable differences.

Several news outlets surmised that Kim's marriage to Humphries had been nothing but a publicity stunt to promote the Kardashian family's brand and their multiple television shows. There were even a few people close to Kim, including a former publicist, who claimed that her short-lived marriage was staged as a way to make some quick cash.

With all of her massive publicity and the accompanying throngs of paparazzi following her everywhere she goes, Kim continued the Paris Hilton road to fortune. Like Paris Hilton, Kim soon ventured out into various businesses with her name as the brand to attract customers.

In February 2008 Kim became the spokeswoman for Bongo Jeans. In March 2009 Kim launched an endorsement with ShoeDazzle, shopping as the cofounder and chief fashion stylist. In addition to opening new DASH stores in both Miami and New York City, Kim Kardashian and her sisters also designed and developed clothing lines for Bebe stores called "Virgins, Saints, and Angels."

Then in early 2012, the sisters launched an international line called the "Kardashian Kollection," which consisted of clothing, bedding, eyewear, and other items. By November 2012 the sisters were launching "Khroma Beauty." The Kardashian name has been on fragrances, handbags, water, and even a prepaid credit card. The empire has officially been assembled.

So just how has Kim been able to keep her post-sex-tape image clean, while remaining a regular fixture in the nightlife scene and at all of the biggest parties and events in Hollywood? She's kept busy and presumably stayed away from alcohol abuse, driving violations while impaired, and shoplifting. Aside from the negative criticism towards her failed marriage, she's technically never done anything horrible. Most impressively, unlike a few of her peers, she's avoided jail time.

Kim has exploited her fame to focus on her many businesses that generate what seems like an infinite income. And while people tend to grow tired of a single person or celebrity over time, as happened with Paris Hilton, Kim has taken a back seat at times to help promote her sisters, her mom, her brother, and even friends. Actions like these will keep the content fresh and the possibilities for earning big money endless.

In 2010 Kim's earnings were the highest among Hollywood-based reality stars, estimated at $6 million, and now according to Forbes in 2014 was worth $28 million. Although Paris Hilton's net worth is estimated at about $94 million more than Kim Kardashian's, no one will argue that Kim has clearly surpassed Paris in the area of fame.

Paris Hilton believes she is responsible for Kim Kardashian's celebrity status and at one point was reportedly "fuming" over her former friend's rise to fame. A source explains, "Paris thinks Kim wasn't a loyal friend and only used her to gain fame and that she is ungrateful for everything Paris claimed to do for her." In reply, Kim said she "couldn't care less." It's a reality star eat reality star world out there. Or something like that.

While Paris Hilton's stardom is on the decline, Kim Kardashian is poised to be around for some time, especially being the mother of Kanye West's child. Where Paris Hilton appears to the public as an attractive woman who uses her money and fame to break the law and get away with it, Kim Kardashian appears to the public as an attractive woman who uses her money and fame to stay within the law—while, of course, still not managing to do anything worthwhile. The court of public opinion is the most important court when it comes to staying relevant and making money.

Paris Hilton played the Fame Game well and got rich as a result. Kim Kardashian played the Fame Game better, and got rich and remains famous as a result. When the paparazzi trail Kim Kardashian, they're likely to capture pictures of her endorsing yet another one of her family's business ventures. When the paparazzi trail Paris Hilton, they're hoping to capture another train wreck in action.

Fame is a double-edged sword that can magnify your presence whether you're on the way up or on the way down. The camera doesn't care, but as its target, you should. Given the choice between Paris Hilton or Kim Kardashian, it's pretty obvious who will remain in the spotlight in the long run.

The Emergence of Tabloid Media Empires and Powerhouses

"People who read the tabloids deserve to be lied to."—Jerry Seinfeld

With me so far? Let's continue with our history lesson. The background info is important.

If you want to know what helped propel useless people like Paris Hilton and Kim Kardashian into the public spotlight, stand in any supermarket checkout aisle and you can't help noticing the lurid tabloid magazines right next to other impulse items like candy, gift cards, and deodorant. (Actually, deodorant is important. Strike from impulse purchase list.)

The whole purpose of tabloids is to embarrass celebrities. The second purpose of tabloids is to make ordinary people feel superior to celebrities. The third purpose of tabloids is to separate money from ordinary people who actually believe they could be superior to someone worth millions of dollars. In this sense, tabloids have been supremely successful for decades.

The word "tabloid" comes from the London-based pharmaceutical company Burroughs Wellcome & Co., considered by some as an early forerunner of a Mexican drug cartel. Back in the late 1880s, people used to buy poorly tested medicines that contained potentially dangerous side effects, but—shockingly—still wouldn't give you an erection for longer than four hours. (I know: I said the E word. But more importantly, four hours should work for most people. Right?) Since most medicine back then came in powder form, people came up with the bright idea of ingesting their medicine up their nose through a rolled-up dollar bill.

This inconvenient method of ingesting medicine proved too far ahead of its time, so the popular Burroughs Wellcome & Co. started compressing powder into small, easy-to-take and more easily absorbed tablets that they trademarked as "Tabloid" pills. They then used this word for all of the company's successfully marketed products.

Soon the connotation of tabloid was applied to other small items and was used in journalism to refer to collections of condensed or "compressed" stories that were both simplified, easy to read stories and printed on roughly 17 by 11 inch paper half the size of a newspaper "broadsheet." (And that would be better rolled around a cardboard tube and hung within easy reach of anyone sitting on a toilet. And was not the quality soft stuff either.)

The checkout-stand publication that reshaped society originated in 1952, when Italian publisher Generoso Pope Jr. bought New York's *National Enquirer* racing tip sheet for $75,000. Before then, America's favorite tabloid focused solely on thoroughbred racing news and the lurid headlines could only have been things like "I Had Sex with Seabiscuit!" or "War Admiral Sires a Centaur That Looks Suspiciously Like J. Edgar Hoover!"

Pope immediately changed the focus of the tabloid from racing thoroughbreds to the bizarre and grisly. Correctly guessing that Americans would gravitate towards blood and guts, this new version of the *National Enquirer* quickly rose to a million copies a week.

Besides catering to the public's base instincts, the *National Enquirer* also created a revolutionary distribution system by selling copies in neighborhood grocery stores all over America. Instead of creating their own salacious moments, Americans could now read about the depraved lifestyles of others at their kitchen tables.

In the early days, the *National Enquirer* fabricated sensational stories and enticing headlines to create sales while attracting customers that still held the naive belief that "they couldn't print it if it wasn't true." Decades later, the idea of fabricating stories would form the cornerstone of popular shows involving Rush Limbaugh, Glenn Beck, and pretty much everyone on Fox News.

The *National Enquirer* also pioneered the idea of annoying celebrities by making up stories about them for the public to believe. Tabloid reporters would pose as bellboys, cops, or even funeral workers to get a scoop on these stars. If they couldn't get a good story legitimately, they frequently just made them up. Did you see the movie *Idiocracy*? It's worth watching.

In 1968 Pope overhauled the *National Enquirer* to appeal to more mainstream Americans who lived in trailer parks and were missing most of their teeth through poor dental hygiene and heavy methamphetamine use. Instead of focusing on weird sex and gore, the *National Enquirer* started emphasizing upbeat stories, supernatural phenomenon, miracle diets, and even more celebrity gossip, since people were starting to get tired of seeing live video on the news showing Vietnamese children getting napalmed in their villages. The unreal is just more compelling, and an irresistible distraction. Circulation jumped to three million as Americans all over the country sought confirmation that they weren't as gullible as they looked. (They failed.)

To compete for the minds of people with too much free time and money on their hands, more tabloids started appearing with original names like *People* and *Us Magazine*. In 1974 these tabloids focused on stories about major stars like Sonny and Cher because people were amazed that anyone who looked like Sonny could actually have sex with a hot chick like Cher. By this time, circulation in the *National Enquirer* had climbed to over five million copies a week, which meant there were at least five million Americans with some small disposable income to burn on whatever.

The tabloids linked the incredibly popular Cher to everyone living and dead, sleeping with everyone but poor Sonny. No matter what bizarre details the tabloids printed, people believed these things about their favorite stars just like they believed their single vote actually impacts the direction of American democracy. (It doesn't.)

Initially, the tabloids treated celebrities with grudging respect. That all changed when the tabloids learned they could trample over the privacy of celebrities and sell more magazines and newspapers in the process. Let's take a moment to pay homage to the gods of unbridled commercialism. But again, it is what it is. Moving on.

The Appeal of Dead Celebrities

On August 16, 1977, Elvis Presley died. The *National Enquirer* managed to publish a picture of Elvis lying embalmed in his coffin and sales shot through the roof, peaking at seven million copies a week. The tabloids knew that celebrity news sold papers, but they suddenly realized that dead celebrities sold even more papers.

Later that same year, Bing Crosby passed away. The *National Enquirer* went to great lengths to get a photo of Bing Crosby in his coffin, even bribing a funeral home worker. When John Lennon's coffin appeared on the cover, the public suddenly pretended to be disgusted while they pushed sales of the *National Enquirer* up to 5.9 million copies a week in 1978.

By 1979 the *National Enquirer* had started adding full color covers and color photo spreads. It may have been because black and white pictures no longer captured an image accurately—unless, of course, it was a "before and after" picture of Michael Jackson's skin color.

In the 80s, tabloid celebrity gossip burst on TV with shows like *Hard Copy, Entertainment Tonight, A Current Affair,* and *We Don't Care about Our Own Neighbors but Tell Us More about a Celebrity.* Suddenly, Americans could learn the latest celebrity gossip without having to read, and sales of newsstand tabloids started to plummet. In 1988, with sales down to 4.3 million, the *National Enquirer* and its sister publication *Weekly World News* were sold for $412.5 million, and then later sold again to American Media.

Suing the Tabloids

With tabloids publishing both real and fabricated stories about celebrities, celebrities started to fight back by suing, making lawyers on both sides exceedingly happy. The first case against the modern tabloids went to trial in 1976 when Carol Burnett sued the *Enquirer* for falsely reporting that she was drunk in public.

Shirley Jones and her husband Marty Ingels went to court in 1977 over the *National Enquirer* headline, "Husband's Bizarre Behavior Driving Shirley Jones to Drink." Paul Lynde unsuccessfully hit the *National Enquirer* up for $10 million in 1979 because "an insider" claimed Lynde was forced to leave the Hollywood Squares because his costars objected "to his drinking and nastiness."

In 1981 Cher actually won a $663,234 judgment against the *Star* tabloid for misappropriation of her image for commercial purposes. Even Elizabeth Taylor sued the *National Enquirer* in the nineties over a headline that read: "While Doctor's Battle to Save Her Life . . . Liz Boozes It Up in Hospital."

In the old days, tabloids had to make up stories. Then they started to dig up dirt on celebrities through every means possible, even resorting to wiretapping phones, which eventually brought down the British tabloid, *News of the World.* (No big loss there.) Nowadays, tabloids have it much, much easier. They can get their information from disgruntled assistants to the stars who willingly sell insider information for extra cash. (If you're willing to pay a little more, you might get some of these insiders to sell their bodies for cash too. And internal organs. And family members.)

The Changing Tabloid Market

For years, tabloids with names like *News of the World, Grazia, People, US Weekly, Star,* and the *National Enquirer* dominated the tabloid market, and provided inexpensive newspapers to housebreak puppies all over the world.

Of course, tabloids just present celebrity gossip news, but there's an entire underground economy that thrives on supporting these tabloids, much like a bra that supports the oversized, surgically enhanced breasts of a washed-up celebrity who thinks bigger boobs will make her more popular. (She's right.)

One of the more prominent entertainment text and photo service providers is the World Entertainment News Network (commonly known as WENN). Headquartered in London (to capture gossip about the Royal Family and their crazy antics living off British taxpayer money), the company also has offices in Los Angeles (to capture gossip about the crazy movie stars), New York (to capture gossip about crazy movie stars who think that moving to the East Coast suddenly makes them more intelligent), Las Vegas (to capture gossip about crazy celebrities drinking, having sex, and gambling), and Berlin (to capture gossip about those crazy former East Germans who still can't adapt to democracy and capitalism). It's a well-rounded, international network of unending lucrative fluff.

WENN provides breaking entertainment news, images, and text features to newspapers, magazines, radio stations, television networks, mobile phone companies, and websites including Yahoo UK Entertainment News and IMDb.com. If they could, they would also sell photoshopped images of celebrities having sex with each other, but that would be considered illegal, so they focus on selling actual images of celebrities having sex with each other instead.

WENN originally launched as an entertainment news wire service in 1989 called the World Rock News Network (WRNN). The company provided music news to MTV, BBC, and ABC. Surprisingly, one of their original clients also included Russia's daily youth newspaper, *Komsomolskaya Pravda,* because nothing says fun and entertainment better than a newspaper that was once the official mouthpiece of the Soviet communist party.

When even stories about the music industry proved less profitable than more important news like knowing which celebrities were sleeping with each other, the company changed its name to the World Entertainment News Network (WENN) and switched to covering the more lucrative celebrity news and photos market. Why risk getting killed trying to uncover photographic evidence of human rights violations in Third World countries supported by Western democracies, when it's so much easier and more profitable to get a picture of Britney Spears stepping out of a limousine not wearing any underwear? No contest there.

Another company that secretly feeds off the celebrity gossip industry is Getty Images, a stock photo agency based in Seattle, Washington. Getty Images supplies stock images for business and consumers with an archive of eighty million still images and illustrations and more than fifty hours of stock film footage. Despite their vast archives, none of the images in the Getty library include pictures that most people would really want to pay to view. (Yes, I am speaking of pornography.)

The Rise of Tabloid Alternatives

Perhaps the biggest threats to tabloid newspapers are celebrity gossip news websites such as TMZ. The name TMZ stands for the historic "studio zone" or thirty-mile demilitarized zone radius from the intersection of West Beverly Boulevard and North La Cienega Boulevard in Los Angeles. Since so many Hollywood executives travel through this area, it tends to be the most heavily guarded areas by the Los Angeles police department, which protects the rich and ignores the poor—unfortunately, like most police departments around the world.

TMZ debuted on November 8, 2005, as a collaboration between AOL (otherwise known as that annoying Internet company that used to send CDs to everyone) and Telepictures Productions, a division of Warner Bros. At the time of the launch, AOL confirmed that the site was a desperate attempt to remain relevant. To that end, the TMZ site would primarily feature Hollywood gossip, including interviews, photos, and video footage of celebrities.

The site was described as "an effort to further feed the current American obsession with celebrities," since we have already established that most Americans are definitively non-obsessed with more trivial matters such as solving poverty, conquering world hunger, and eradicating infectious diseases. TMZs managing editor is Harvey Levin, a lawyer-turned-journalist who claims that TMZ does not pay for stories or interviews. Speaking like a typical lawyer, (my sincere apologies to the rare "good" lawyer out there) Levin admits that TMZ does "sometimes pay sources for leads on stories," which to any rational mind is basically the same thing as paying for stories and interviews.

A companion TV series, TMZ on TV, debuted on September 10, 2007. TMZ on TV's unofficial goal should be, "to further dumb down the average American to the point where their intelligence could be easily mistaken for a houseplant." This goal is what George W. Bush was really referring to when he landed on the aircraft carrier USS Abraham Lincoln and proudly stated "Mission Accomplished!"

TMZ's huge advantage over tabloid newspapers is that they can report and deliver celebrity news almost as quickly as it happens. In comparison, tabloids must remain limited to a fixed publishing schedule, and celebrities rarely misbehave exactly on cue (but—thankfully—predictably enough to spawn the billion-dollar celebrity gossip industry).

On July 28, 2006, TMZ.com was the first to report that actor Mel Gibson had been arrested for driving under the influence of alcohol. As part of this report, TMZ included the original eight-page report written by the arresting officer, before the officer was allegedly instructed by his superiors to omit inflammatory details about Gibson's alleged anti-Semitic comments and behavior.

What shocked the American public was that Mel Gibson had been caught driving drunk, not that the police department had engaged in a cover up to lie about the truth (since police corruption isn't anything new to anyone who has been living longer than a few years in any country on the planet).

On November 7, 2006, as TMZ.com continued their gallant quest to report breaking news on the trivial, TMZ was the first to report that pop singer Britney Spears had filed a petition for divorce from then-husband Kevin Federline. This had immediate global impact; guys all over the world began to fantasize that they might nail Britney in bed one day if they really got lucky.

Then on May 3, 2007, TMZ was the first to break the story that socialite Paris Hilton would be sentenced to forty-five days in jail for driving with a suspended license—after losing her license as a penalty for driving under the influence four months earlier. This again had global impact; guys all over the world began to fantasize that they might

Mel Gibson at *American Gangster* industry screening in 2007
(GL/PR Photos)

nail Paris in jail one day if they got lucky enough to work in the woman's prison as a security guard. On February 22, 2009, TMZ released a police evidence photo of pop singer Rihanna's bruised and battered face after ex-partner Chris Brown reportedly beat her up. Then guys all over the world could fantasize about beating Chris Brown up so they could nail Rihanna one day. And so on and so on. Not to jump to conclusions, but there may be a pattern here.

TMZ first broke the news of Michael Jackson's death on June 25, 2009, with a scoop that beat even the major broadcast and cable news outlets by almost three hours. TMZ was also the first to receive the coroner's report of the singer on February 8, 2010, proving Propofol dosage and negligence killed the legendary pop star. Of course, there were conspiracy theorists who were still claiming that Michael Jackson was actually still alive and hanging around with Elvis Presley in Las Vegas.

The Rising Credibility of Tabloids (and the Decline of Traditional News)

As the popularity of tabloid newspapers, websites, and television shows sky-rocketed, the traditional media outlets soon found themselves facing declining ratings. Rather than focus on more in-depth reporting, these outlets decided to focus on more frivolous topics that didn't require any reporting at all.

On September 14, 2011, popular TV host Anderson Cooper decided to go hard news and showed viewers his first-ever spray tan. To lend additional credibility to his reporting, Cooper relied on the advice and expertise of Jersey Shore's Nicole "Snooki" Polizzi. It was a riveting clip of national importance.

While the traditional media embraced trivia as news, the tabloid gossip news started shifting towards actual reporting that the traditional news media had long since abandoned as unprofitable. As tabloid competition began to heat up, the *National Enquirer* decided to become more journalistically responsible and fact-check their articles, while the major news media outlets went the other direction. Instead of fabricating stories, the *National Enquirer* now required two independent sources for each story.

In a fascinating turn, the *National Enquirer* actually began breaking real news stories. Their reporters rummaged through Secretary of State Henry Kissinger's trash to find classified documents in 1975, uncovered proof of Joan Kennedy's alcoholism, exposed governmental waste, and discovered crucial evidence in the O. J. Simpson trial. In the meantime, the March 17, 1975 cover of *Time* magazine showed a half-naked picture of Cher. It was Twilight Zone in our media world.

And there were tabloid stories of genuine international impact. On February 24, 2009, TMZ.com broke the story that out of the $1.6 billion Chicago's Northern Trust Bank received in federal bailout money (which they never requested and were hesitant to accept), most of that cash went towards entertaining clients in Los Angeles at venues like the House of Blues that featured performances by Chicago, Earth Wind and Fire, and Sheryl Crow along with gift bags from Tiffany & Co.

Shortly after TMZ.com published the story, United States Congressman Barney Frank demanded that Northern Trust repay the money it received in the bailout (or perhaps at least give him a cut). Northern Trust CEO Frederick Waddell quickly sent a letter to members of the House Financial Services Committee, stating that the bank would repay the money "as quickly as prudently possible." When Northern Trust finally repaid the TARP money on June 17, 2009, taxpayers received a 14 percent return on the investment, beating all major market indices over the same time period. Whether the government will spend the money wisely to benefit the nation or simply waste the money through lack of oversight of and outright corruption remains to be seen. (Can you guess the likely outcome?)

In 2010 former presidential candidate John Edwards had an affair and a child with mistress Rielle Hunter. The first news outlet to break the story? The *National Enquirer*, the tabloid whose former reputation was based on stories about Big Foot cooperating with the CIA as a spy and space aliens beaming instructions directly into the White House to inform the president of a fabulous new diet to lose weight by eating candy bars. (I didn't buy the candy bar part; it's just not realistic.)

The Pulitzer Prize board even made the *National Enquirer's* news staff eligible for the coveted prize in two categories: investigative reporting and national news reporting. Besides forcing Edwards to finally admit he had fathered a child, the *National Enquirer's* revelations also led to a federal investigation into whether Edwards' campaign broke any laws by continuing to pay Hunter after she stopped working for the campaign. That's because we all know it's completely legal for people to collect a paycheck after they stop working for an employer. Such people are usually just called "union workers." (Yes I went Washington again. Sorry.)

While the *National Enquirer* was earning a Pulitzer Prize nomination for investigating John Edwards, *Time* magazine chose to run a story about football (the American kind that involves steroids, not the soccer kind that also involves steroids) for its February 8, 2010 cover story. In the spirit of investigative reporting to support a free press, *Newsweek* took a sexy photograph of Sarah Palin posing in shorts, and made that their November 11, 2009 cover story. This is serious journalism!

Another illustration is the popular show *The Daily Show with Jon Stewart*, which provides more insight into world events than traditional news media like the *New York Times* and CBS News. Ironically, *The Daily Show* specializes in political comedy and satirical news while airing on the Comedy Central network. When a comedy show provides more insightful news coverage than the news, perhaps the last laugh is on the long-cherished belief that traditional news media outlets actually care about reporting the truth.

Viva Las Vegas! Lessons from the Sin City

"Las Vegas is sort of like how God would do it if he had money."
—Steve Wynn

Celebrity gossip sites and tabloids follow celebrities in their natural habitat, which usually involves Hollywood, New York, Miami, and, of course, the Betty Ford Clinic. However, one city that has attracted its share of celebrity news due to its proximity to Hollywood is Las Vegas, located in the arid state of Nevada.

Nevada was the first state to legalize casino-style gambling. They were also the first state to unofficially legalize organized crime, money laundering, and burials of murder victims in shallow graves on the outskirts of the desert. Yet how did Las Vegas become the entertainment powerhouse of the world when every city, from the smallest corrupt town along the Mexican border to the largest corrupt capital of the United States, offers escort services, call girls, strip clubs, and topless dancers?

It didn't come just from legalized gambling designed to siphon Social Security checks from senior citizens (who need their often-dwindling funds more than any of us). Nor did it come from gut-busting buffets that throw away more food every day than the entire population of the African continent eats in a decade. (And gives us plenty of cholesterol.)

To truly understand the power of Las Vegas in the entertainment world, we have to delve into a little bit of history. Fortunately, it's a familiar history of sex, drugs, and paparazzi, so we will all stay interested.

The History of Las Vegas

At midnight on October 1, 1910, Nevada passed a strict antigambling law—one that even banned the Western custom of flipping a coin for the price of a drink. The *Nevada State Journal* newspaper in Reno proudly reported: "Stilled forever is the click of the roulette wheel, the rattle of dice, and the swish of cards." In that same issue, the *Nevada State Journal* also reported that world peace had now descended upon the universe for a thousand years and that the first two international peace conferences were scheduled for July 28, 1914 (the day World War One began), and September 1, 1939 (the day World War Two began).

Three weeks later, gamblers set up underground casinos because no matter how you spin it, morality and ethics aren't nearly as profitable as vice. Illegal gambling happily flourished until 1931, when the Nevada Legislature officially made gambling legal again, although nobody could tell the difference.

Originally, Nevada legalized gambling to raise money for public schools, which is like a church running a brothel to raise money for Sunday school. I'm not complaining. After all, brothels need good institutional backing. Today, more than 34 percent of the state's general fund from legal gambling goes straight into public education after passing through the hands of prostitutes, drug dealers, and corrupt politicians.

In return, Nevada's public school system has rewarded voters by getting ranked last of all the fifty states for three years in a row. Nevada school children have even been known to sell their textbooks to pawn shops and put that money in a slot machine to ensure that they will continue having a school that they won't want to attend.

Las Vegas actually thrived during the Great Depression. Not only were there plenty of jobs in the casinos to whet the public's appetite for losing money faster than a government agency, but there were also plenty of jobs in the construction industry, like building the Hoover Dam (and taking leftover concrete to encase the feet of rival mob figures to make their deaths look like they accidentally drowned while jet skiing on the Colorado River—except jet skis hadn't been invented yet. Minor detail.)

During World War Two, the military set up what would later become Nellis Air Force Base. This air base brought in a sudden influx of military personnel that helped fuel the Las Vegas hooker market for years to come.

In 1941 hotelman Tommy Hull built the El Rancho Vegas Hotel-Casino. Originally designed to accommodate the growing bed demand caused by a surplus of military personnel with a lack of hotel rooms for them to privately bang a hooker, the success of the El Rancho Vegas triggered a building boom. This boom only recently ended with the completion of the giant, billion-dollar CityCenter project that finally brought the number of hotel rooms equal to the number of prostitutes in Las Vegas.

Organized Crime Brings Entertainment (and Nobody Saw Anything)

The most celebrated resort was the Flamingo Hotel, built by mobster Benjamin "Bugsy" Siegel, a member of the Meyer Lansky and Luciano crime organizations and an admired friend of many Hollywood stars. Six months after he opened the Flamingo, Siegel was murdered by a shotgun blast as he sat in the living room of a home in Beverly Hills, California. Police ruled his death "an accident."

Las Vegas soon built its reputation as an adult playground where people from all over the world could come to get VD. To attract visitors, casinos started offering entertainment such as singers, comedians, strippers, instrumentalists, dancers, and those really cute escorts who will show up at your hotel room whenever you need some company late at night.

To separate themselves from the competition, casinos began promoting unique stage spectaculars as their main entertainment feature. The Stardust casino imported the Lido de Paris from France, which was acclaimed by critics as even more fabulous than the original Paris version because at least the Las Vegas performers shaved their armpits and took showers.

The Tropicana Hotel bought the American rights to the spectacular Folies Bergère—so spectacular that most Americans don't even know how to pronounce its name. The Riviera Hotel offered gay singer Liberace a then unheard of salary of $50,000 a week. The Riviera was run by a man named Gus Greenbaum, who had formerly run the Flamingo Hotel. When Gus Greenbaum and his wife were found in their home with both of their throats slit open, police ruled their deaths "an accident." So many accidents in Las Vegas.

During the 50s and 60s, casino lounges also provided continuous entertainment from dusk to dawn at no charge to the customer except for the cost of one or more overpriced and highly-diluted drink. Soon these lounges became major entertainment attractions, filled with well-known names like Don Rickles, Buddy Hackett, Shecky Greene, Alan King, Louis Prima and Keely Smith, the Mary Kaye Trio, and many others that only your grandparents will remember to this day.

In contrast to other casinos promoting big-name entertainers, Binion's Horseshoe casino opted to focus solely on gambling. Then former Binion's Horseshoe owner Lonnie "Ted" Binion was found dead in his Las Vegas home. The cause of death appeared to be a drug overdose, a shotgun blast to the back of the head, multiple stab wounds in the back, decapitation with a chainsaw, and fourth degree burns over 90 percent of his body caused by an exploding car bomb that went off when he turned the ignition key. Shall we say it together? Police ruled his death "an accident."

Publicity Stunts and Celebrity Infatuation

As Las Vegas grew, casinos competed for Social Security dollars from senior citizens dragging oxygen tanks behind them, East coasters willing to gamble away all the hard-earned cash they had generated by excelling in math in their private schools while still failing to realize the odds were against them, and gullible tourists who actually thought they were special because casinos gave them free drinks while they played the slot machine.

While each casino offered main and secondary shows as lures to bring in customers, their offerings all began to blur erratically like the mind of Mel Gibson (when giving another drunken, anti-Semite rant as he propositions a Jewish female police officer). Between competing magic shows, musical acts, topless dancers, and comedy acts, every casino offered something different. Yet they all tended to offer the same thing, which felt like everyone was just selling thirty different flavors of vanilla. That's when casinos started running publicity stunts.

Caesars Palace ran one of the most notoriously famous publicity stunts in Las Vegas history. On New Year's Day in 1968, Caesars Palace invited people to watch daredevil Evel Knievel attempt to jump the famous fountains in front of Caesars Palace on his motorcycle.

Evel Knievel jumped 151 feet across the fountains, but upon landing, he lost control of his vehicle. As horrified spectators looked on, Knievel somersaulted over and over again, suffering a shattered pelvis, fractured hip, and smashed right femur. Surgeons had to rebuild his leg with a two-foot-long, three-inch-wide strip of steel, and his injuries put him in a coma for twenty-nine days.

The Caesars Palace crash brought Knievel instant fame. ABC-TV immediately bought the rights to the film of the jump since they knew the American public would be easily amused watching someone almost get killed. ABC-TV later tried to purchase the film rights to the My Lai massacre in Vietnam and the Kent State massacre where National Guardsman gunned down unarmed American college students, but the American military outbid them and the actual film footage has never been seen since.

Fans immediately clamored for Evel Knievel to repeat his stunt but this time either land properly or go all the way and spread his DNA across the asphalt. (We never said fans were sensitive.) Since Evel Knievel could barely walk and nobody else thought risking death was worth the price of fame (performing unnatural sexual favors is the preferred method for becoming famous), the casinos had to attract

attention in other ways. To do that, the casinos turned to the most popular celebrities of the day.

People love celebrities. Then again, people have loved pet rocks,
Hello Kitty, and the New Kids on the Block, which proves most people
aren't that smart in the first place. What makes celebrities so attractive
is the unnatural desire for ordinary people to feel honored just to see a
celebrity in person. Even if the celebrity didn't do anything of importance (which is something celebrities specialize in doing twenty-four
hours a day), people still wanted to see them live. If people could see a
celebrity actually doing something, that makes the appearance of that
celebrity all the more exciting.

A second reason casinos love celebrities was that celebrities are often
powder kegs of emotion that have all the stability of nitroglycerine. Put
a celebrity in public and chances were extremely high that celebrity
would do something foolish. The dumber the act or behavior, the more
free publicity the casino gets

Since people are happy seeing a celebrity in person and celebrities
often attract free publicity through their moronic behavior, the casinos
soon found their answer to generating publicity: get more celebrities
into the casinos as either as guests or performers, and wait for something exciting (dumb, idiotic, crazy) to happen.

Frank Sinatra and His Nonexistent Mafia Connections

In September 1951 Frank Sinatra made his Las Vegas debut at the Desert Inn. A month later, the second season of *The Frank Sinatra Show*
began on CBS Television. Few people remember that Frank Sinatra ever
had a TV show because his persona projected an arrogance that people
wouldn't accept from a television celebrity—that is, until *American Idol*
introduced the public to Simon Cowell.

Despite his lack of success as a television celebrity, Frank Sinatra
still proved popular as an entertainer in Las Vegas, frequently associated
with various Mafia figures who—of course—were always completely
innocent of all charges levied against them by the FBI. I believe it. As
part of the "Rat Pack" that consisted of Dean Martin, Peter Lawford,
Joey Bishop, and Sammy Davis Jr. (the token black guy long before it
became fashionable to have a token black guy), Frank Sinatra ruled the
Las Vegas Strip during the 1960s.

People often came to Las Vegas just to see Sinatra. In fact, more people came to see Sinatra than actually left Las Vegas. (Their bodies are still buried somewhere in the desert for crossing the mob.) Under the protection of the mob (a protection that doesn't exist and never has in Las Vegas), Frank Sinatra soon became a Las Vegas icon. If anyone wanted to cross Frank Sinatra, they had to be more powerful than him and his nonexistent Mafia backers. That person turned out to be an eccentric, sometimes naked billionaire who urinated in glass jars (yes we mentioned this already but I am fascinated) called Howard Hughes.

Howard Hughes had a history of enmity with Sinatra dating back to the time when Sinatra starred in several movies for Hughes's RKO Pictures movie studio. Unlike most people who thought celebrities were perfect in every way, Hughes wanted to put Sinatra in his place.

Hughes has just bought the Sands Hotel and Casino when Sinatra showed up to enjoy himself. As a Las Vegas icon, Frank Sinatra claimed near royalty status in every casino he visited, but this time he had a falling out with the Sands management after the casino cut off his credit under direct orders from Hughes.

Furious, an angry and drunk Sinatra drove a golf cart through a plate glass window at the Sands, threw chips in the face of a casino employee, and defied hotel security officers who tried to quiet him. Next he staggered into the Garden Room, the Sands' twenty-four-hour restaurant, where he found casino manager Carl Cohen, and overturned his table.

Even back then, such outrageous behavior from a celebrity generated tons of publicity. Frank Sinatra soon stopped performing at the Sands and appeared at Caesars Palace instead. Yet rather than suffer from his temper tantrum, Frank Sinatra simply made himself more popular than before. Unknowingly, Frank Sinatra helped usher in the era of celebrity and publicity gimmicks. Thank you, Frank.

Elvis Presley in Las Vegas

The first time Elvis Presley performed in Las Vegas, he appeared at the New Frontier hotel, billed as "The Atomic Powered Singer." Already popular with teens, Elvis Presley was not the typical Las Vegas Strip entertainer. Since the typical Las Vegas crowd consisted of a unique class of senior citizens who thought the world was a better place forty years ago, they tended not to like anything new.

Elvis wouldn't gain fame from appearing in Las Vegas. (Las Vegas, like the rest of show business, only wants you after you're already famous so they don't have to mail as many press releases letting people know how famous you really are.) Instead, Elvis parlayed his fame as a singer in movies. In 1963 he appeared in the hit movie *Viva Las Vegas*, which costarred Ann-Margret. The movie became a huge success, but not because it was critically acclaimed and selected as worthy of preservation by the Library of Congress. Instead, *Viva Las Vegas* was deemed successful because it cost only $1 million to make but earned $5 million in revenue.

Of course, once Elvis became famous in the movies, he became even more famous as a singer, which makes absolutely no sense when you think about it. However, that's how the Fame Game works. Get famous in your area of expertise. Then get more publicity doing something you're not that good at. Become famous for doing that, and people will suddenly "discover" you for what you were really good at in the first place.

When Elvis performed his first show at the International Hotel that had just opened in 1969, he sold out his show for the next seven years. In one twenty-nine-day period, Elvis entertained 101,509 guests, of which 101,508 had probably just lost money gambling in the casinos. Whenever Elvis performed, one in two visitors to Las Vegas saw his show, and most of them even stayed sober when they did it.

In 1971 the International changed its name to the Las Vegas Hilton. Decades later, Paris Hilton would forever tarnish the Hilton hotel brand, but until that occurred, more people saw Elvis perform at the Las Vegas Hilton than anywhere else in the world. (Of course, if people tried to watch Elvis perform in Istanbul or Budapest, they wouldn't have seen him at all because he was never there.)

When Elvis died (although some would argue that he's still alive, performing Friday nights in Las Vegas as an Elvis impersonator so people won't recognize him), he helped establish Las Vegas as the one place you could see a celebrity without stalking them in Los Angeles. Elvis helped turned Las Vegas into the entertainment capital of the world. Hollywood might create celebrities, but Las Vegas was where you could see them in person without their bodyguard shoving you to the ground and smashing your camera on the sidewalk.

(Max Espinoza/Ruben Gerard

While both Frank Sinatra and Elvis were already famous before appearing in Las Vegas, the Emerald City of Nevada would soon find they could create celebrities on their own. Among the most famous Las Vegas celebrities were two German magicians called Siegfried & Roy.

Siegfried & Roy and Their Not-So-Tame Animals

Siegfried and Roy met on a German ocean liner in 1959 when Siegfried worked as a cabin steward and Roy worked as a waiter. Skipping over the lurid details of what they did after they met and got familiar with each other in the privacy of their own cabins, Siegfried started performing magic for some of the passengers and eventually got his own show with Roy as his assistant.

Unbeknownst to the crew, Roy had smuggled a cheetah named Chico aboard the vessel, and that's how Siegfried and Roy became known for performing magic around wild animals capable of mauling you to death in front of a sold-out audience. (More on that later.)

After developing their show using ocean liner passengers as their test audience, they started performing around the world with occasional appearances in Las Vegas. Eventually they started becoming so popular that even Las Vegas wanted to leech off their growing fame. That's how they wound up with their own show at the Frontier Hotel and Casino where they stayed for seven years and not once bothered to tip the bartender.

In 1990 Steve Wynn, manager of The Mirage Hotel and Casino, hired the pair for an annual guarantee of $57.5 million. In 2001 they signed a lifetime contract with the hotel. Then in 2003, that contract almost ended when Roy Horn (who represents the "Roy" portion of Siegfried & Roy) was attacked by one of his white tigers named Montecore.

A woman in the audience reportedly tried to reach out and pet the white tiger, and Roy stepped between the white tiger and this foolish woman. The tiger then grabbed Horn's neck and dragged him off stage (to protect him from further exposure to the woman). And that was the last time Siegried and Roy performed with their white tigers ever again.

What Siegfried & Roy taught the world was that Las Vegas wasn't just a place where you could see famous celebrities, but also a rare place where people with actual talent could be turned into celebrities after decades of hard work.

Celebrities Behaving Badly

While nobody really wanted to see Roy Horn get mauled by a white tiger, people do enjoy the train wrecks celebrities make of their lives while visiting Las Vegas. As a result, people often come to Las Vegas to see celebrities perform and possibly see their favorite ones doing something crazy that they could film and put on YouTube.

Robin Leach (the entertainment celebrity reporter with the annoying voice who somehow managed to turn the audio equivalent of fingernails on a chalkboard into his distinctive brand) loved to party in Las Vegas. On May 31, 1999, Leach began engaging in questionable acts with several female companions at a table in the Delmonico Steakhouse at the Venetian. Many of his female companions peeled off their clothes, which neighboring diners assumed was just part of the show for buying a two-drink minimum. One woman even stretched out naked on the table while her companions spread whipped cream and chocolate all over her body. Just a day in the life of Vegas.

Waiting for celebrities to misbehave was unpredictable, so casinos turned to more predictable events to attract an audience. If there's one thing people in Las Vegas enjoy most, it's cheering for two people to beat each other up. Celebrities often turn out at such boxing events, which makes boxing matches another draw for the average person who might catch a glimpse of their favorite celebrities picking their nose. On June 28, 1997, Mike Tyson was disqualified after the third round after biting reigning champ Evander Holyfield twice on the ear. The bizarre finish stunned the crowd who had expected a show, but not one bordering on the edge of cannibalism.

Another bizarre event occurred during the Evander Holyfield's boxing match with Riddick Bowe. (Conspiracy theorists likely believe Evander Holyfield might be orchestrating these strange events as a publicity stunt to draw more attention to himself.)

During the seventh round, James "Fan Man" Miller swooped into the ring via a motorized paraglider to protest what he claimed was violence in spectator sports. The cords of his chute tangled in the overhead lights and one of his legs got caught in the top rope of the ring. In response to his act of protest, fans dragged him to the ground and beat the living pulp out of him, which proved that violence wasn't just confined to sporting events.

While boxing still remains popular in Las Vegas, a new way has emerged for people to beat the daylights out of each other while still pretending it's a sport. Called mixed martial arts or MMA, the Ultimate Fighting Championship promotes fights in Las Vegas between some of the top-ranked fighters in the sport who devote their lives training to punch someone in the face.

Boxing and fighting is just one more vehicle that Las Vegas uses to promote itself as the entertainment capital of the world. Within a few square miles, you can see practically any type of show you want (with the obvious exception of anything of cultural or historical significance). By offering so much entertainment that seems within walking distance (but really isn't), Las Vegas has something for everyone, unless you're looking for a really good public library system.

Modern Las Vegas

Las Vegas is now more than just gambling, quickie marriages, and getting laid. It's now about gambling, quickie marriages, entertainment, and getting laid. See the important difference? Las Vegas thrives on entertainment the way a cannibalistic zombie thrives on living flesh. Like most of show business, Las Vegas will give you the chance to showcase your talent, but until you start becoming famous, they won't give you all the really cool stuff like your own multimillion dollar theater with your name on it so you can go back to your twenty-year high school reunion one day and ask, "Hey, who's the loser now?" (Ok, we covered this already. I guess it's my own high school issue.)

In the old days, Las Vegas wasn't run or controlled by organized crime. Today, Las Vegas still isn't run or controlled by organized crime. Instead, it's controlled by various personalities who are minor Las Vegas celebrities on their own.

You can't miss one of the most famous casino owners because he has his last name plastered on the front of a major luxury hotel. Steve Wynn played a pivotal role in rebuilding the Strip by refurbishing the Golden Nugget from a dumpy, seedy casino where men went just to bang hookers into a high-end, luxury casino where men went just to bang hookers. He later built The Mirage, Treasure Island, Bellagio, Wynn, and Encore. Incredibly, he did it all by himself with just his two bare hands and the help of a talking gerbil who advised him on the architecture. (Seriously. I have interviewed the gerbil.)

As of March 2012, Wynn is the 491st richest man in the world with a net worth of $2.5 billion. If you were to ask him if money can buy happiness, he'd probably laugh in your face and then have his security guards throw you off the top floor of one of his hotels just for his own amusement.

Ron Tutor may not be a household name like Steve Wynn, but he heads the Tutor Perini Corporation, one of the largest general contractors in the United States that has yet to be indicted for massive government fraud and corruption. With annual revenue of approximately $3.7 billion, the Tutor Perini Corporation works on many construction projects throughout the United States and Canada where most people still speak English (except for those pesky people in Quebec and New Orleans who still speak French). The company specializes in civil infrastructure, healthcare, industrial power, hospitality and gaming, and anything that can make a quick buck.

Some of Tutor's famed projects in Las Vegas include McCarran Airport, Encore Las Vegas, Planet Hollywood, Red Rock Resort and Spa, Trump International Tower, Cosmopolitan, Palms Casino, and the CityCenter project that currently holds the record for being the largest privately-held property to be foreclosed on by Bank of America.

Just as equally unknown to most of the public are the Maloof Brothers. In 1994 the Maloof family bought the Fiesta Hotel in Las Vegas for $8 million. In 2000 they sold it for over $185 million. They invested the money into the creation of The Palms Hotel and Casino, which later helped them dispose of their excess wealth through continual operating losses.

Initially, the Palms became the hot spot for young people whose parents had too much money on their hands and not enough time for proper childrearing. MTV filmed several specials at the Palms including the MTV Video Music Awards, *Spring Break*, and *The Real World* (which is something you'll probably never see in your own life, so it's not that real after all. Or let's hope that's the case).

Despite being better known as one of the few cities where it's legal to break as many of the Ten Commandments as possible, Las Vegas plays an important role in the show business industry. To attract as many suckers (I mean visitors) as possible, Las Vegas depends on entertainment.

By studying Las Vegas, you can see where older performers go before they die. The next time you think of Las Vegas, you can think beyond the sexually suggestive advertisements and focus on the power of fame, and how it helps both the famous person and the venue that the person appears at.

Fame is a two-way street. To be famous, you have to provide a benefit to others. In return, others will create the illusion that you're famous and more important than you really are so you can act inappropriately and make a roaring ass out of yourself in public—and at the same time, promote them in return. That will generate more fame, and that's what show business is really all about.

CHAPTER 2

How to Become and Stay Famous

"Talent is God given. Be humble. Fame is man-given. Be grateful.
Conceit is self-given. Be careful."—John Wooden

How to Become a Celebrity

Think back to your school days. Wasn't there one boy and one girl who were always more popular than everybody else? Fortunately, the most insufferable ones often graduate, enter the real world, become a nobody, lead a life of soulless despair, endure multiple loveless marriages and subsequent expensive divorces, become raging alcoholics, gain loads of weight, get arrested during various midlife crises (enough, you get the point), and in general stumble through life wondering why they could never achieve any measure of fame outside of school. So there's almost always a happy ending.

In any social setting, whether it's at school, work, church, synagogue, your cricket or bowling team, a self-help group for people obsessed with everything wrong with Washington (never been there!) an AA meeting or even your local orgy, some people will always be more popular than others. If life were completely fair, then you would always be the most popular person—but life isn't always fair. (Not my most original offering, but sadly true) If it was, then your fellow countrymen would elect you to rule with an iron fist, surrounded by a population who adore you and laugh under pain of death at even your bad jokes, but there can only be one North Korean dictator at a time. So you have to create your own fame in a way that doesn't involve torturing political dissidents. You have to create fame all by yourself.

We all want some measure of fame in our lives. At the simplest level, fame is nothing more than being recognized and appreciated for who you are and what you do. At the more complex level, fame lets you tell off your boss, quit your job, and spend all your time and money on drugs and hookers like Charlie Sheen did.

The dictionary defines fame as "the condition of being known or talked about by many people." Of course, there's a fine line between fame and being a nuisance. Fame is when people you don't know like you (and continue liking you even if they do know you). Being thought of as a nuisance is having people dislike you whether they know you or not. Think how many people like some hypothetical celebrity named—let's say—Paris Hilton. Now think of the smallest positive whole number, and chances are you have hit on the correct figure.

Fame is nothing more than a popularity contest, just like political elections and executive promotions. You can whine about the fact that some people will always be more popular than others or you can do something about it, such as driving the most popular person out to the desert and leaving her there. However, a more constructive and less criminal solution is to learn how to become popular yourself. (Then you too can learn to become suspicious the next time somebody asks if you would like to take a long ride out into the desert late one night.)

To become famous, you must have a reason, even if that reason is trivial, pointless, and even seems (and is) irrational. **Fame is a byproduct of action.** If you don't do anything, you can't get famous. But as long as you do something interesting that people like, you can. If a former Minnesota film student and MTV production assistant named Dane Boedigheimer could create an oddly disturbing orange cartoon that became popular on YouTube, there's nothing stopping a live human being like yourself from achieving your own measure of fame, whatever legal way you decide to pursue it.

If you want to become a doctor, you go to medical school. If you want to become an engineer, you go to engineering school. If you want to become a liar, you go to law school. In many common fields, there's a distinct path you need to follow if you want to achieve a specific goal. No matter who you are, if you want to achieve a goal with a well-worn path to its door, you just have to follow the right steps and you'll get there. These are linear paths that many of us take.

Unfortunately, fame doesn't work that way. There is no one best way to become famous. Depending on what you want and who you are, your path to fame can be completely different from another person, even if you have identical goals.

Instead of following a recipe to bake a cake, chasing after fame is like having to make up both your recipe and the cake you want to make at the same time, and then making it in public in front of drunken crowds. This method is sure to lead to a seriously crappy cake, and in the same vein chasing after fame is almost certain to lead to failure—or directly to prison, depending on your level of desperation and sense of self worth.

Basically there are three common paths to fame:

+ Pursue a career with celebrity status.
+ Became famous accidentally.
+ Engineer your own fame.

High-Status Celebrity Careers

Some professions offer high visibility by their very nature—such as the work of professional actors, politicians, models, athletes, TV news reporters, singers and, of course, international spies for Her Majesty's Secret Service. In ordinary life, look at who the most popular people are at school, work or other social settings such as your local PTA or drug cartel. The people with the most fame in real life are those who choose positions that automatically give them a higher profile over other people.

In high school, it's almost a cliché that one of the most popular boys in high school will be the quarterback of the team (unless he really sucks). Likewise, it's also a cliché that one of the most popular girls in high school will be a cheerleader (even if she sucks. Not going to make the obvious joke here because my editors won't let me. Have to maintain *some* decorum here). That's because anyone who becomes quarterback or cheerleader puts themselves in a higher profile position regardless of their actual talent.

In a social setting such as a committee, one of the most popular people will likely be whoever runs that committee, even if that person happens to be a pedophile. (Ask the Catholic Church about the logic of that one.) Positions alone can automatically elevate you to a higher social status over others, thus making you more popular by default.

If you want to be more popular at work, volunteer to lead worthy projects. If you can't be the project leader, be the brownnosing project assistant that everyone looks down on. **Don't worry what other people think of you. Focus on putting yourself in the spotlight through**

high-profile jobs, and your position alone will elevate your visibility so people can't ignore you. They may dislike or even hate you, but they can never ignore you, and that's what fame is really all about.

Ask yourself why Tom Cruise, Lady Gaga, and even Mother Teresa are so well known. It's not necessarily who they are but what position they put themselves in. Is Tom Cruise the best actor in the world? Probably not. (Anyone ever see *Mission Impossible 2* or *Cocktail*?) The reason why Tom Cruise is popular is because he's a movie star and people see his movies, good or bad, all over the world. It's just that simple. He is visible; therefore he is famous. (I am the Descartes of the Fame Game.)

In comparison, a great actor who only appears in Broadway plays may be the best, but far fewer people will see that actor or even know who he is. Talent means far less than simply putting yourself out there. Comedian Woody Allen once said, "Eighty percent of success is just showing up." By getting rich through making movies, Woody Allen not only made himself popular, but he also made it possible for him to date teenage girls within his own family without getting into trouble with child protective services.

The basic steps for this path to fame are simply this:

+ Find something you really want to do.
+ Find a high-profile position that lets you do what you really want to do.
+ Immerse yourself in it.

And for the most important part:

+ Produce results as if you were already famous.

Finding something you really want to do means you'll have the motivation to keep pursuing your dream despite the inevitable setbacks that will jolt you back to reality, like Courtney Love driving drunk and coming down from a heroin high. The biggest mistake people make is pursuing something they aren't passionate about. It's hard to keep your motivation up if you're easily discouraged, and if you give up too soon, you'll never taste the success you so want to rub in the faces of everyone who doubted you.

Imagine a former politician becoming a porn star. He would likely love being a porn star and having sex with different women while getting paid for it. Put a little obstacle in his way like telling him "No," and he'll be highly motivated to find a way to get paid to have sex with a beautiful woman anyway. That's what passion and motivation can do for you.

Now imagine this same politician trying to become a celibate priest. No matter what the ultimate reward might be (such as getting into heaven), this politician would find it hard to remain celibate because *not* having sex with different women every weekend isn't what he's passionate about. In fact, he hates it and becomes a very sad figure in priestly garb, moping and dejected. As a result, such a politician would easily give up at the first sign of "No" and likely return to being a politician and misappropriating your tax dollars to pay for his mistresses once more.

Once you find something that you're passionate about, the next step is to find a position that will put you in the spotlight. Why be a slut and have sex with multiple men when you can become a porn star and get paid to have sex with multiple men? The difference between a slut and a porn star is fame.

Lady Gaga and Madonna could just as easily have turned their passion for singing into performing as backup singers for a band. Instead, they took their passion for singing to pursue a dream of becoming the main singer everyone wanted to see. The difference between a backup singer and the headlining singer is fame (and a few more shekels).

Once you've identified something you're passionate about and have found a recognized, top-level position, the last step is to throw yourself into that job. At this point, many people shrink back in terror and believe they're not ready for such a distinguished position. Here's what we have to say to that argument: "Are you stupid or what?"

Guess what? Nobody's ready for a more prominent and important position than his or her current job. **The way you get ready is to go out and do it regardless of any fears you may have.** Even if you screw up completely (and you will, at something, so that should take that fear away), you'll still get the fame you seek anyway.

If you stay only within your comfort zone, you'll never get anything more than what you already have. **The pursuit of fame is the continuous risk of looking foolish every time you put yourself in the spotlight.** Winners learn from their mistakes and keep going forward. Losers are people like your boss, your ex-spouse, and your annoying relatives who avoid challenges because they're too insecure to risk looking foolish.

Do you want to become a complete and utter failure like these people who will do nothing of importance the rest of their lives besides die and fertilize a cemetery to create greener grass? (And we really don't know for sure that you will be the right kind of fertilizer anyway, so even that might elude you.) Or would you rather become so famous one day that you could stand over the grave of a psychotic boss who once made your life miserable and urinate on his tombstone without getting thrown out because you're a celebrity?

Look at the following table that provides examples for how the high status celebrity path might work in different situations:

If you look carefully, you should notice a distinct pattern. To achieve any prominent position, your main action is to start doing something that produces results to give someone a reason to put you in the elevated position you want.

Imagine if you were in a position of power either through your own raw talent and abilities or, of course, because you slept with the right person. Which one of the following would you want to help put in a higher-profile position?

A. Someone who wants to sing

B. Someone who already sings in a band

C. Someone who already sings in a band and has distributed their songs over the Internet

D. Someone who already sings in a band, has distributed their songs over the Internet, and has developed a large and loyal following

E. Someone who already sings in a band, has distributed their songs over the Internet, has developed a large and loyal following, and makes a six-figure income through sales of albums sold over the Internet

F. Someone who wants to have sex with you

If you answered F, you're absolutely right! However, people put in exalted positions eventually need to produce results (or sleep with someone else higher than you), so from a business perspective, it's not practical to help someone who just wants to have sex with you.

Instead, the second correct answer should be E. Just having a top-level job doesn't mean that people in these occupations will automatically attain celebrity status. (Everyone knows who 007 is, but how many

PASSION	POSSIBLE HIGH-PROFILE POSITION	CORRECT ACTION	INCORRECT ACTION
★ Sports	Football quarterback, baseball pitcher, basketball player with tattoos, hockey player with teeth	Practice skill and get so good you can attract an agent. Get a good agent and make your agent work for his money, try out for teams, find a team that needs your particular skill, produce positive results in games to attract attention. Learn how to seize the moment and be an entertainer	Sleep with the guy who works at Foot Locker, date a woman whose only knowledge of sports is the number of athletes she's slept with, play sports video games on your Xbox while living in your mother's basement
★ Acting	Movie or TV actor, model, voice-over actor, improv performer, stand-up comedian	Audition for everything you can, put together and star in your own plays or short films	Wait to be "discovered," act as a costumed character in a theme park where little kids will kick and punch you while their parents take pictures
★ Singing	Singer of hit songs as a solo artist or lead singer of a band	Develop your voice, audition for high-profile singing positions, start your own band, write and record songs, distribute your songs on the Internet, develop a specialty in certain types of music	Avoid singing in public, refuse to practice and improve, sing songs that most people don't want to hear (polka, Hungarian folk songs, communist military marching songs)
★ Taking advantage of gullible people	TV evangelist, politician, lawyer	Make yourself famous, promote yourself as a specialist, ask for money, ask for more money, ask for even more money because God needs cash	Stay within the law, do what's ethical, be honest, care about people and be willing to help them (Had to throw this in but you know what I mean)

people know who 006 or 008 are? Those two spies are getting screwed out of their fame by James Bond. It's a travesty!)

In many cases, people in high-status careers are just as unknown as everybody else, which can really piss them off when they realize all their good looks aren't helping them impose their will upon others. If you choose a highly respected position as your path to fame, you also need to produce results. The more successful you are on your own, the more likely you'll achieve fame when others realize they can make a quick buck off your efforts by helping you become even more famous.

Given a choice between helping a raw novice or a seasoned veteran who is already producing results, it's a no-brainer that people in a position of power will only want to help those who are already producing results. Since—shockingly—power and brains don't always go hand in hand, you can see why it would be important to make their decisions about you as easy as possible.

Accidental Fame

You can't prepare for accidental fame; you can only take advantage of it. Accidental fame relies completely on luck. Just ask Pamela Anderson, who went with her friends to a BC Lions game in Vancouver. During the game, the stadium screen showed her wearing a Labatt's T-shirt, causing the crowd to cheer and wet their pants (at least the guys did anyway). Her photographer boyfriend later produced a Blue Zone Girl poster for Labatt's. This poster helped launch her career and by October 1989 she appeared as the cover girl on *Playboy* magazine.

Now there are thousands of blonde, big-breasted women all over the world, but Pamela Anderson just happened to be in the right place at the right time. If you or I went to a football game wearing a Labatt's T-shirt, our chances of becoming famous would be about as low as the collective IQ of all the Kardashian sisters put together.

Accidental fame can happen to anyone, which is how people with no talent can suddenly wind up becoming stars on reality TV shows. Of course, accidental fame can disappear just as quickly, which is how stars on reality TV shows can go back to being nobodies the moment their TV show gets cancelled.

Anyone can achieve fifteen minutes of fame by being in the right place at a right time. If played right, you can turn accidental fame into a

Pamela Anderson out in Manhattan, N.Y., 2006
(*Janet Mayer/PR Photos*)

lifetime career like Pamela Anderson. You just may need big breasts to do it. (Or a really good plastic surgeon.)

Accidental fame is, however, an opportunity for those savvy enough to take it. The basic steps to successful accidental fame are:

1. Be in the right place at the right time (completely out of your control).

2. Exploit your fame as quickly as possible (completely within your control).

For Pamela Anderson, fame came out of nowhere just from wearing the right T-shirt and getting a cameraman to put her image on the stadium screen so everyone could stare at her breasts, which is what sports is really all about. What Savvy Pamela (and her boyfriend at the time) did to cement it was to immediately parlay it into something more concrete, taking advantage of her accidental fame by creating their own Blue Zone Girl poster for Labatt's. Initially, the company rejected this poster, but when it proved popular, they officially endorsed it.

Savvy Pamela then went on to appear on the cover of Playboy (and her boyfriend who helped her went on to obscurity when his suddenly famous girlfriend dumped him.) **The key to accidental fame is to take advantage of it as soon as possible before people forget who you are.** The other key to fame is to never help Pamela Anderson.

When Chesley Sullenberger, the pilot of US Airways Flight 1549, took off on January 15, 2009, he wasn't thinking about becoming famous. Yet when his jet carrying one hundred fifty passengers hit a flock of geese, both engines suddenly went out. With no place to land, he ditched the crippled jet into the Hudson River. Miraculously, all one hundred fifty passengers and four crewmembers survived. Suddenly, Sullenberger was a hero, and he didn't even have to exploit and dump Pamela Anderson's old boyfriend to do it.

Besides having his face plastered across newspapers, magazines and websites around the world, Sullenberger also found himself throwing out the first pitch at a San Francisco Giants baseball game and attending Barrack Obama's presidential inauguration ceremony. In the parallel universe that is Hollywood, I would imagine that publicists urged Sullenberger to crash land a helicopter, a hang glider, and a space shuttle to keep his crash landing finesse in the public eye, but thankfully Sullenberger chose another method.

Sullenberger authored a *New York Times* best seller titled *Highest Duty: My Search for What Really Matters*, describing how his life prepared him for the moments of his heroic exploits. Then Sullenberger followed up with a second book about leadership titled *Making a Difference: Stories of Vision and Courage from America's Leaders*. Sullenberger plans to write a third book that explains how he managed to maintain his fame by writing books-and not pissing it away on partying like most other suddenly famous people do.

Although opportunities for Sullenberger's brand of heroism normally don't present themselves more than once in a lifetime, Sullenberger found another way to maintain his popularity. Much like Savvy Pamela, he understood that accidental fame is fleeting and took immediate advantage of his stroke of luck to carve himself a niche. As long as he doesn't do something stupid like start working with Savvy Pamela or shoplift like Lindsey Lohan, Chesley will likely maintain his moderate level of success that arose one day from a single event

In your own life you can't predict how you might suddenly find yourself achieving accidental fame. Maybe you'll capture film footage of Big Foot. Maybe you'll buy boots for a homeless person and have your picture taken by a tourist that gets shared all over the Internet. Maybe you'll find yourself in the middle of a bank robbery when the robbers trip over your prone body and spill all their stolen money on the floor in a video that wins the top prize on *America's Funniest Home Videos*. You can't plan for or predict accidental fame, so stop trying. Yes, right now. That means you.

Just remember that if any measure of accidental fame comes your way, **take advantage of it.** Think of accidental fame as a masochist just begging to be exploited, used, and tossed aside like an old condom. Accidental fame can crack open the door to celebrity, but you have to be quick enough to slip through before the door slams shut and crushes your nuts in between.

Accidental fame can thrust you in the spotlight ahead of everyone else who has been trying to achieve fame for years, but don't worry about their jealous glances and envious sarcasm about how you just got lucky. It's not your fault that accidental fame came your way—but it *will* be your fault if you don't use that accidental fame to propel yourself into greater visibility.

Suppose you're in charge of a project at work that has no chance of getting approved. Suddenly, a meteor flies out of nowhere and crushes your competition underneath its massive bulk. Because your competition has now been taken out by an Act of God (see, prayer really does work sometimes!), your incompetent project suddenly wins approval and your company gets a huge contract as a result. But don't create the meteor yourself, because then you will be in jail and won't get the change to capitalize on your opportunity.

Now that you have your moment, how should you exploit it? Ask your boss for a raise. Ask for your boss's job. Ask to sleep with your boss's daughter. Strike while your fame is fresh so anyone who opposes you will look like an idiot due to poor timing. You have a very limited window of opportunity with accidental fame, so act quickly.

Sometimes life only gives you one chance. Don't blow it. Just look at how many reality TV stars disappear from the spotlight the moment their TV show gets cancelled. Do you want to be a loser like Jon Gosselin (who achieved fame through the show *Jon and Kate Plus 8* and lost it just as quickly when he left the show)? Or do you want to be a winner like Kate Gosselin, who got divorced from a loser like Jon Gosselin and managed to maintain her limited amount of fame by appearing on other reality TV shows as a host and contestant? The choice is yours.

Engineering Fame

Not everyone who chooses a praiseworthy career like acting, modeling, or singing achieves fame, and not everyone gets lucky achieving accidental fame. The vast majority of people have to create and engineer their own fame. If this sounds manipulative, you're right! **Fame is nothing more than manipulating the perception of the public to see you in a positive light.**

If this bothers you for whatever reason, just realize you're being manipulated all the time through advertisements, TV and radio commercials, and even the colors used in fast-food restaurants (which usually just inspire me to leave as quickly as possible and CALL HAZMAT. Manipulation is part of life. Being manipulated is just one of the unspoken articles that our Founding Fathers buried inside the Constitution of the United States. It's a great country, damn it, and we will take full advantage.

Engineering fame basically means turning yourself from a nobody who people in Hollywood will refuse to talk to into a celebrity who people in Hollywood will talk to as long as they can make money by associating with you.

The first step to engineering your own fame can be as simple as choosing a prominent position of some kind, but that's not absolutely necessary. After all, there are only a handful of athletes, actors, singers, and models who achieve massive fame. Most people in those careers achieve moderate or no fame at all, which really makes all those acting classes they're taking at night seem like a complete waste of time and money.

The basic steps to engineering fame are:

+ Create something useful that others will want.

+ Deliver it.

+ Promote it.

+ Build your following.

Ironically, this is also the same series of steps Jim Jones used to build his cult in Guyana and persuade them all to commit suicide by drinking cyanide-flavored punch, but that's beside the point. In the immortal words of Spiderman, "With great power comes great responsibility." In other words, use your fame for good, such as generating more cash for your bank account so you can buy expensive sports cars, fly in private jets, and consume the finest liquor and weed that money can buy.

Lady Gaga began her singing career as Stefani Joanne Angelina Germanotta, which is a name only a mother could love if she were trying to buy a vowel on *The Wheel of Fortune*. As a singer, Stefani was just one of many people singing. To separate herself from the rest of the unimaginative singers out there, she changed her name to Lady Gaga. Nobody remembered any performance by Stefani. People did remember performances by Lady Gaga. (This just goes to show you the power of branding to our gullible American public. Just change the name and you create a whole new image in the eyes of the public. Thank heaven for gullibility.)

Next, Lady Gaga ran into a performance artist named Lady Starlight who helped create her onstage persona based on David Bowie and Queen. Instead of just singing on stage, Lady Gaga started dressing in outlandish costumes and becoming more of a visual performer than just a singer. Lady Gaga's name and onstage performances (her original brand) soon attracted the attention of a record label, and the rest is history.

Would Lady Gaga have ever gotten a record contract if she had remained Stefani and just sang on stage instead of performing bizarre dance and visual art as well? Maybe, but my money would be on the fact that her new stage name and wildly outrageous costumes helped propel her into success far faster.

Lady Gaga followed the four steps of engineered fame:

1. She created songs that people liked to hear.

2. She sang and performed her songs on stage in a way that set her apart.

3. Her outlandish costumes and performances on stage made it easy for people to spread the word about her.

4. The more fans she got, the more they helped introduce her to others.

How can you engineer fame in your own life? The exact same steps still work, except instead of manipulating the public, you'll be manipulating your neighbors, which can be even more fun since you can see their befuddled looks every day when they walk their dogs past your house. (Of course, my neighbors just bring the dogs over to poop on my lawn. Have to start manipulating!)

Suppose you want to become more famous in your local community. First, create something useful, such as a petition to improve your local library or add a traffic light to a dangerous intersection. Next, deliver your proposal to your local government. Make sure you publicize your proposal in the local newspapers and radio talk shows. Attract followers who support your proposal, and congratulations. You've just engineered yourself some local fame.

Just as with accidental fame, you can parlay this little bit of engineered fame to even greater fame. After submitting a proposal to local government, maybe run for a government position. Based on your followers, you might get yourself elected to public office or at least associate yourself with a more powerful politician. That's the power of fame!

When you look behind the scenes of most celebrities, you'll find that most of them actually engineered their own fame even if they originally chose a well-publicized position or achieved accidental fame. Despite never appearing in a TV show or movie worth watching, actor Ashton Kutcher got his start by winning a modeling competition in Iowa.

After a short stint modeling in New York, Ashton soon moved to Los Angeles and got roles on television shows and movies that were mostly as forgettable as the wedding vows Tiger Woods made to his wife before he cheated on her. On MTV, Ashton Kutcher started his own series called *Punk'd* where he was the host.

Ashton took his accidental fame as a winner of a modeling competition and turned it into an acting and producing career. He also embraced Twitter and was the first person to gain one million followers. No matter what you think of Ashton Kutcher, you can't take away the fact that he was also smart enough to manipulate his fame into sleeping with actress Demi Moore and Mila Kunis. Ashton engineered his fame while other actors with more talent simply became alcoholics or drug addicts and now have trouble unzipping their pants whenever they urinate in the Los Angeles public parks.

Ashton Kutcher turned his good looks into fame and fortune by constantly putting himself in the spotlight. And aspiring actor, Mario Armando Lavandeira, Jr., had an even stranger path towards engineered fame that doesn't involve sleeping with Demi Moore or Mila Kunis.

After trying to break into show business as an actor, Mario decided to start a blog. Now most people start blogs about pointless topics like what they ate for dinner that night or how to balance the national budget in a sane and rational manner through tax cuts and reduced government spending. (Yes I tried to do that last one once and quickly admitted defeat once I discovered I had torn out all my hair and created a me-shaped hole in my wall in frustration.) Mario started blogging about celebrities, because he aspired to be one of them. Then he changed his name to Perez Hilton, a neat play on "Paris Hilton" that played off of Paris's visibility at the time but had more intelligence behind it.

Within six months, *The Insider* TV show described his blog as one of "Hollywood's most hated Websites" due to the comments he made about various stars. By 2009 Alexa ranked Perez Hilton's blog as the 491st most visited website in the world, which meant his blog actually became more popular than many pornographic, piracy, and malware-infested sites combined. (I know, quite the stunning coup.) Perez used his fame as a blogger to appear as a guest on various television shows while also starting a radio show and publishing a book.

The difference between Ashton Kutcher and Perez Hilton? Besides the fact that Ashton Kutcher would rather have sex with Demi Moore while Perez Hilton would rather have sex with Ashton Kutcher, **both engineered their own fame by creating a product that people wanted.**

In Ashton Kutcher's case, his youthful good looks were his content. In Perez Hilton's case, his celebrity blog was his content. Both then delivered their content and promoted themselves through other forms of media. Is such content meaningful to society in any way, shape, or form? Of course not, but that's not the point. Fame and developing a fanbase is the point. Ashton Kutcher created his followers on Twitter while Perez Hilton created his followers through his blog.

Ultimately, engineering your own fame is the only sure route to success. Luck plays a part in every person's career, but you must still be ready to take advantage of that opportunity and nurture your own fame.

The Common Denominators of Celebrity

No matter how you become a celebrity, there are several common characteristics that all celebrities share. If you want to become famous, you'll have to adapt these same traits. In your own life you need to be:

- ✦ A workaholic
- ✦ A hustler (in a good way, not the vagina-stretching ways seen in Hustler magazine)
- ✦ Brand-conscious
- ✦ Alert to publicity opportunities
- ✦ Visually good looking or interesting
- ✦ Someone with a support network
- ✦ A natural-born leader
- ✦ Narcissistic (sorry, but it's true)

Notwithstanding the cliché of celebrities lounging around swimming pools surrounded by bikini-clad women, most celebrities are actually workaholics. Because they love what they do, they find it easy to practice their craft, hone their skills and develop their talent. Because many celebrities also love drugs, sex, and alcohol, they also find it easy to become drug addicts, sex fiends, and alcoholics too. But—yet again—we meander. Damn you, ADD!!

This is where your passion comes into play. If you love something, you'll find it easy to spend more time doing it. If you don't love something, you'll spend less time developing that talent and fall behind someone else who loves what they do. Most aspiring Hollywood fortune seekers love money and hate hard work. As a result, they wind up with no money and lots of hard work doing menial jobs in the hopes of hitting it big one day. (Refer back to the clueless hopefuls detailed in the beginning of chapter one.) Such fortune seekers might as well dream about finding an oil well in their backyard or, as in my case, dreaming of eating free pizza around the clock and never gaining a pound.

Most celebrities are also hustlers in the sense that they're willing to tirelessly promote themselves and their careers. Such hustlers rarely take no for an answer, which makes them admirably persistent. (Or unbearably annoying, depending on your point of view.)

Most importantly, celebrities understand their brand, which is their public persona and their lifeline to success. When celebrities fail to remain within their brand, they often just fail. A reality TV star like Jon Gosselin developed a brand as the father of eight kids. As soon as he left the show following his divorce from Kate Gosselin, his brand went from a loving father of eight children to a total loser who nobody would entrust with a puppy, or want at their parties.

Celebrities know who they are and work tirelessly to promote their image. Most people don't know who they are and waste time trying to promote themselves in whatever way they think will make them famous. The end result is that they go nowhere and never become famous unless they give up and start appearing in porn movies. Always an option for some.

Since fame relies on publicity, celebrities stay alert for any opportunity for exposure. This is why celebrities tend to support charities that coincide with the latest news. A hurricane hits New Orleans and celebrities are quick to donate money, but only after making sure the press will dutifully report it. If space aliens attempted to conquer the planet, you can be certain celebrities would be endorsing charities to help the unfortunate victims with post-traumatic stress disorder or whatever.

Celebrities are also concerned about their appearance. Even if they aren't good looking, they make sure they remain visually appealing. Lady Gaga may not be the most attractive woman in the world, but she's certainly one of the most interesting because of what I will call her signature "insane asylum style." (The meat dress made us all kind of sick, but everyone was talking about it, so whatever, it worked.) Probably the only costume Lady Gaga won't wear is one that makes her look like a normal person. But at this point, even if she did, it would have its own shock value.

Most importantly, celebrities develop a support network. Celebrities know they can't do it alone, so they build a team of people to keep their celebrity publicity machine operating twenty-four hours a day, seven days a week. This can mean sending out tweets through Twitter, responding to e-mail messages or opening up letters to make sure none of them contain anthrax—or even worse, scary pictures of middle-aged nude fans who should never, ever, take off their clothes in public.

Keeping a celebrity in the spotlight is hard enough for a team, but it's overwhelming for a single person. Initially, you will have to do everything yourself, but as you grow, you can afford to outsource your work to child labor in overseas countries. Then you can feel good that you're supporting a local economy by paying kids the equivalent of five cents a week to help keep you in the spotlight. Good for you.

Celebrities also tend to be natural leaders who know how to influence others, though maybe not to the point of convincing an entire nation that it would be a really swell idea to invade Poland. Part of being famous is the ability to convince other people that they should adore you for being famous. If they don't, then there must be something seriously wrong with their mental health. Too many cousins marrying each other on their family tree—that must be it!)

One major negative celebrity trait is that they tend to be narcissistic, which means they only care about themselves and see the world exclusively through the narrow lens of their own self-interest. If they didn't care about themselves, nobody else would either, so they have to focus on themselves at all times. This is why so many celebrities get the reputation for being hard to deal with.

And truthfully? Average people with no initiative can be harder to deal with. Would you rather put up with being around supermodel Gisele Bundchen or that surly cashier at Starbucks who makes minimum wage, yet still manages to scorn you while messing up your order.

I can guess what your answer would be. We can therefore conclude that narcissism is everywhere and if you are narcissistic, you might as well try to parlay it into fame so people will be forced to put up with you and pretend to love it. (Instead of complaining to the manager or throwing the Starbucks back in your face.)

Turning Yourself into a Celebrity

If you want to become a celebrity, you need to choose a path. Do you want to depend on luck to achieve accidental fame or do you plan to pursue a highly regarded career in acting or singing? Do you want to engineer your own fame? Whatever path you choose will determine your next step, which still means having to engineer your fame to greater heights.

Being a celebrity means creating a product for the public to consume. Even if that product is something as useless as just being a socialite and appearing at parties, that's still something that plenty of people will willingly pay to see. It's a big, big world out there and people sometimes need their stars to make things feel smaller and more accessible—and to vicariously enjoy their beauty, clothes, trips, social events and, of course, little puppies with diamond collars. Even our good buddy Paris Hilton understood this basic fact.

Once you've defined a product to deliver, you need to find a way to start delivering it without waiting to be "discovered." **Never wait for permission to pursue fame** or else you'll risk waiting forever like someone waiting at the Department of Motor Vehicles. By delivering your product to your fans, no matter how few they may be, you can get early feedback on what works and what doesn't work.

Recruit a celebrity team. These are the people who take care of the details of promoting you so you can focus on the more important task of developing your brand. After all, it's all about you and always will be about you, except for the percentage your agent or manager extracts from your income.

Finally, develop a viable business model for your celebrity status. How will you make money? Remember, show business is a business, which explains why the ratio of lawyers and accountants to celebrities in Hollywood exceeds one hundred to one.

You are a business and you need to be a sustainable one. The more money you can make on your own, the more likely someone will help you become famous so they can take 10 to 15 percent of everything you make after you become a celebrity. Not the most idealistic truth but a truth nonetheless. If this bothers you, Hollywood fame may not be for you. Just go out and do some good in the world and be genuinely happy and fulfilled for the rest of us.

So the five basic steps to becoming a celebrity include:

STEPS	EXAMPLES
★ Step 1. Define your goal, the reasons why you need fame, and develop your fame game strategy.	Depending on your goals and objectives you can choose from: ✦ Celebrity career ✦ Accidental fame ✦ Engineered fame Or combination of all of the above, but always including engineering your own fame.
★ Step 2. Define your genre(s) and develop a pipeline of creative projects.	Public speaker, activist, actor, musician, artist, writer, comedian, athlete, socialite, or expert (in a given field). When choosing your genre it would help to be realistic about your talents and capabilities.
★ Step 3. Define your target audience and start growing your fanbase.	Start with your social media, website, and blog and venture into print, radio, TV, and online media to build and engage your fanbase.
★ Step 4. Recruit and build your celebrity team.	Find producers, managers, publicists, booking and endorsement agents, and your brand ambassadors or at least a few die-hard believers and fans that will help you on the way.
★ Step 5. Develop the business plan, PR, sales and marketing plan and execute it.	Keep your eyes on the bottom line. Know where your cash is coming from and make sure you don't run your brand into the ground before you have a chance to spread your wings. Don't forget to reward and share your success and its spoils with your team.

Step 1 is the step that most people skip or overlook; however, it can fundamentally change your career. It helps to know why you need fame and what fame and success mean to you personally before jumping into the water. Once you have a clear understanding of what you are after, your path to fame will become much more clear.

Step 2 is where a handful of people separate themselves by consciously deciding what product they'll offer to the public based on their own assessment their strengths and talents Even if those talents seem mundane, trivial or even outright useless to others at first glance, they can—surprisingly—still lead to success. In just one example, Kim Kardashian may have great talents that no one knows about, but as I just implied her fame has zero to do with them.

Step 3 is where most fortune seekers fail. They think they'll achieve a fanbase after they become famous, but the truth is that you need to start working on your fanbase the second you decide to be a winner in the Fame Game. Not only will you know much better who your audience is and what makes them tick; you are creating troops and ambassadors that will tell others about you and promote you by the mere fact of being your fan. It's pretty cool how it works once you know how to do it.

Steps 4 and 5 are the two steps most people never think about, which explains why most people never achieve any measure of fame other than getting drunk, passing out, and having their friends post pictures of their drunken stupor on Facebook. (No judgment on that type of fame. We have all been there and different strokes.) You need to prime your publicity-making machine now before you're famous. Then you'll be ready to promote yourself as soon as it happens. Like developing a fanbase, you need a well-oiled publicity team before you can become famous. If this sounds weird, then this might explain why you're not already famous, smarty-pants. If it sounds counterintuitive it's actually not. Where fame is concerned, putting the proverbial cart before the horse is the way to go.

Step 5 is the one step nearly every failed fortune seeker misses. The real question isn't how you will make money, but how will you make money for someone else? The moment you figure out how you can make money for someone else, others will eagerly help you become famous by latching on to a percentage of your income.

Your fame is a business. If you go out of business, you become a nobody like many reality TV stars who were never stars in the first place, but horribly loud and annoying people who happened to be on TV. If your business thrives, then your fame and wealth will thrive as well.

You can develop fame in pursuit of show business or in your ordinary life. Become famous in your school or workplace. Then become famous on a worldwide level so you can have money and visibility and never be able to pick your nose in public or swing a golf club into someone's car window again. (At least while not looking your best.) Or feel really, really good when walking by your high school tormenter, ex-boyfriend or girlfriend who dumped you or that nasty boss or coworker.) Fame may be fleeting, but that doesn't mean you can't rub it into the noses of people who tried to discourage you from achieving your dream. Right? Right?? Who's with me?

The Celebrity Life Cycle

"I already am a product."—Lady Gaga

All celebrities are a product, just like a box of cereal or a carton of milk. The only difference is that people throw out cereal or milk when it gets too old—and this, naturally, can be harder to do with people. Every product (and celebrities in particular) has a life cycle. By understanding the stages of any product lifecycle, you can define where you might be at and then make the best decisions for that stage. The alternative is to remain ignorant about product lifecycles and wind up being quickly forgotten like all those poor people who were the first people eliminated on reality TV shows like *Survivor*.

The first step in any life cycle is the beginning. (I know, I'm just brimming over with rare insight here.) In the celebrity world, the beginning is where you finally break through to the public. As far as the celebrity is concerned, he or she has worked hard for years. As far as the public is concerned, the celebrity suddenly became an overnight success, which again underscores the sheer power of perception.

After a star is born, the second stage involves **growing and maintaining the newly won fame**. A celebrity might start out as a minor D-list star. Then by shedding an exoskeleton, tossing ethics aside and maybe taking a visit to the silicon gods, the celebrity might evolve into a C-list star, then a B-list star, until possibly reaching the much-vaunted A-list celebrity status.

Upon reaching any level of celebrity, the third and final stage of the lifecycle involves **a value and reality check**. That's where the celebrity must evaluate changing conditions to maintain his or her status as a celebrity. Most celebrities are only as good as their last performance, and those who don't change with the times won't keep up.

A value and reality check lets celebrities reinvent themselves to create a new "celebrity birth" and begin the life cycle all over again. Failure to do so means that the celebrity gradually fades out of the public's eye and becomes nothing more than an obscure answer to stump contestants on game shows like Jeopardy.

Basically, the celebrity life cycle goes through these predictable stages:

1. Celebrity breakthrough (product introduction)
2. Celebrity growth and maintenance (product marketing)
3. Celebrity value and reality check (product evaluation)
4. Celebrity decline, where they crash back to Earth and realize they weren't such big shots after all, while their enemies laugh their asses off at their sudden loss of status in show business (product termination) Okay, that last bit is maybe just me writing on an empty stomach. What can I say? And what the hell happened to the pizza guy? Did he go to Nicaragua first on the way to my house?)

Here it is, my biology book Visual Aid:

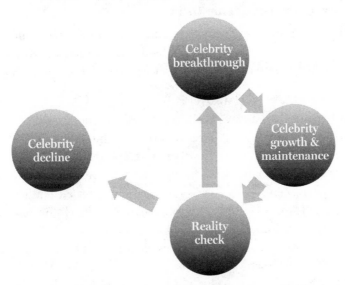

The Celebrity Life Cycle that often ends in rehab, fatal drug overdoses, or murder/ suicide, which explains why so many people will do anything to become a celebrity.

Think of the life cycle of any product such as the latest iPhone. First, Apple introduces a new model (product birth). Second, Apple promotes the latest iPhone (product marketing). Finally, Apple evaluates their sales and customer feedback to determine what to offer next (product reality check). Then they release a new version that repeats the cycle all over again.

Fame never lasts forever. (Twinkies, on the other hand, do last forever and will likely be found with cockroaches as the only two items left on Earth after humanity destroys the rest of the planet.)

To see how transient fame can be, see if you can correctly answer the following question:

What happened to the majority of contestants who appeared on reality TV shows like *Survivor, American Idol,* and *Project Runway*?

A. They remained famous and now have a sandwich named after them.

B. Their fame gradually faded, but now they have several illegitimate kids named after them.

C. Their fame gradually faded until they had to resort to working back in a minimum wage job again. And now have a DWI warrant named after them.

D. They remained famous and beloved, but only in remote areas of the world where cannibalism is still practiced. And only as a tasty main course low in saturated fat and high in Botox.

Obviously the correct answer is B, C, or D.

Most reality TV show contestants are barely memorable even when they first appeared on TV. After a year or two, the public quickly forgets about these "stars" because a new batch of "stars" suddenly appears. If a toddler can't focus on anything for longer than five seconds, the average person can't remember celebrities for much longer either. The phrase "out of sight is out of mind" is never truer than in Hollywood. Only I would add "pretty much instantly."

In your own life, you can see how fleeting fame can be. The most popular kid in high school typically graduates and then spends the rest of his life returning back to his old high school football games, trying to recapture the glory of his past. Instead of being acknowledged as popular, he's now escorted by the police off the school grounds for being a creepy old man.

Life constantly changes. Even major celebrities like Madonna and Julia Roberts see their popularity rise and fall. As soon as Madonna finishes a tour after releasing a new album, people start forgetting about her. As soon as Julia Roberts no longer appears in a film currently in theaters, people start forgetting about her. As soon as rap singer Chris Brown stops punching Rihanna in the face, people start forgetting about him.

If fame never lasts, how do celebrities maintain their position in the spotlight without constantly sleeping with the right people? First of all, they often do sleep with the right people— or at least people who are famous themselves, powerful, or just very photogenic. Second, they know that fame goes through cycles, so they prepare for the inevitable change in two ways:

+ They reinvent themselves to start a new cycle.
+ They create multiple, parallel cycles.

When Madonna first started out, she closely mimicked another successful singer named Cyndi Lauper. Why do we still put Madonna in the spotlight while largely ignoring Cyndi Lauper? Both Madonna and Cyndi Lauper changed their image with each new album they released. Both artists still managed to produce hit singles, but Cyndi Lauper gradually ran out of hits while Madonna continued generating new ones. Besides creating more hit singles than Cyndi Lauper, Madonna went one step further. **She courted controversy.**

Madonna's hit song "Like a Virgin" caused conservative organizations to protest its theme of premarital sex and corrupted family values. While such conservatives often practiced premarital and extramarital sex to corrupt their own family values, the last thing they wanted was to be reminded of their own failings and hypocrisy. Nevertheless, the controversy helped keep Madonna in the spotlight.

In January 1989 Madonna signed an endorsement deal with soft drink manufacturer Pepsi. In one of her Pepsi commercials, she debuted her song "Like a Prayer," which included a corresponding music video featuring many Catholic symbols, such as stigmata and cross burning. More shockingly (to conservatives who are easily shocked), the music video included a dream about making love to a saint, thereby leading the

Vatican to condemn the video (while looking the other way as Catholic priests molested boys all over the world. Told you I was coming back to this.) Religious groups sought to ban the commercial and boycott Pepsi products. Even though Pepsi revoked the commercial and canceled her sponsorship contract, the controversy kept Madonna in the spotlight.

During her 1990 Blond Ambition World Tour, Madonna deliberately aimed to push people's buttons, be provocative, and break useless taboos. Once more, religious groups provided Madonna with free publicity by protesting her performance of "Like a Virgin" when two male dancers caressed her body before she simulated masturbation. The Church of England and the Catholic Church criticized her performance as unrealistic (since many church leaders already know very well what masturbation looks like. Ok. I'm done now.) Of course, Madonna was risking little because we all know exactly how much weight the Catholic Church has on teenage preferences in music.

In 1990 Madonna released a music video for her song "Justify My Love." The music video featured scenes of sadomasochism, bondage, same-sex kissing and brief nudity. Once more, the conservative, religious groups protested Madonna by giving her more free publicity. I think at that point she sent them all nice fruit baskets with handwritten thank-you notes.

Madonna faced backlash during a 1993 tour in Puerto Rico when she rubbed the island's flag between her legs. It's apparently not as safe to go after patriotic symbols as religious ones. In 1994 she appeared on *The David Letterman Show* where she handed him a pair of her underwear and asked David Letterman to sniff them. She also unleashed a barrage of profanity that had to be edited so that people at home, who normally cursed vehemently in front of their children, wouldn't be offended by the same words when spoken on their television sets.

But she realized and adjusted. To tone down her sexual renegade image, Madonna quickly adopted a more subdued image. When her ninth studio album, *American Life* proved to be her poorest seller, she quickly put herself back in the spotlight by French kissing Britney Spears during the 2003 MTV Video Music Awards. Much safer ground here.

With Madonna, every new album and world tour represents another chance to reinvent herself to the public with a new look and style. By using controversy, she continues to remain popular while still managing

Madonna at the 1995 MTV Video Music Awards in New York, NY

(Terry Thompson/PR Photos)

to produce hit singles. In comparison, Cyndi Lauper's hit singles soon dried up and she remained free of controversy, and thus free of publicity as well.

However, Madonna didn't just rely on her music. She also created multiple, parallel cycles.

First, Madonna began appearing as an actress in movies, just like Cyndi Lauper. But while Cyndi Lauper had the misfortune of appearing in poor films, Madonna had the better luck of appearing in both poor and popular films such as *Desperately Seeking Susan*, *A League of Their Own*, and *Evita*.

Besides appearing in movies, Madonna also contributed songs to the soundtracks of popular movies such as *Dick Tracy* and *Die Another Day*. By constantly appearing in movies or forcing captive theatergoers to listen to her singing in other movies, Madonna kept herself in front of the public like an interrogator waterboarding an innocent prisoner. She just wouldn't go away but stayed everywhere. (That's when I began having nightmares about thousands of giant Madonnas chasing me around dark alleys and making me sing "Material Girl." But that's a story for another time and place.)

Starring in movies or just providing songs for movies created a new parallel cycle for Madonna. Not content to leech off the movie industry, Madonna turned her sights on the book and music publishing industry as well.

In 1992 she formed her own entertainment company, Maverick, consisting of a record company (Maverick Records), a film production company (Maverick Films), and associated music publishing, television broadcasting, book publishing, and merchandising divisions.

That same year, Madonna released a book titled *Sex*, which (Can you guess?) consisted of sexually provocative and explicit images. The media immediately condemned the book with a strong negative reaction, but of course it went on to sell 1.5 million copies at fifty dollars each in a matter of days, most likely to the same uptight critics who were publically condemning it (I'm sure just for "research"). Since 2003 Madonna has also written and published multiple children's books so kids can learn how to spell words like "whore" and "slut."

If you look at Madonna as a product, you can see how she relies on her main life cycle of music, but has created multiple, parallel life cycles to keep her in the spotlight:

+ Studio albums and world tours (main life cycle)
+ Movie actress (parallel life cycle)
+ Movie soundtrack contributor (parallel life cycle)
+ Book author (parallel life cycle)

The moment the public starts forgetting about her in one life cycle, Madonna pops up in a different one, much like a sexually provocative Whack-A-Mole. No matter how many times you try to erase her name and image from your mind, she keeps popping up again and again.

Relying on a single product life cycle is dangerous because there's always a chance that this life cycle will end and resist all attempts to reinvent itself. Cyndi Lauper had just a handful of hit albums before her life cycle faded. Although Cyndi Lauper also pursued acting, her acting life cycle also disappeared like a Playboy bunny being kicked out of the Playboy Mansion the day after her thirtieth birthday.

To maintain your fame, you need to be like Madonna, except for the part about having sex with Sean Penn, Warren Beatty, and half the men in North America. Not only must you constantly and successfully reinvent your main life cycle, but you also need to spread out by creating multiple product life cycles.

The chance that your main life cycle will fade is high, but the chance that all your life cycles will fade simultaneously is about as low as the odds that the Arabs and the Israelis will declare peace in the Middle East. Pretty darn low.

Once you understand that reinventing your product life cycles is critical, and creating multiple life cycles is just as crucial, you can focus on the three stages of each life cycle: breakthrough, growth, and reality checks.

Celebrity Breakthrough Strategies

What happens when a nuclear bomb goes off? Besides killing a lot of Japanese civilians, a nuclear bomb explodes with a force that's undeniable even to the thickest-skulled moron on the planet. That's what your celebrity product life cycle must also do in the beginning. Not kill a city full of any civilians, but blow up in the public's consciousness in a way that nobody can ignore.

How can you blow yourself up (figuratively, not literally)? You use one or more of three possible breakthrough strategies:

+ Budget-driven (buy your way to fame)
+ News-driven (take advantage of current news)
+ Product-driven (create something that goes viral)

A **budget-driven strategy** basically buys your way to fame like a multimillionaire politician who earns more than 99 percent of the population, lives off a family trust fund, and claims that he represents the "common people," who apparently also have assets worth over $100 million in the bank.

Think of any politician. (You might want to mentally cleanse yourself first. I will pause for one moment to allow you to do this. Ok, let's continue.) Politicians spend millions of dollars campaigning for a job that only pays them a few hundred thousand dollars a year. Then these same politicians want us to believe they're capable of balancing a budget, so figure that one out.

My unremittingly sarcastic anti-Washington Tourette Syndrome aside, there is indeed a logic to the madness. Through the miracle of trust funds and donations, politicians can raise themselves up from the complete unknown to a well-publicized complete unknown. With enough money for television advertisements, billboards, posters, and brochures, it's possible to promote yourself to fame without demonstrating any talent or ability whatsoever. That's how we currently elect our political leaders, and that's how the Fame Game works.

When you have a limitless war chest of money, you can buy your way into the upper social circles and the public consciousness. Then by proximity to rich and powerful people who can make decisions, you can parlay your friendships into lucrative publicity opportunities.

Extreme wealth alone attracts fame. At the simplest level, the richest kid in school often attracted positive attention just because they could afford to drive around in the fanciest cars, wear the most expensive clothes, go on the best trips and generally wear their wealth everywhere like an automatic free pass. For better or for worse, people are irresistibly attracted to the golden aura that great wealth seems to automatically confer.

At work, the person with the most wealth typically is the boss. Not only do they have more money than most people, they also have more power. In the workplace, people with the most money and power can behave in ways that the rest of us—as mere peasants, office rebels or hopeful brownnosers—could never get away with. (Well, could totally get away with but not while remaining employed.)

In your community, the person with the most wealth can regularly ignore traffic laws, cheat on their income taxes, and order the assassination of associates under the excuse of "it's just business." Wealthy people in all areas of life can promote their status every second they're around you. That's one reason why so many people want to be rich.

Being rich automatically gives you a certain measure of fame in the same way that being pretty automatically gives you a certain measure of attention. The more wealth you have, the more publicity you can buy for yourself.

If you wore a bad hairpiece and acted obnoxiously, people would shun you in public. However, if Donald Trump wears a bad hairpiece and acts obnoxiously, he gets his own TV show. What's the difference between you and Donald Trump? How about a few billion dollars?

Without money, Donald Trump would just be another lunatic screaming about conspiracies. With money, Donald Trump is still another lunatic screaming about conspiracies, but he's a celebrity and people pay attention. He might be one of the most lampooned people on the planet, but gets his points across and has lots of fun with all of his attention and displays of power. (So does your average toddler or cat but that's another story entirely.)

Besides multimillionaire business people and politicians (who as we have shown are often one and the same), a third class of people able to buy their way to fame is the offspring of celebrities.

Actress Kate Hudson got her big break by being the daughter of actress Goldie Hawn. Actress Drew Barrymore got her big break by being born into the Barrymore family that includes film legend John Barrymore. Actor Nicholas Cage got his big break by being the nephew of noted film director Francis Ford Coppola. Actress Carmen Electra got her big break by posing nude in *Playboy* magazine, so it's nice to know that some people can still get famous in Hollywood the old-fashioned way by taking off their clothes in front of the right people.

Anyway, have you discerned the subtle pattern here? By spending enough money, you can elevate yourself from a nobody to a nobody who's actually famous.

While everyone can spend money, not everyone has lots of money, mainly because they are not famous yet. Another catch-22! So, a second way to create fame is through a **news-driven strategy**. Since major news events always capture attention, the simplest way to exploit this is to latch on to the biggest news stories of the day.

Wolf Blitzer was generally unknown to the public until he reported from the Persian Gulf in 1990-91 during the first Gulf War as CNN's military affairs reporter. This live TV war coverage made him a household name. Blitzer followed up on his fame from the First Iraq War as CNN's White House correspondent covering the 1995 Oklahoma City bombing, which earned him an Emmy. With his coverage of notable disasters involving mass suffering and loss of human life, Wolf Blitzer went from being a relative nobody to a news journalist celebrity. That's what a news-driven strategy can do for you too!

If you don't have a major budget and can't piggyback your status with the latest news, you can pursue a third breakthrough strategy by **creating a product that goes viral**. The easiest way to trigger a viral effect is through humor and sex (giggling while having sex doesn't count).

In 1999 two brothers named Evan and Gregg Spiridellis formed a digital entertainment company called JibJab to take advantage of a new video creation and delivery tool known as Adobe Flash (which hackers have also found to be good for infecting computers with viruses). After creating and releasing a few humorous videos, they released a very funny 2004 presidential election video called "This Land is Your Land," which became a viral hit even though—amazingly—it didn't contain any sex.

Back in 1984 Charlie Schmidt took a video of his orange cat, "Fatso." In this video, Charles manipulated Fatso to make it look like he was playing the piano, which meant that he had more musical talent than many recording artists out there. When YouTube appeared, Charles uploaded his video of "Fatso" and it became an instant viral hit.

Others took clips of the original "Fatso" video and added it to the end of videos showing people stumbling, falling, or doing something equally stupid (like dating Kim Kardashian). Then the clip would end with "Fatso," now dubbed "Keyboard Cat," playing off the hapless person.

However, the best strategy to fame is a combination of these three angles: money, news, and creativity. If you only rely on one or two of these breakthrough strategies, you might not get the full effect right away. For example, suppose you create a viral video. Your video may take so long to achieve a critical mass that the message in your video will lose relevance. Even worse, somebody else might recognize your good idea, repackage it, and steal the initiative from you. Don't wave that aside, it happens every day.

Now, if you create a viral video that's creative and tied to a news event, such as the JibJab video that was linked to the 2004 presidential campaign, your chance of instant success is much better. Toss in a marketing budget and you can buy your way to publicity, or at least buy a hit man who can break the kneecaps of anyone who tries to steal your idea and pass it off as their own. (No, I can't help you with that one. I just make clean, good-natured fun of people from the safety of my laptop.)

Remember, the secret to fame is the best use of your money (to buy your way to popularity), news media (to take advantage of current events), and creativity (to create something that others will want). So how can you use these three strategies in your own life to boost your popularity? Money can often buy votes (illegally, of course, but it works) and even buy a prostitute (illegally, of course, but it also works. Well, that actually depends on the quality of the prostitute. But I digress again.) However, the best use for your money is to pay others to help promote you.

Want to be more popular at work? Buy a dozen doughnuts every Friday for all your coworkers to enjoy. Even the smallest gifts can make you more popular among coworkers even if they are just a stubborn bunch of sour grapes. Then while they're greedily stuffing their faces with your sugary snacks that will give them diabetes, you can sneak into their desks and steal all of their work so you can take credit for it before they can. (Did I just say that? I mean they will like you more.)

By buying your coworkers something as simple as a doughnut, you can make yourself more popular. The next time people think about who to give a promotion to, they'll ask themselves who's more qualified? Your coworker who recently completed night classes at Harvard to earn an MBA, or the guy who bought everyone doughnuts once a month? As most businesses think rationally and logically, they'll have no choice but to give the next promotion to the guy who bought them doughnuts. That's how major business decisions are made in corporate America. That is yet another basic tenet of the Fame Game. **Everything at its core is personal.**

Want to be more popular at school? Money may be an issue, so you can focus on a news-driven strategy instead. Suppose your school is playing a sporting event against an archrival that consists of other students who are much like yourself and your classmates, but who you've been trained to hate because they belong to another school. (This is how schools teach kids how to hate people in other countries so it's easier to declare war against them. Who said kids aren't learning anything in schools these days?)

Since most high school students are more concerned about upcoming school sporting events than learning, uh, pretty much anything, they might appreciate someone who can find humiliating photographs on the Internet of their archrival's sport team. If you could post pictures of the other school's sport stars getting drunk, having sex with a donkey, attending a Star Trek convention, or any other humiliating activity, you could become a hero among your classmates just because you found a way to turn a current event into a publicity-making opportunity for yourself.

Want to become more popular in your church, synagogue, mosque, or Buddhist temple?

Use your creativity. Come up with an interesting sign and slogan that demonstrates your religion's foundational beliefs, such as forgiveness and love for your neighbor. Now use those foundational beliefs to create the best anti-homosexuality sign your church members have ever seen to demonstrate your hatred for anyone who chooses to live a different lifestyle than you do. You'll be more popular among the most hardened, conservative members of your church in no time. See how easy?

Celebrity Maintenance and Growth Strategies

Remember when you first broke through to the public with the force of a nuclear bomb that they couldn't ignore? Guess what? If you don't do anything, your fame will dissipate as quickly as the alcohol in your wine cellar if you invite Mel Gibson over for dinner.

As soon as you gain fame, you have to learn to cultivate it. It's like taking the energy of a nuclear bomb and harnessing it to generate electricity so you can power electric chairs and kill people individually instead of haphazardly en masse through random bolts of lightning. It's just more civilized that way, and of course more effective.

To nurture and maintain the fame of any lifecycle, you need to do the following:

+ Develop a creative pipeline.

+ Attach yourself to news cycles.

+ Use long magazine lead times to publicize yourself regularly.

+ Develop a fanbase.

Fame always starts with one life cycle first. The biggest mistake people make is thinking that once they get famous, people will love them forever, when in reality even their own relatives often tire of them and thankfully stop inviting them to every painfully boring family event. (Yes, I may be speaking from experience here.) Show business cranks out new stars every year. As soon as a new star appears, the older stars start rotting like fish left out on the kitchen counter for too long, unless they start to parlay what made them famous into other areas.

The only way old stars can maintain their fame is by creating a product pipeline. Your first product is what gets you famous. A rap singer like Jay-Z got famous for having a hit album. A movie star like Jennifer Lawrence got famous for appearing in a hit movie. A singer like Bobby Brown got famous for hitting Whitney Houston.

Many celebrities become one-hit wonders and disappear so quickly that nobody would recognize their picture on the back of a milk carton. To avoid getting lost in the **purgatory of forgotten fame,** you must constantly develop new products in your pipeline.

After the first hit album, singers like Jay-Z keep producing more hit albums. Each new album represents another product in the pipeline. In comparison, the story of "Octocrazy" and her rise to fame reads: An already out to lunch mother of six gives birth to octuplets, bringing her grand total of children to fourteen and her public persona to Bellvue. (And hopefully to the ongoing attention of child protective services.)

Create multiple products in your pipeline and you'll always have something new to keep yourself in the public's eye. Let your product pipeline dry up and your fame will soon wither away like the overworked skin of Hugh Hefner's scrotum.

Remember, your fame is a product like a box of Wheaties. Just as cereal companies introduce new products or redesign the packaging of their existing products, you also need to keep your products fresh and introduce new ones all the time. Otherwise you'll risk falling into obscurity like reality TV star Heidi Montag, who simply vanished from the spotlight altogether shortly after her show went off the air.

Besides constantly refreshing your creativity product pipeline, you also need to follow the news cycles. Headline news automatically grabs people's attention whether it's good news ("Detroit records zero homicides in a three-minute time span!") or bad news ("Detroit records twenty-nine homicides in a three-minute time span!"). By shifting that attention to you, you can further strengthen your brand while inflating your ego.

Starting a charitable foundation or donating money to an existing charity is one common way people put themselves in the spotlight. A hurricane wipes out a beachfront town? Look for the first celebrity to get his or her picture in the newspaper handing out bottles of water to the victims. Everyone on Wall Street starts talking about a looming fiscal crisis? Wait for a celebrity to endorse the first politician who proposes a plan that the public actually supports and believes might work (even if it doesn't). An alcoholic drunk driver plows into a bunch of innocent people waiting in line at a concert? Look for dozens of celebrities to suddenly check themselves into rehab.

By associating yourself with the positive aspects of the news headlines (and distancing yourself from the negative aspects), you can **piggyback off the public's desire to know more about a specific event while also promoting yourself at the same time.** Celebrities who perform at the halftime show during the Super Bowl do it for free. That's because they know being seen by millions of people is far more valuable than getting a paycheck that they'll probably just blow on drugs, hookers, or alcohol.

Even ordinary people know the power of associating themselves with the news. When the city breaks ground for a new library (that most people will never visit in their lifetime) or a new hospital (that most people can never afford to visit in their lifetime), politicians suddenly show up wearing hard hats and holding shovels while dressed in business suits. Now everyone associates the building of the library or hospital with that politician and vice versa (instead of the grainy video footage of said politician sneaking into a brothel).

Every news headline offers another opportunity for publicity. If the Humane Society issues a report about the number of dogs and cats people abandoned every year, donate money to help stray animals and get your picture taken holding a puppy or kitten to show that you care (even if you're deathly allergic to puppies or kittens). No matter what happens in the news, you can find a way to use current events to turn the spotlight back on you—where it should always belong.

But while every day brings a different headline news story, don't rely on capitalizing on the news all the time. You don't want to look like you're constantly exploiting current events (even though you are). Instead, you want to look like you just "happened" to be there, not like you were using the news to keep your image in the public's mind like a bad song that they can't get out of their heads.

A more traditional way to stay in the news is to get stories about you planted in magazines ahead of time. While you probably don't want to be the topic of a story about the most corrupt politician in your city, you do want to be the topic of that news story if you're the one rooting out corruption (and hiding your own use of graft from the public spotlight).

Unlike newspapers, magazines can't rely on a constant source of news since magazines tend to appear monthly. As a result, magazines need to plan their issues several weeks in advance. Celebrities often give interviews in magazines so that a particular issue appears at the same time as a major event such as a movie release. Sometimes celebrities just magically appear on the cover of a magazine to attract readers with incredibly important information like how they care for their cat or how they lost twenty pounds by eating nothing but chocolate doughnuts for a week—just coincidentally when their movie or album comes out.

Celebrities appear on magazines to promote themselves and to promote the magazine. If your image can't promote the magazine, they have no reason to promote you in return. Again, its quid pro quo. That's the way show business works.

So if you want to appear in a magazine, you need some measure of fame so that your fame can promote that magazine. Suppose you recently gunned down three intruders trying to invade your house. Now you could appear on the cover of a magazine like *Guns & Ammo* (showcasing your weapon of choice).

And you don't have to be a celebrity to build your fame through a magazine. While major magazines want celebrities on their covers, every magazine still needs authorities to lend credibility to their other stories. For example, suppose you're an expert on natural herbal medicines. If a magazine prints a story about how people can stay healthy, you can give a quote explaining how you use natural medicine to boost the performance of athletes without triggering tests checking for banned substances. People will read the story, see your name printed as an authority, and now you have instant credibility.

Simply find the types of magazines your target audience might read and contact the magazine's editors with your expertise and how it's newsworthy. If the magazine can use your information, a writer will ask you some questions and in a few months your name and quote will appear in that magazine. Seeing your name and quote in print will suddenly make you seem more credible, even if you're totally incompetent. That's the power of the printed word. It's a beautiful thing!

Getting your name in print through newspapers, magazines, or even websites requires the acceptance of others. Since not every magazine or newspaper editor can recognize the greatness within your soul, you may have to start promoting yourself by developing your own fans.

Start a blog, open a Twitter account, create a Facebook page, post videos on YouTube, and do everything you can to promote yourself whatever your field of expertise may be. As long as you create something interesting or useful that other people will want on a consistent basis, people will start becoming fans of your work. Over time, people will spread the word about you.

Your fame can even jump across national borders. South Korean rapper musician PSY uploaded his "Gangnam Style" music video on to YouTube in 2012, which quickly became the most watched video in history with over one billion views. His sudden fame through the Internet proved that people all over the world would mimic dance moves from a rap singer from South Korea but refuse to mimic the study habits of a typical student from that same country.

As you become more famous, you can keep promoting yourself through bigger media forms until you achieve world domination, or at least the measure of fame that you want. Cuban dictator Fidel Castro really wanted to be a baseball star, but wound up becoming dictator of an impoverished island nation instead. If he can achieve fame in his own way, then there should be nothing stopping you from taking over a Third World country if you want to make a name for yourself as a dictator too.

Celebrity Reality Check

Before your fame has had a chance to percolate, simmer, and eventually go flatter than the brain activity of reality TV star Tila Tequila, you need to conduct a reality check. That means realizing that your fame won't last forever because people tend to have the attention span of a mouse on crack with ADD. To keep yourself famous, you must keep feeding your fame machine in the same way that you have to keep providing fuel to a nuclear reactor. (With the same pizazz, of course.) Stop providing fuel to your fame machine and you can become a nobody faster than the first contestant kicked off of *American Idol.*

Fame depends on freshness because even the most exciting celebrity can get old-both literally and figuratively. One way to maintain your fame is to keep doing what made you famous, only make it different. That's why author J. K. Rowling kept publishing Harry Potter books to maintain her creativity pipeline. When that series ended, she started writing adult books instead. While you don't see adults lining up to read her latest adult book, J. K. Rowling is at least keeping her name out there without embarrassing herself by getting intoxicated in public and smashing into a car like Nick Nolte. (Don't you love all of my analogies and real life illustrations? And so many to choose from!)

Besides doing the same thing in different ways like J. K. Rowling, Madonna writing children's books in addition to producing another music album, or Lindsay Lohan pissing off another judge instead of actually acting, a second way to maintain your fame is to branch out into other areas. Even if you completely embarrass yourself in a field where you have no talent whatsoever, you can just use the publicity to bring attention back to yourself.

Everyone knew Mike Tyson as a great boxer, but careers in professional sports barely last longer than Hugh Hefner in bed. (Ha! Good one! . . . No?) Following the sad demise of his boxing career, Mike Tyson kept himself in the spotlight in other ways than just fighting in public, snorting cocaine, and assaulting women.

First, Mike Tyson starred in a one-man show. Next, he started his Mike Tyson Cares Foundation to help underprivileged kids from growing up and wrecking their lives (like Mike Tyson did). He also appeared in a documentary about his life that explained how a kid from Brooklyn could grow up and bite the ear of an opponent and get a tattoo across his face. By exploiting his fame as a boxer, Mike Tyson branched out into other fields and kept himself in the public spotlight. **Like any product out there, it's all about diversifying your brand to give it staying power.**

The smart celebrities conduct constant reality checks to determine when their fame might start to fade. The clueless celebrities (of which there are many more) simply assume that they are inherently famous so their existence is all that they need. Fortunately for them, such clueless celebrities can become famous in homeless shelters as "that idiot who was once on TV and now doesn't have enough money to buy clean underwear."

In your own life, you're already famous in a certain way through your own reputation. Whether that's positive or negative depends on who you are. Identify what makes you memorable in the eyes of others and find a way to get famous in your own world, whether that means doing a great job at work or taking all the credit from someone else (who actually may have done the great job at work) Try to be as objective as possible when evaluating your fame areas in your circles.

Next, maintain your fame by creating something on a regular basis. Keep yourself relevant by attaching yourself to the news somehow so when people think about radiation leaks in crippled power plants in Japan, two-headed pigs born in Malaysia, or mad cow disease contaminating beef supplies across the United States, people will automatically think of you!

Finally, keep your feet grounded in reality so you don't let fame go to your head. Branch out into other areas and reinvent yourself to keep up with changing times. You don't want to look like a great disco dancer in the age of rap. You want to be Madonna who changed her style of music from 80s rock to the more soulful music of today to remain relevant, than branched out into what we will call literature because we are praising her. **Change is the only constant and the more you control your own change, the more you'll control your own fame and ultimately your own fate as well.**

Meet the New You—Your Brand

"The only thing that's worse than being blind, is having sight but no vision."—Helen Keller

Helen Keller said it all. Think of any popular celebrity and you can often summarize their reputation in a single word or sentence. When you see George Clooney, you may think "handsome." When you see Megan Fox, you may think "sexy, but deserves to have a giant robot step on her head." When you see Britney Spears, you may think "singer who can't sing and also deserves to have a giant robot step on her head," which proves yet again that talent is often somewhere in between incidental and inconsequential to the Fame Game.

Now look in the mirror and ask yourself, "When complete strangers look at me, what words immediately come to mind?" If no clear-cut, descriptive word or phrase pops up, then you've got a bigger problem than having someone stalk you. Until you can present yourself in a way so anyone can define you within the first few seconds of seeing you, you're missing the number one component of fame and that's a **brand.**

A brand is both an ID that identifies who you are (although it won't let you buy liquor or get into an adult bookstore if you're under twenty-one) and a story that tells what you have to offer (which doesn't require any actual reading, so it appeals to the masses). We see branding everywhere from the second we get up, from highway billboards to store windows to your co-workers dress for the day: are they trying to project competent or artistic or sexy? Branding is in everything we do.

The key is to know what you project and control it. When you think of Federal Express, you immediately think of shipping packages overnight. When you think of the United States Post Office, you immediately think of long lines, slow service, even slower delivery of packages, along with postal workers ready to snap if you dare complain about how awful their service might be. Notice that two different organizations can have the same purpose, yet present completely different identities. That's the difference that a brand can make.

If you don't define and deliver a positive association with your brand (like Federal Express), you'll risk presenting a negative association with your brand (like the United States Post Office). In the Fame Game, the worst negative association can be people not knowing or caring who you are in the first place, which is why serial killers and pedophiles will get more publicity than you ever will if you don't take steps to define your brand right now.

What Branding Does for You

In the business world, everyone hands out business cards, making business cards the only paper product flushed down the drain more often than toilet paper. In the acting world, actors hand out their headshots. Need I say ditto?

The reason is that a business card or headshot doesn't uniquely identify who you are and what you have to offer. All a business card or headshot does is tell the world that you have a business card or a headshot and can afford to waste money printing them in the hopes that they might actually do something for you.

Business cards and headshots are pointless in getting people interested in you. The real purpose of business cards and headshots is to let others know how to contact you only after they're already interested in you. The next time you're trying to pick someone up in a singles bar, hand that person a business card or headshot and walk away. Then see how many times you get laid. (Answer: zero times, unless that person has a business card or headshot fetish.)

Any idiot can get a business card or headshot, and many of them do. What will separate you from the idiots is your brand. Here's what a brand needs to do besides telling who you are and what you have to offer:

+ Attract attention to yourself

+ Target a certain fanbase

Make it easy for others to make a decision about you based on what you have to offer.

When Lady Gaga walks out on stage wearing a dress made out of raw meat, it definitely gets your attention even if you don't even care about her music (or raw meat). Until you get someone's attention, nobody will care about your actual talent, so your brand must grab people's attention right away, and **the quickest way to do that is to be visually interesting.**

A raw meat outfit is visually interesting whether it's on Lady Gaga or Lassie. (Except on me. I made one at home and tried it on. The results were not good.) In fact, some people would prefer to have sex with Lassie rather than Lady Gaga, but they still know who Lady Gaga is, which tells you how powerful her brand can be in drawing attention to herself. Of course, Lady Gaga's visual brand tends more towards the "freak of nature" extreme. Doesn't matter, it works very well for her.

Before she became known as Lady Gaga, Stefani Germanotta struggled to get attention as an artist in New York City. People often confused her with Amy Winehouse, despite the fact that Stefani didn't overdose on drugs and alcohol on a regular basis. To avoid these comparisons, Stefani dyed her hair bleach blonde.

After becoming bleach blonde (I know, blond jokes are old and tired, and here's another one!!) *and lowering her IQ by double digits as a result,* (sorry, couldn't resist. Let's continue) Stefani soon found herself being compared to Christina Aguilera. Interestingly, such comparisons actually helped Stefani by giving her publicity that she wouldn't have gotten otherwise. But only somewhat: while comparisons helped draw attention to Stefani, always being compared to someone else can only generate a limited amount of fame. What Stefani needed was her own brand that would uniquely distinguish her from Amy Winehouse and Christina Aguilera.

After she changed her name and created elaborate stage themes and costumes, Stefani finally found success as Lady Gaga. Suddenly people who didn't care about the music of Stefani Germanotta became passionate followers of Lady Gaga, which proves once and for all how susceptible most people are to a strong brand, talent completely aside. (That was my nice way of saying we are easily led by nature.)

Not only has the persona of Lady Gaga transformed Stefani from just another singer to a famous musician, but her mix of theater, fashion, and music has turned her into one of the most well-known cultural icons on the planet. She manages to maintain her popularity by wearing outlandish costumes that most parents would see as signs of mental illness in a child. Whether she's wearing sixteen-inch high heels while meeting President Barack Obama at a Human Rights Campaign fundraiser or laying in a coffin while her backup singers carry her on stage, Lady Gaga's brand is distinctively weird enough for people to admire her gumption while simultaneously staring in utter disbelief at her costumes that look like they were created by alien, psychotic fashion designers on LSD.

Another example of this extreme "freak of nature" style of branding is the band KISS, known more for their extravagant outfits and black and white makeup than their actual music. After the band formed in the 70s, just three months after playing their first show the band members started wearing full-face makeup. Their costumes and makeup defined the KISS brand.

After more than ten years of success in the 70s, KISS tried to perform unmasked in the 80s. They released seven albums during that time, but struggled to find the same success because people expected them to appear in their outrageous hair, makeup, and outfits. Without their signature styling, they lost their strength of presence.

It wasn't until 1996 at the Grammy Awards that KISS reunited with their original lineup and dressed up in full makeup for the first time in more than ten years. This gimmick of costumes and face paint once again helped return KISS to their former glory in the public's eye, again demonstrating the power of a successful brand and that we are all just Pavlov's dogs. (Remember the famous psychology experiment about conditioning where his dogs would start salivating when Pavlov entered the room just because they associated him with feeding time? And he wasn't even wearing a meat dress. That, my friends, is us. We are creatures of conditioning.)

Just as Lady Gaga used to be compared to Christina Aguilera, another singer named Nicki Minaj is being compared to Lady Gaga. Like Lady Gaga, Nicki Minaj has created a visual brand by wearing bright, neon colors and a lot of pink, to the point where she refers to herself as "Barbie" and calls her legions of fans "Barbz" (while other people call her legions of fans much less flattering names that often include lots of colorfully insulting four-letter words).

If you'd rather not turn yourself into a freak of nature just for fame—give it up now! No, just kidding. You can still create a visually distinctive brand that grabs the public's eye. Television host Larry King represents an example of a subdued visual brand consisting of his wrinkled face, dark framed glasses, suspenders, and air of sardonic authority that I am desperately trying without success to mimic here. Larry King also tends to marry women young enough to be his granddaughters' gold digging friends, but that's less important to his brand than his shriveled, scrunched up, wise demeanor. (Maybe I just need more wrinkles. There must be a plastic surgeon here in LA that will add wrinkles? Am sure they have a plenty lying around.)

Anyway, when you flip through the channels and see Larry King's withered face glaring out at you from behind dark framed glasses while wearing his colorful suspenders, you can't help but notice him and wonder if he needs Viagra. Whatever you think of Larry King, you can't ignore his visual appearance as much as you might want to.

On the flipside, anyone remember actress Jennifer Grey? Ok, anyone under 35 remember Jennifer Grey? Here's another question: Anyone who remembers Jennifer Grey from mega hit movies like *Ferris Bueller's Day Off* and of course *Dirty Dancing* wonder what ever happened to her after that? Answer: She got rid of her famous slightly oversized "I'm your cute little sister" honker and traded it in for a generic ski slope nose that made her totally unrecognizable. See her much later on guest starring on an episode of *Friends*? Recognize her? No? That's my point. Probably on the advice of a dumb agent who thought her nose wouldn't translate out of teenage roles, she got rid of her most visually striking feature, and it killed her brand overnight. (Ready for the contrast? Actress Mayim Bialik rose to fame in the early 90s in the hit NBC show *Blossom*, refused to get rid of her slightly oversized honker, and is now a star of the hit show *The Big Bang Theory*. She also happens to be a neuroscientist. Girl knows what she's doing.)

A distinctive brand is key with reality stars as well. Although reality TV stars often become famous by acting like idiots and parading around like the psychological train wrecks that they are, they also need a distinctive brand to separate them from the rest of the train wrecks on reality TV.

When MTV premiered *Jersey Shore*, the show focused on the "guido" and "guidette" look. Out of that entire cast, Snooki quickly distinguished herself with her appearance as a short, tan Italian with a wild "poof" haircut. Besides this distinctive look that would have made her a prime target for a serial killer in any neighborhood in America, Snooki further branded herself by defining her image with an "animal print" look.

While animal prints are nothing new, the pink and purple zebra and cheetah styles suddenly seemed branded just for Snooki. She sold animal print merchandise including slippers and perfume with animal print labels. To further define her brand, she marketed all of her social media accounts with animal print patterns as well. Now when people think of animal skins, they automatically think of Snooki. She saw it and capitalized on it. And *believe me,* if she can, so can anyone.

Another member from *Jersey Shore* also found a way to differentiate himself from the rest of the cast. Mike "The Situation" Sorrentino made sure everyone knew him for one thing: his abs. Besides his descriptive nickname as "The Situation," he also defined himself through his phrase "GTL," which stands for "gym, tan, and laundry." With such distinctive branding, The Situation soon expanded his brand to include endorsements for Devotion Vodka and Reebok Zigtech shoes. He also published a ghostwritten autobiography, produced a rap song and a workout DVD, and created a vitamin line for GNC. To expand his presence beyond *Jersey Shore,* he appeared on the reality TV show *Dancing with the Stars.*

Jersey Shore first premiered in 2009 and by 2010 Sorrentino had made more than $5 million, making him the second highest paid reality star after Kim Kardashian, which pretty much destroys the theory that studying and getting good grades in school will earn you the most money.

Every brand needs to attract attention because the more eyeballs you can get staring at you (even if they are crazy eyeballs), the more fame you'll get. However, a brand must do more than get everyone staring in your direction. Your brand must also target and appeal to a specific type of fan.

When Lady Gaga wears a meat dress, she's appealing to a young crowd that enjoys the outrageous use of food as a form of clothing, ignoring the millions in Third World countries that starve and die every day because they have neither food nor clothing.

People who find Lady Gaga's meat dress appealing are different from people who find Larry King's wrinkled face appealing. Lady Gaga's brand and Larry King's brand both attract attention, but they're reaching two different groups of people. Larry King is trying to reach people who enjoy seeing televised interviews (and, of course, rapier wit just like mine) while Lady Gaga is trying to reach younger people who want to rebel against society. By supporting Lady Gaga's outrageous theatrics, such people can feel like they're rebelling against society but without risking tear gas or a clubbing by the police to do it. If Lady Gaga wanted to appeal to senior citizens, she might wear a dress made up of Metamucil and Viagra. (Certainly would inspire less nausea than the meat dress.)

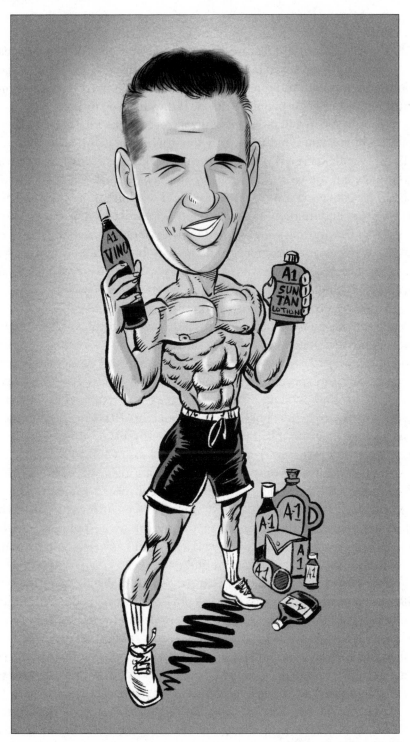

Max Espinoza/Ruben Gerard

The most important feature of any brand is that you will never appeal to everyone, so don't even bother. Instead, your brand must target a specific demographic. And once you know your target market, your brand must make it easy for people to decide if they like you or not.

When you're driving on the highway and want something cheap to eat in a hurry, you'll naturally gravitate towards a fast food restaurant like McDonald's, even if you know the food is kind of disgusting and will eventually kill you years later. (But sometimes we can't resist a synthetic potato fry cooked in tons of fat. Yummy.) If you have more time and are willing to spend more money, you might skip a fast food restaurant and eat at a sit down restaurant like Red Lobster or Olive Garden. Instead of taking a chance on a local restaurant, a name-brand restaurant makes it easier to decide what you want and what you'll get. **Your own personal brand is no different.** It's a quick identifier that makes you stand out.

And gives people the information you want them to get. When people see a musician like Marilyn Manson dressed in gothic black, only the most demented person would think they're about to hear polka or country music. That's because the Marilyn Manson brand immediately tells people what to expect. When people see a half-naked Britney Spears prancing around on stage with an albino python wrapped around her neck, everybody is too busy staring at her breasts to expect to care much about her singing. Britney Spears' early brand of an adorable, innocent young woman from the Mickey Mouse Club transformed to a sexy, provocative, good-girl-gone-bad, resulting in her 100 million dollar perfume line along with her successful record company (while lip-syncing her own songs). After a number of meltdowns resulting in extremely negative publicity, she withdrew from the public spotlight and re-emerged with new albums and a show in Las Vegas, entertaining people who have lost money in the slot machines.

Your brand simply makes it easy for people to decide whether they like you or not. (If they like you, they obviously have good taste. If they don't like you, then they're obviously brain dead. But even if they don't like you at first, if your fans make you famous enough they may end up following you anyway.) You'll never appeal to everyone. Instead, **focus on appealing to a specific group of people who will like what you have to offer.** Then your brand must advertise to that type of person.

Imagine if Larry King showed up one day wearing a meat dress. (He would look even scarier than me in a meat dress.) That would draw attention, but it wouldn't attract his type of audience. Now imagine if

Lady Gaga wore an ordinary shirt with suspenders. Her type of audience would find this boring even though it would be different. Create the wrong brand and you'll attract the wrong type of people. Create the right brand and you'll attract the people willing to give you money, and those people are always the right audience for you.

Defining Your Own Brand

So how can you apply these principles to your own life to become more popular at school or work? Now that you know the importance of a brand, you need to consciously define the one you want to cultivate for yourself:

DEFINING YOUR BRAND	EXAMPLES
★ Define your image	*"Freak of nature"*—Lady Gaga, dress outrageously *"Distinctive but Normal"*—Larry King, dress distinctively but within normal social bounds *"A-hole with a British accent"*—Simon Cowell, speak your mind arrogantly with a distinctive speech pattern *"Bad boy"*—Johnny Depp, Colin Farrell, behave in a way that makes people cringe, but secretly wish they had the guts to do it too *"Womanizer"*—John Mayer, be smooth and friendly with multiple members of the opposite sex *"Train wreck"*—Lindsay Lohan, constantly get in trouble with the law *"Tragic hero"*—Charlie Sheen, act like a victim of circumstances even if you created them *"Sexy mama"*—Jennifer Lopez, exude sexuality no matter what your age *"Ditzy blonde singer"*—Britney Spears, play up a stereotype
★ Define your target audience	Are you targeting athletes, corporate executives, teens, men, women, science students, blue-collar workers, or retirees? Where do they live? What do they like and dislike? What is their education and level of income? You want to know your fans and how to reach and engage them better than they know themselves.
★ Define what you have to offer	Make sure your brand defines and is consistent with what you have to offer, while giving your target audience what they want.

First, decide if you want to act like a "freak of nature" or a "distinctive but normal" person. There's no right or wrong choice here, but whatever choice you make, you'll have to live with it. It's a long-term commitment that should go with your personality, taste and comfort zone.

If you don't like the idea of dressing like a mental patient on Halloween every day, you probably wouldn't want to choose the "freak of nature" approach. Likewise, if you find ordinary life too drab, then you might want to avoid the "distinctive but normal" approach. (Then you can shock your parents by showing them that dressing like a transvestite serial killer really can make you more money than going to medical school and becoming a doctor. Break it to them gently.)

If you're in show business, you might prefer the "freak of nature" approach to draw attention to yourself in a hurry. Think of Elton John, David Bowie, and Lady Gaga dressing up in costumes that look like they came from *Plan 9 from Outer Space's* prop department.

If you're not in show business, this "freak of nature" approach might simply get your boss, parents, and teachers calling 911 to get you psychological help as quickly as possible. In regular life, you may need to brand yourself with the "distinctive but normal" look, such as Larry King's glasses and suspenders or the late Steve Jobs' black turtleneck sweaters. Larry King plays up the establishment, while Steve Jobs' black turtlenecks gave him a creative genius vibe.

To get an idea of how to look distinctive without looking like a freak of nature, study how actors brand themselves. And notice how if an actor brands him or herself too narrowly, they'll get typecast for certain roles.

Actress Eva Longoria became a success when she appeared on the comedy/drama *Desperate Housewives*. Because she achieved success playing a certain role, the public expects her to appear in similar roles. That shows the public's lack of imagination, but also demonstrates that once you've defined a brand for yourself, you're often stuck with that brand—whether you like it or not.

Without relying on visual gimmicks (can anyone imagine Lady Gaga appearing in a movie wearing a meat dress?) actors portray their brand through their roles. Angelina Jolie's brand is the "tough sexpot" as seen in films like *Gone in Sixty Seconds*, *Tomb Raider*, *Mr. & Mrs. Smith*, and *The Tourist*.

Samuel L. Jackson's brand is the "badass muthafucker" as seen in films like *Pulp Fiction, Snakes on a Plane, The Avengers,* and *Django*

Unchained. Yet actors sometimes actors try to broaden their brand by choosing roles that play against it, such as when Samuel L. Jackson played a wheelchair-bound manipulator in *Unbreakable* or the slightly odd bluesman in *Black Snake Moan.* However, when you see Samuel L. Jackson, you normally expect to see him portray the Badass Muthafucker because that's what the Pavlovian public wants to see.

The public's mantra can be summed up like this: "Give me the same thing, only different." **You want your brand to be versatile enough to be different, but not too narrow to be restrictive.** Lady Gaga defined herself by wearing outlandish costumes, not meat dresses, so thankfully for us she's not restricted to wearing pork chops or rib eye steaks for the rest of her life.

Next, decide on your target audience. If you want to become more popular with executives at work, you probably wouldn't want to show up wearing a lamb chop. However, you could go to a subtler extreme and wear a business suit with a bowtie. That bowtie could separate you from everyone else who wears a regular tie and looks like just another replaceable cog in the corporate machine. Or channel Jobs and go "black sweater artsy."

Knowing your target audience is one step, but the next step is knowing what you can do for your target group. Samuel L. Jackson's brand appeals to people who also want to be Badass Muthafuckers. Rather than risk acting out that persona in real life and getting punched in the face, people prefer to live vicariously through Samuel L. Jackson's roles instead.

Your brand always provides your fan base with something they want. For fans of Mike "The Situation" Sorrentino, they would also love to get paid millions of dollars to work out, look good, and party all day. Since they can't do that without eventually losing their jobs or getting kicked out of their parent's house, they follow The Situation's brand as an alternative.

Knowing what you offer your target group is the final step to defining your brand. Maybe your school or workplace is full of oppressive teachers/co-workers and a backwards administration/boss. Your brand could be the rebel who specializes in exploiting the latest technology- thus circumventing the teachers and making them look like the backwards Neanderthals that they really are.

Your brand must grab people's attention, appeal to a specific target audience, and give that target audience something that they want, **even**

if they don't know what they want until you give it to them. Do that and you'll put yourself miles ahead of everyone else who just relies on talent to get ahead and can't figure out why they're going nowhere because nobody knows or cares who they are.

CHAPTER 3

Digital Age: Fame Reloaded

"Fame is proof that the people are gullible."—Ralph Waldo Emerson

Celebrities of the Digital Age

Great quote again!! Thank you, Quote.com! So you weren't born a rich socialite with nothing better to do than pose in front of the mirror every day while the most pressing issue on your mind is whether you look better in mauve or indigo. (I have a slight preference for indigo.) You may also not be famous enough to have casinos in Las Vegas hire you to perform or have celebrity tabloids care about following your every move. Take heart! There's still a way for you to get famous without relying on luck.

First of all, the techniques that work for celebrities, or people who are already leeching off their accidental relationships with celebrities, may not apply to you. Socialites like Paris Hilton and Kim Kardashian have a sizable head start over the rest of us because they can each devote their entire banal existence to thinking up new ways to stay in the spotlight, while spending money they didn't earn to do it.

In the meantime, the rest of us have to fight rush hour traffic as we curse out our bosses and fantasize about winning the lottery so we can quit our jobs and then buy the company that once employed us, fire our boss and finally change the dress code. (Bring on Meat Dress Fridays! Ok, am getting off my meat dress kick.)

Remember, the key to the Fame Game is to selflessly and tirelessly promote yourself. (Selflessly promote yourself. Interesting. Time for more coffee.) In the old days, the best you could hope for would be to stand on a soapbox on the corner of a busy intersection and shout incomprehensibly at people passing by. If you were lucky, someone would actually listen to your illogical ramblings and give you a job as a commentator on Fox News.

To boost your public exposure (and we don't mean the kind that involves flashing open a trench coat while wearing nothing else underneath), you could travel to different intersections around the city, or even visit different cities altogether. Of course, this would take time. The moment you left one area, the people there would probably forget everything about you.

Fortunately, the old days are gone forever, although many of our country's ultra-conservative keep trying to bring them back. Today, there's a new way to climb on your soapbox and make a public spectacle of yourself to a global audience.

In the old days (the ones those pesky conservatives keep obsessing about—give it up already!) you had to publish a book, magazine, or newspaper article to reach a literate audience.

In the old days, you had to beg for airtime from your local radio or TV station to contact people across the city, country or even the globe. Today, that's no longer a problem because of a certain communication medium that allows even starving children in Bangladesh to receive ads for penis enlargement pills twenty-four hours a day from the convenience of their home. That communication medium is the Internet.

The Internet as a Promotion Medium

As reality TV shows already prove, anyone can be a star. You don't have to be talented, you don't have to be rich, and you don't even have to be good-looking. You just have to be you. (Of course it doesn't hurt to be talented, rich, and good-looking, but it's not crucial.)

Kate Upton began her career like so many other gorgeous women by looking in the mirror one day and asking herself, "Do I want to go to college for four or more years, study hard, and earn a college degree so I could get a job doing something difficult that could benefit society like researching a cure for cancer? Or do I want to take off most of my clothes in front of a camera and make a lot of money?"

The answer, not surprisingly, led her into modeling for Damien Haumpy Garage, Dooney & Bourke, Guess, Beach Bunny Swimwear, and Victoria's Secret. In 2011 she even appeared in the *Sports Illustrated Swimsuit Issue* in the body paint section where she was named Rookie of the Year. As part of a global conspiracy to make most women on the planet feel fat and unattractive so they'll buy more beauty products from magazine sponsors, she has also appeared in magazines such as *Complex* and *Esquire*.

But good looks can only get you so far in show business as far as the casting couch. That's because Hollywood is already crawling with thousands of gorgeous, attractive women capable of modeling a swimsuit, and many of them even started out biologically as men. (They mostly live in West Hollywood, but you get the point.)

Given the tremendous competition of beautiful women and the short shelf-life of any female in show business who's over twenty-five years old, Kate Upton decided to rocket herself to super stardom (over the outstretched talons of a thousand other gorgeous women who cry slut) by using the Internet as a promotional tool.

In April 2011 she released a video of herself doing the Dougie at a Los Angeles Clippers game. This video soon went viral and dramatically increased her popularity. On April 30, 2012, a bikini-clad Upton performed the "Cat Daddy" by The Rej3ctz in a video directed by Terry Richardson. Like her previous Internet video, this one also went viral, amassing almost 750,000 views in the first twenty-four hours.

Although Kate Upton was already a successful model, shaking her boobs on an Internet video separated her from the pack of other models, clawing equally hard for fame and fortune. What's the difference between Kate Upton's breasts and the breasts of an equally well-endowed swimsuit model whose name you've never heard of? Got it? That's right, you can see Kate Upton's breasts jiggling on the Internet, and that makes all the difference in the world.

So you may be asking yourself, "What if I don't have breasts that some horny, middle-aged Hollywood producer will want to fondle and make me a star?" The answer is simple. Take away Kate Upton's plump pair of breasts, (which would surely feel like two velvet pillows sandwiching your ears if you should happen to rest your head on her chest after an exhaustive night of hot sex—but again, I digress. Oy.) and what do you have left that might appeal to people around the world? Your brand and the Internet. You just need to let the global presence of the Internet amplify who you are.

When the social network MySpace first became popular, comedian Dane Cook used it to promote himself. Using MySpace (despite the fact that it would soon lose its "coolness" factor to Facebook in a few years)

Dane gradually built a loyal following who would attend his comedy shows wherever he went. As the crowds swelled, comedy club owners started booking Dane Cook more often. That's because comedy club owners only really care about comedians who can attract more people to their clubs so that they will buy two or more exorbitantly priced alcoholic drinks and stagger back home. Then the entertainment industry soon took notice and offered Dane appearances on HBO.

Unlike comedy clubs, HBO doesn't even make money selling alcohol, unless you count beer commercials depicting hot young women having a great time drinking (the commercials always seem to end right before they rush to the bathroom to throw up all over their shoes, though. Damn, I keep waiting for that and am invariably disappointed.) But the point is clear. If you only drink the right kind of beer, you too can meet hot chicks in a bar.

It's the silver lining to our media-addicted times. **If you promote yourself on the Internet, you too can create your own global audience, who can start putting money in your pocket right away. Fame really can be as close as the nearest computer.**

The Formula for Internet Fame and Fortune

The formula to rocket yourself to stardom and global fame is actually pretty easy. The problem is that the path to fame can be short and simple for people with no talent (think of all the cast members on the latest reality TV show), but long and arduous for people who actually deserve the fame and fortune (that less talented hacks are currently enjoying) that should be rightfully yours.

The path to Internet fame is no different from the path to getting drunk. (I told you it was easy!) Anyone can find the path that leads into a bar, but just because you follow that path doesn't mean that you're going to find a nymphomaniac swimsuit model inside, just waiting for you to show up so she can get laid. (Just like the beer commercial promised. A pox on false advertising!) Likewise, the path to Internet fame is simple, but there's still no guarantee that you'll ever become famous as a result. What I can guarantee is that if you follow these three simple steps, at the end of the day, you'll have a shot at it.

PATH TO INTERNET FAME	TIPS
★ Step 1. Brand Yourself and Create Content.	Brand yourself with something original and catchy. Whether it is your look, your talent, your message, or preferably all of the above, translate that in your website, blog, and social media.
★ Step 2. Promote Yourself.	Take time to promote your content and product in order to get your brand name out there.
★ Step 3. Go Back To Step 1 and Do It Again.	See what works and what doesn't and build on that.

Branding is most important, but we're not talking about the kind that involves pressing searing hot metal against your flesh because you think tattoos don't mutilate your body fast enough. What we're talking about is choosing that one, single most attractive idea of yourself that you want to promote, and then sticking with it even if your friends laugh and your mother wrings her hands in worried concern and urges you to give up your crazy ideas and become a doctor like your brother. (Not speaking from experience here at all of course.)

When you think of any celebrity, there's always a single idea that stands out as that celebrity's brand. Sylvester Stallone is an action hero. Ellen DeGeneres is a comedian. If Ellen DeGeneres became straight or Sylvester Stallone got a sex change operation and turned gay, they could get married and adopt an unwanted child from China who might become a comedic action hero like Jackie Chan.

Think of any celebrity and test our theory. Go ahead, I dare you. Get off your couch, put down your Twinkie and your remote, think about it for ten or twenty seconds, and you should see how branding works for all celebrities in every aspect of show business.

Taylor Swift is a country singer. Jon Stewart is a comedian talk show host. Kristen Stewart is an actress. David Beckham is a soccer player (or as they call it everywhere else, a football player, but let's see how great David Beckham would be if he had to defend against Peyton Manning on fourth and ten on the twenty-nine yard line with three seconds left in the Super Bowl).

That's what branding does for you. It condenses your whole reason for being (or as the French say, "reason for being," after they suck up their pride and demean themselves to speak English because French is the only language that contains seventeen different ways to say "We surrender!" to the Germans).

The attention span of the public has shrunk over the years to the point where it can only hold one thought about a person before getting distracted like a baby staring at a shiny set of car keys dangled in the air. What will that thought be when people think of you? (Think quickly! People are already getting distracted!) Whatever that thought might be, that's your brand and that's what you need to promote to make yourself stand out among a sea of mediocrity.

Try the following exercise to define yourself by filling in the blank:

"When people think of me, they think I'm _____."

Examples to fill in the blank:

- Sexy (Mila Kunis)
- Smart (Albert Einstein—notice we couldn't name anyone in Hollywood?)
- Strong (Mike Tyson)
- A great actress (Meryl Streep)
- A former child actress in serious need of psychological help (Miley Cyrus)
- Handsome (Brad Pitt)
- More handsome than Brad Pitt (George Clooney)
- A handsome actor who we pretend isn't really in a bizarre cult (Tom Cruise)
- A funny black man (Chris Rock)
- A black man who used to be funny (Eddie Murphy)
- A complete waste of a human life (Lindsay Lohan)
- A swimsuit model with a PhD in quantum physics (Nobody—see how a brand has to be believable?)

Once you can define your brand in one or more distinctive word, it's time to promote your brand to the general public on the web. Remember, your promotions must continually reinforce your brand because people can only hold one thought in their mind at any given time.

So how do you promote yourself? **You start with creating something useful.** (Ok, useful might be stretching it. Create *something*.) That could be a YouTube video, a cartoon, a blog post, or a batch of really great brownies you'd be willing to sell really cheap to the first person who contacts you on eBay. Develop a promotional vehicle for your brand.

Next, **your promotion needs to be predictable** so people know what to expect from you in the future. If you're creating YouTube videos of people getting mauled in the crotch by rabid Chihuahuas in funny situations, then you'll need to keep uploading videos on YouTube that show people being mauled by Chihuahuas during weddings, birthday parties, or congressional hearings.

Whatever method you use to promote yourself, make sure you can keep it up on a regular basis between now and whenever you become famous and can afford to hire other desperate Hollywood fortune seekers to do all the hard work instead. You don't want to promote yourself in a YouTube video one week, write a blog post the next week, and draw a cartoon to post on your website the third week. This would be like a major network trying to promote a sitcom by airing a show on television one week, airing a second show over the radio the next week, and printing the script for the third show to sell as a book on the third week. Your potential audience will only get confused-most of the public is already confused enough, and your brand would get lost.

Since most of the general public actually has to work to make a living, they don't have time to evaluate your brand for longer than a few seconds. If it's not interesting to them at first glance, they'll move on and find something else to do.

Here are some of the many ways you can promote yourself over the Internet:

+ YouTube videos

+ Podcasts

+ Cartoons, still and/or animated

+ Blogs

+ E-books

+ Live webcam broadcasts involving beautiful women who will charge people $2.95 a minute to watch them take suggestions

+ MP3 files

+ Photographs (except for the really naughty ones you keep encrypted in a hidden portion of your hard drive)

+ PDF files

+ Websites

+ Facebook pages

+ Twitter

+ E-mail

+ Online forums

+ Hacked NORAD computers that allow you to start World War III at the touch of a button unless everyone on the planet agrees to elect you dictator of the planet for life (I loved *War Games*! Great movie. See it if you haven't.)

In fact, the number of ways you can promote yourself over the Internet is only dwarfed by the infinitesimal number of ways Hollywood can ignore you if you sit around and wait to be "discovered." Think about that one for ten seconds. Knowing that, put a smile on your face and let's get started!

How do you know which method you should try to maximize your chance for fame? You don't. Isn't the pursuit of fame exciting? Don't worry. If you have half a brain, you can probably figure out the best way to promote yourself based on what your content might be. Take this sample question to see if you have the brainpower to figure out the best way to promote yourself on the Internet:

Q: If you wanted to promote yourself using video, what would be the best Internet method to do so?

A. YouTube

B. Twitter

C. MP3 files

D. I just want to be famous, why do I have to do anything to
   earn it?

If you answered, D, congratulations! You already have the mindset
of the average Hollywood fortune seeker. Of course, that's not going to
get you anything but a full-time job waiting tables at a dumpy restaurant late at night, but at least you can still cling to your dreams as you
count the remaining days of your life before you give up and move back
home with your parents.

(If you can't figure out the correct answer on your own, then you
probably should just put this book away, crawl under the nearest rock,
and wait for evolution to pass your gene pool by. Or alternatively, audi-
tion for a reality show.)

Now that you understand that you need to deliver interesting
content that people will want regularly (and can actually deliver said
content regularly without giving up in despair), you actually need to do
it. When will fame come knocking at your door?

Maybe never, but as long as you truly enjoy what you're doing and
can hold down a job that actually pays the bills while you wait, fame
might come sooner than you think. Then again, it might come a lot
later than you think. Anyway, the point is that there are no guarantees
in life, so just do the best you can, and keep trying as hard as you can.
Nobody said generating your own fame would be easy, especially if you
don't have a great pair of breasts or perfect six-pack abs to go along with
them. But as we have demonstrated, you don't need them.

To help give you hope before the realities of show business stomp
the life out of your dreams once more, let's take a quick tour of some
people who succeeded in promoting themselves to fame and fortune.
You know you're better and more talented than these people, so now's
the time to go out and prove it.

YouTube Celebrities

Perhaps one of the most famous YouTube celebrities is singer Justin
Bieber. While searching for evidence that the world would soon be
wiped out by the coming Apocalypse in 2008, American talent manager, Scooter Braun, came across Bieber's videos on YouTube.

Finding all the evidence he needed that the world indeed was going
to hell in a hand basket, Braun soon became Justin Bieber's manager.

Shortly afterwards, he likely began building an underground bunker to protect himself from the inevitable fallout, once it became known that he was the guy who helped propel Justin Bieber into the public consciousness.

YouTube lets anyone with a camera (and no sense of public shame) put themselves in the public eye for anyone to see. No matter who you are, you too can be discovered, as long as someone actually finds your YouTube video clip buried among the million and one other hopefuls trying to do the exact same thing you're trying to do.

What will separate your YouTube video from all those other losers who don't possess a fraction of the talent that you have? **You need your video to go viral so people will eagerly share it with others.** Basically, you're getting other people to help spread your fame because your video makes them happy or evokes some other strong emotion that will encourage them to promote you without realizing it. Even if none of your videos go viral, a steadily growing collection of videos will gradually build your following to the point where you could start fleecing them like a TV evangelist.

Keenan Cahill shot to fame by posting videos of himself lip-syncing to popular songs using an iMac. (That's because PCs suck. All the cool kids—and even cooler adults—are using Macs. Pass this along.) After gaining millions of views and subscribers, he attracted the attention of music producers. Soon he appeared in videos with many big-name celebrities, including Jennifer Aniston, 50 Cent and DJ Pauly D, as well as on multiple television programs. Since becoming famous, he has started releasing original music.

Unlike all those mentally unhinged characters you see gaining fame on reality TV shows, Keenan Cahill has actually worked hard to earn his place in pop culture. He suffers from a rare genetic disorder called Mucopolysaccharidosis (MPS type VI). In comparison, most celebrities suffer from a more common disorder better known as "ego."

The first video that garnered Keenan international attention was his cover of Katy Perry's "Teenage Dream." Legions of adoring fans shared the video of his lovably goofy take on Perry's ode to teenage love, and Cahill suddenly found himself a celebrity.

The video even found its way to Katy Perry herself. In a single week, the video went from six hundred thousand views to three million and now has over fifty-five million views to date. Since then, Cahill has

Keenan Cahill at Q102 Jingle Ball in 2011 in Philadelphia, PA
(Paul Froggatt/PR Photos)

collaborated with some of the biggest names in music including videos with Justin Bieber and The Wanted. For a kid who spent the better part of his childhood shuttling between hospitals, suddenly he had no limits on who he could become and what he could achieve. The moral of the story? The next time you pick on a kid at school, that kid could become an Internet celebrity and make you look like the chump that you really are for picking on him in the first place.

In addition to Cahill's successful YouTube channel and appearance on E!'s *Chelsea Lately*, Cahill has also appeared on CW's *America's Next Top Model* with Tyra Banks, NBC's *America's Got Talent* with Nick Cannon, and ABC's American Music Awards performing with LMFAO, Justin Bieber, will.i.am, and David Hasselhoff.

He has created viral campaigns for the San Francisco Giants, the New York Knicks, Smartwater (starring Jennifer Aniston), and Wrigley Gum (with Serenading Unicorn). In other words, this kid has done more in his life than 99 percent of the critics in your life who keep trying to discourage you. Kidding aside, this one's pretty inspiring.

So stop listening to the judgmental losers in your life and become a success to really shut them up for good.

Another YouTube sensation is Charice. In 2005 Charice joined *Little Big Star*, a talent show in the Philippines loosely patterned after *American Idol*, except with more sympathetic judges who actually try to help others and not insult them as a way to make themselves feel better than everyone else.

Proving that talent shows often ignore people who actually have talent, Charice only placed third in the *Little Big Star* competition. An avid supporter, Dave Dueñas started posting a series of her performance videos on YouTube. Eventually, these videos received over fifteen million hits, turning her into an Internet sensation. Her fame on the Internet grew so rapidly that she could have even filmed a video of herself, giving the finger to all those judges on *Little Big Star* who didn't vote for her.

Over the next few years, she appeared on many American TV shows, including the Oprah Winfrey show. She has performed with Celine Dion and was cast in a recurring role in the television series *Glee*. On the show, she plays an exchange student from the Philippines named Sunshine Corazon, who presents serious competition against the lead character.

Twitter Sensations

In 2009 Justin Halpern started a Twitter account called "S**t My Dad Says," which shared the thoughts of his seventy-four-year-old curmudgeonly father. His tweets included short bits of wisdom such as: "I lost 20 pounds . . . How? I drank bear piss and took up fencing. How the f**k you think, son? I exercised."

Eventually his tweets proved so popular that people started sharing them with others. Like a shark that can smell blood a mile away, Hollywood quickly sniffed out his growing fame. It goes without saying that show business only likes associating with winners so they can look like winners too. It's high school all over again.

Harper Collins quickly offered Justin a book deal. When the book became a best seller, CBS turned his book into a situation comedy starring William Shatner (the guy who could never act in the original *Star Trek* series, and who always got the hot alien babes). Just by setting up a Twitter account and sticking to his brand of "S**t My Dad Says," Justin turned his sense of humor into a career as an author due to the support of over three million followers on Twitter.

If you think becoming an Internet sensation is something other people can do but you can't, you might be humbled to know that Jason Scott opened a Twitter account in 2007 to post tweets supposedly written by his cat, Sockington. Obviously cats can't write, but then again, neither can most Hollywood directors, yet they take credit for writing screenplays all the time. So the thought of a cat writing on Twitter shouldn't come as a surprise to anyone.

Between 2007 and January 2009, Sockington's Twitter account grew to ten thousand followers. In February 2009, Twitter started recommending the Sockington account to all new users, which added between five hundred to five thousand new followers a day. By 2009 the account had half a million followers. By 2010, Sockington had over one and a half million followers, making him the ninety-eighth most popular Twitter feed. If a cat can attract so much publicity on Twitter, what are you waiting for? A hamster to shame you with more followers than you have?

Jason Scott even plans to sell T-shirts with Sockington's face on it and may soon score a book deal. Given a choice between giving a book deal to an unknown author with the literary skills of Hemingway or

Faulkner, or a popular cat with millions of followers who will likely turn it into a best seller overnight, can you guess which option book publishers will consider?

Facebook and All-Around Social Media Celebrities

While Sockington's tweets are obviously imaginary (sorry. I know how shocked you must be), Lil Bub's fame is based on reality. Lil Bub's owner publicizes her photos and content through Facebook, YouTube, Instagram, and Twitter. Because of the popularity of her pictures, Lil Bub has grown a huge following, allowing her owner to open up an online store and sell Lil Bub Merchandise. In addition, Lil Bub has also appeared on *The Today Show* and other morning programs.

Lil Bub is what is known as a "perma-kitten." That means she'll stay kitten sized and maintain kitten-like features her entire life, not unlike many men or women who never grow up, act immature and live with their mothers for their entire lives.

Physically, Lil Bub is a dwarf, which means her limbs are disproportionately small relative to the rest of her body. She has short, stubby legs and a weird, long, serpent-like body. Her lower jaw is very short compared to her upper jaw, and her teeth never grew in so she's as toothless as a redneck NASCAR fan hooked on meth.

Despite her physical condition, Lil Bub maintains a healthy appetite and eats both dry and wet food with no problems. Additionally, Lil Bub is a polydactyl cat, meaning she has extra toes. She even has one extra toe on all four of her paws and her front paws even have two opposable thumbs, which might indicate that the cat species is starting to evolve and will eventually become capable of opening their own cans of cat food for a change.

Her most prominent features are her big, bulging, wonder-filled green eyes. Some think she can see into the future, although whatever future she sees, she's not telling for fear it might upset somebody. (Hint: By the year 2304, the Chicago Cubs still will have failed to win the World Series.)

Lil Bub was the runt of an otherwise healthy litter from a stray outdoor mother. She just was born with several genetic mutations that make her special or a freak of nature, depending on your point of view. Despite the fact that she can't talk, write, or even move to Los Angeles in hopes of striking it big in Hollywood, Lil Bub has managed to become more famous than most people on the planet.

Knowing that animals can become Internet sensations, you can openly weep at the fact that cats can get more followers and fame than people, or you can realize that if a housecat can become famous on the Internet, there should be nothing stopping you. What are you waiting for? A cockroach to become the next Internet sensation before you do? A marigold to become more popular? The opportunities are freely available to everyone. It's up to you to take advantage of them now.

Courting Fame through Social Networks

"We're all publishers now, and the more we publish,
the more valuable connections we'll make."

—Peter Cashmore, founder of Mashable

In the old days, celebrities seemed unreal since you could only see them in the movies, on TV, or in magazines and newspapers. Seeing a celebrity in person back then was as unlikely as seeing Lindsay Lohan studying a twelve-step program today. (Or counting to 12 at all?)

In those days when celebrities only appeared as images in movies or magazines, nobody knew much about their private lives, let alone their thoughts or opinions. In fact, most people liked celebrities precisely because they didn't know their thoughts or opinions. Just think how much you would like most of your relatives or coworkers if they would just stand there and shut up.

When news of any celebrity appeared, it usually came filtered through newspapers and magazines. Such media moguls had to decide if printing a story about a celebrity was more important than printing a more newsworthy story, maybe one teaching people about the mass slaughter that took place in Rwanda in 1994. When having to decide between telling the public something that might disturb their beliefs and soothing the public with a pointless story about a meaningless celebrity, the story about the celebrity always won.

Today, the filtering mechanism, the time delay, and the limited distribution of newspapers and magazines are gone. Instead of feeding carefully crafted press releases and stories to reporters in the hopes that they would print a flattering story about a celebrity days, weeks, or even months later, celebrities are taking matters into their own hands. Letting celebrities control anything on their own can be as dangerous as giving congressmen unlimited access to hookers, but in today's world, celebrities can now reach their raving fan base immediately without going through the middleman of newspaper and magazine publishers. For better or worse.

With Twitter, celebrities can post their meaningless opinions to the world. Now their followers can feel like their favorite musicians, actors, and comedians are talking directly to them in the same sense that putting little kids on the laps of shopping mall Santa Clauses gives children the feeling that they're talking directly to the man who forces elves to make toys for them in the off-season and never gets in trouble for violating child labor laws.

With Facebook, fans can bask in the delusion that they're "friends" with celebrities like singer Taylor Swift or super model Tyra Banks. In return for befriending celebrities on Facebook, fans can receive the latest information direct from the celebrities themselves, often before the gossip magazines and tabloids can print a story that most people will never bother reading anyway.

The Internet, and social media networks in particular, has basically wiped out the middlemen of newspapers and publishers. Now celebrities have direct access to their fan base without the drawbacks of having someone constantly asking them for an autograph. Celebrities are embracing social media networks for three reasons:

Social media networks often create celebrities, such as Nora, a piano-playing cat whose videos on YouTube are more popular (and useful) than anything produced by a congressman or Supreme Court justice. After achieving fame through luck or actual talent, social media networks then help keep celebrities in the spotlight.

In the old days, celebrities only appeared in the spotlight when they did something interesting such as appearing in a hit movie, winning a major sporting competition without the benefit of performance-enhancing drugs, or crashing their car into a tree while screaming

REASONING	BENEFITS
★ Shameless Self-Promotion	Twenty-four-hour public exposure at their own leisure. Free publicity. Being both the source and the delivery network for breaking news about themselves.
★ Damage Control	Being able to respond to negative publicity and give their side of the story, even if their side of the story is totally illogical and indefensible, like Arnold Schwarzenegger trying to explain that it could just be a coincidence why his housekeeper's son looks so much like him. (Can't blame the guy for trying.)
★ Making Money	Making money by shamelessly exploiting their fans, squeezing even more cash out of people whose retirement plan involves lottery tickets and slot machines, or demanding more money from the brands they endorse and for gigs they book. Celebrity social media pages are like billboards, and have the potential to earn lots of money with the right size following.

a drunken tirade against people of Jewish descent. As soon as that moment had passed, celebrities often found themselves forgotten by the general public.

Since celebrities crave attention like rock musicians crave drugs, they quickly realized that social media networks could satisfy their desire for fame by giving them their own spotlight to shine on themselves as many times as they liked (which is usually every day).

Social media networks also give celebrities the power of controlling public opinion. With paparazzi ambushing celebrities in hopes of capturing a picture of a famous person picking their nose, and gossip magazines hoping to dig up embarrassing stories of their past when they appeared in soft-core pornography and had sex with farm animals, celebrities have no control over what the public reads or sees about them. However, by embracing social media networks, celebrities can now control the message and even respond to negative publicity.

Between 1992 and 1994 the actress Nicole Eggert played a sexy lifeguard in the TV show *Baywatch*. When the celebrity tabloids published unflattering pictures of Nicole showing the weight she had gained

Max Espinoza/Ruben Gerard

since her last *Baywatch* appearance, Nicole responded by releasing a humorous video of herself in the same *Baywatch* swimsuit, except this time noticeably showing her extra weight flapping in the wind like Rush Limbaugh's jowls bouncing up and down as he wolfs down another hot dog. By mocking the criticism about her weight, Nicole turned a potential public relations disaster into a cause for celebration that gained her support from the public, generating additional positive publicity.

Social media networks let celebrities craft their own image. That can include sharing naked pictures, stories about hemorrhoids, and the results of their latest HIV test. If anyone else told you this type of information, you would probably ease away and suddenly have somewhere else to be, but if a celebrity tells you this same type of information, you would probably gobble it up eagerly and ask to hear more.

Perhaps the most important reason celebrities are flocking to social media networks like alcoholics rushing to an open bar (I am on an analogy roll here . . . forgive me) is because of the new opportunities to make money without doing much to deserve it. For celebrities, this is absolutely irresistible.

A company called Ad.ly has developed an entire business on monetizing Twitter. When companies want to advertise through Twitter, they contact Ad.ly. When celebrities want some quick cash to further exploit their fame that they probably don't deserve, they also contact Ad.ly. Then Ad.ly matches celebrities with company products, and pays celebrities to Tweet about that particular advertiser's products. The celebrities have already built up a huge Twitter following, so Ad.ly helps these celebrities turn their fans into unwitting targets for advertisements.

Since launching in 2009, Ad.ly has created over twenty thousand endorsements for well-known companies like Sony, Old Navy, Best Buy, and other name brands. Ad.ly currently has more than five thousand celebrities in its Twitter network to market the brands that request the company's services. Even if you're not a celebrity but have a large Twitter following, Ad.ly will pay you to Tweet their client's products, although as a non-celebrity, you'll get paid much less for doing the same (or more) amount of work. The amount of money you can get paid depends on the number of followers you have and the amount of your fame.

Advertising through Twitter eliminates the middleman of newspapers and magazines, plus it includes a celebrity endorsement at the same time. Even better, the ads go directly to a celebrity's fan base for guaranteed exposure that doesn't break any laws. Place an ad in a newspaper or magazine and even though thousands of people might buy that newspaper or magazine, all of them might not look at that particular ad. Force-feeding ads to followers on Twitter guarantees they'll see the ad whether they like it or not, although you still can't line the bottom of a bird cage with a tweet from your favorite celebrity, even if that's where it really belongs.

Now think of a reality TV star like Kim Kardashian. Kim Kardashian has millions of people who follow her on Twitter. This massive captive audience wasting time following Kim Kardashian's daily thoughts represents a huge marketing windfall. And a source of great amusement and disdain from other countries who come to the correct conclusion that we are just willfully dumbing ourselves down.

Through companies like Ad.ly, Kim Kardashian can tweet about a product and get paid $10,000 to $15,000 per tweet due to her massive outreach. Celebrities like Kim Kardashian can post sponsored tweets with a #sponsored hash tag, or they can do a more secretive endorsement deal where they simply gush about a product, knowing that a percentage of their gullible followers will immediately rush out and buy it.

Every celebrity specializes in tweeting about certain products. Kim Kardashian typically focuses on products that she would use such as makeup, clothing brands, and food products. (Obviously she wouldn't bother promoting products she would never use like books, chess sets, or brain teaser puzzles.) She simply chooses which products she wants to Tweet about and when, and how many sponsored tweets she wants to post. The purpose of her tweets is to get her followers to click on the links and buy something, putting money in her pocket while emptying money out of their own.

E! reality star and former Playmate Kendra Wilkinson earns an average of $11,765 per sponsored tweet, which allows her to make money without taking her clothes off any more. Congrats, Kendra! With more than one million followers, she has her choice of the ads she wants to promote such as electronics, weight-loss and fitness products, Facebook apps and jewelry.

Like Kim Kardashian, Kendra doesn't post sponsored Tweets every day because even followers of a Playboy centerfold can only tolerate so many ads when all they want to see are breasts and crotches. Kendra also works her ads into a conversation so they don't seem obvious, such as, "Examining my breasts right now that are larger than a Samsung Galaxy smartphone!" However, look for a "#ad" tag, which indicates that the tweet is an advertisement designed to sucker you into making more money for Kendra or any other celebrity getting paid to advertise a product they probably don't use themselves.

Grammy-nominated hip-hop artist Soulja Boy has millions of followers and earns close to $10,000 per tweet. Kim Kardashian's sister, Khloé Kardashian, gets paid about $8,235 to tweet to her three million followers. Former *The Hills* star Audrina Patridge earns $1,764 per tweet while *Jersey Shore* star JWoww pockets $2,353 every time she posts a sponsored tweet.

While hardworking people are breaking their backs working in manual labor jobs, celebrities make much more just by turning their followers into unwilling ad recipients.

Twitter is just one of many ways that celebrities are making money through social media networks, but it's not the only way. Ray William Johnson doesn't have an agent, a contract, or a TV show, yet he's making one million dollars a year from his own series that appears on YouTube.

Ray William Johnson's YouTube videos have more than 1.5 billion total views, which translate into five million views every week. Given that Google pays up to $9,000 for every two million views, he has now earned a fortune by completely bypassing the traditional TV networks that still think they can dictate their programming schedule to a captive audience.

According to the *Wall Street Journal*, more than 780 million people now watch YouTube every month, which is more than many cable TV networks. Until cable TV networks start offering short videos of cats riding robotic vacuum cleaners or guys getting hit in the crotch with tennis rackets and soccer balls, they won't be able to compete against YouTube's voyeuristic appeal. How can anything possibly compete?

As more people look for entertainment beyond the traditional TV networks, producers no longer have to go through the TV networks to broadcast their content. If you want to bet on the next industry to go belly up faster than a neglected tropical fish, watch the TV network industry flop as badly as Blockbuster Video, Kodak, and Borders bookstores.

Besides getting a cut of the revenue generated by ads that appear on YouTube videos, YouTube content producers can also advertise their own merchandise to make even more. If prostitutes and drug dealers could advertise on YouTube, the revenue generated could pay off the national debt in three seconds. (Until the politicians dig the country into another trillion-dollar hole one second later. Been awhile, have you missed my Washington commentary?)

Besides promoting themselves on YouTube, musicians are now getting a share of the advertising revenue from their music videos, although not always as much as they would like. Being musicians, they're already used to having record labels, promoters, and managers screw them over, so having YouTube do it to them isn't anything different.

Instead of downloading MP3 files, many people are skipping traditional music stores like iTunes and going straight to YouTube to listen to old music and discover new recording artists. Combine music videos on YouTube with young people listening to music on smartphones and tablets and you can see how YouTube has become a new force for promoting yourself to the world while making extra money at the same time.

Dangers of Social Media Networks

The whole point of social media networks is to control your message to the public in a way that's impossible through magazines and newspapers alone. Besides having a conversation with your fans, you can respond to their comments and call them names if you really meet someone who deserves to be insulted.

Yet you have to use social media consciously and deliberately. As Democratic US Congressman Anthony Weiner discovered, (collective sigh and eye roll here) exposing yourself on social media can be a double-edged sword, especially if you have a last name that suggests the body part you're going to expose to the world.

On May 27, 2011, Anthony Wiener thought women would love to see nothing more than a middle-aged man in his underwear. Following this brilliant line of deductive reasoning, he sent a picture of his erection through his underwear to a twenty-one-year old college student who was "following" his Twitter posts. Although he quickly removed the message, claiming that hackers had broken into his account (as if hackers even cared who he was), screen shots of Weiner's original message and the photo of his erection were captured and sent to conservative blogger Andrew Breitbart, who published them on his BigJournalism website the next day.

The Anthony Weiner sexting scandal, dubbed Weinergate, demonstrated once more that people entrusted with spending taxpayer money often have no higher maturity level than a drunken college fraternity member, yet they still get better pension and health care benefits than the rest of us. (I'm back!!) On June 1, Weiner gave a series of interviews denying sending the photo, but could not say "with certitude" that the photo was not of him. Of course, he never explained how someone could get a picture of him in his underwear in the first place.

Eventually when Anthony Weiner realized that most people aren't as stupid as he is, he finally admitted to sending the erection photo along with other sexually explicit photos and messages to women both before and during his marriage. This admission made his wife realize she had married a loser instead of a lifelong meal ticket like other congressmen's wives had done.

On June 16, 2011, Weiner announced his intention to resign from Congress. Even today when you look up Anthony Weiner in the Congressional records, you can see that his face has been replaced by a photo of his crotch, since that's the only part of him that contributed in any way to the workings of the American economy.

How to Take Advantage of Social Media Networks

Now that you've seen how celebrities and people who shouldn't be celebrities (Kim Kardashian) use social media networks to promote themselves, you might be wondering how you can take advantage of social media networks as well.

First, **you have to give people a reason to become your fan.** That means if you're not lucky enough to become famous just by acting like a moron on a reality TV show, you have to provide something of value to the public instead. This all goes back to your brand: who are you? If you can't answer that question, you either don't have a brand or you might already be suffering from premature memory loss.

For example, Lance Armstrong's brand used to be that he won the Tour de France seven times, which made him the perfect spokesman for athletic events and organizations. Now after admitting that he lied about taking performance-enhancing drugs, Lance Armstrong's new brand as a liar would make him the perfect spokesman for lawyers and politicians.

Once you know your brand as a weight-loss guru, a real estate investor, or a TV evangelist who keeps asking for more money while spending it all on himself, you'll know what type of people to target and how to present yourself to attract your target audience. Then you need to start promoting yourself on one or more social media networks.

Think of all those bored office workers trapped in cubicles in office buildings all over the world. What would they want to see instead of doing the actual job they were paid to do? It's a captive audience in many ways. Once you can visualize your YouTube video through the eyes of a bored office worker who has nothing more to look forward to than making it to the next weekend, you can better understand what type of video you should produce.

If your product relies on a combination of text, still images, and short videos, then Facebook might be the best social media network to use. Of course, you can always combine social media networks and promote yourself in multiple ways such as tweeting on Twitter, posting updates on Facebook, and uploading videos to YouTube. Initially, this might seem like a lot of work, so you can always start with one social media network and then branch out into others when you can afford to hire high school and college kids to do all the trivial work for you.

To promote yourself through social media, you need the following:

+ **A brand that defines what you have to offer.** Your brand not only attracts the right people who want what you can deliver, but also weeds out the obvious idiots who can't see your greatness. This way you won't waste your time on people who are foolishly unwilling to give you money.

+ **A product of some kind (tweets, videos, pictures, etc.) that gives people a reason to keep coming back for more,** like gambling addicts who keep going back to casinos despite losing all the time.

+ **A predictable schedule for delivering your product so people will keep coming back.**

While Twitter, Facebook, and YouTube may be the three most popular social media networks (at the time of this writing), these aren't the only social media networks around. Pinterest and Polyvore target the fashion industry, LinkedIn is best for public speakers and business gurus, and MySpace targets musicians.

The size of a social media network is far less important than whether it will reach the people you want to attract. (You know, the old quality over size thing.) While you can post pictures of yourself on Facebook, with its one billion users (most of whom don't have much of a life or else they wouldn't waste it checking their Facebook status every five seconds) posting those same pictures on Instagram might actually get you more attention since Instagram is dedicated to sharing pictures while Facebook is not.

Once you've decided which social media network to exploit first, the next step is to promote yourself. First, promote your social media presence outside of the social network, such as making your blog or website direct readers to your Twitter or YouTube postings. Now if people like your blog or website, they might follow you on Twitter or watch your YouTube postings regularly. If they don't like your blog or website, then you don't care if they get hit by a car since they aren't going to help you anyway.

Second, **keep your social media presence focused, useful, and interesting.** For example, if your brand is teaching people how to lose weight while eating chocolate sundaes and cheeseburgers, then everything you write or record must be related to losing weight.

To attract and keep the attention of people who not only can't remember what they ate for breakfast that morning, but can't remember what they just did three seconds ago, you need the following:

+ Attractive, sexy pictures of yourself
+ Useful or interesting information spiced with sex and/or humor whenever possible
+ Frequent updates

To grab the attention of people who visit your social media page, post an interesting, attractive picture of yourself that defines your brand. Nobody wants to see an ordinary guy sitting around in his underwear, but lots of people (mostly guys) would like to see an attractive woman sitting around in her underwear. Remember, **sex always attracts people.**

Any attractive, sexy picture of yourself will grab someone's attention. The important point is that if you're going to post a picture of yourself on the Internet, make yourself look your best and not like some slob covered in grease from working on his car the night before.

But while people might be drawn to your picture, they won't keep coming back unless you provide them something of interest. Unless you're a porn star, supermodel or centerfold, you might not always want to promote sex as your content.

After sex, **humor** is the second most popular way to attract people. Everyone likes to laugh, especially if they can laugh at someone they hate like their boss or rival coworker. Find a way to make people laugh consistently and you will keep them coming back.

If you can't rely on sex and you can't make it funny, then the third best option is to **give your audience useful information.** If you're an athlete, you might give tips on how to exercise, eat right, and circumvent tests to catch blood doping. If you're a financial guru, you might provide information on how to make money and squirrel it away in offshore banks to avoid paying taxes. As long as you're providing useful information, people will keep coming back for more, even if it has nothing to do with sex and doesn't make them laugh.

Finally, you can't provide useful information once and expect people to keep coming back. To keep your fans coming back for more, you need to provide a steady stream of information on a consistent basis. Give someone sex, humor, or useful information once a month and you'll risk losing people who don't have the patience to wait that long. After a month in this day and age, they might have no idea who you are or why they were ever interested. **Give someone sex, humor, or useful information every day and you'll keep people hooked.**

Think of your social media presence like the comic strip section of the newspaper. Every day the newspaper prints another cartoon, knowing that people will have to get the next day's edition of that newspaper to read it. Of course, people could just find the same cartoon on the Internet, which explains why most people are only interested in newspapers when they need something to cushion a package. The point is that you need fresh content to keep your audience coming back for more. How often you need to provide fresh content depends on your audience and how hard you really want to work.

Tricks to Promoting Yourself on Social Media Networks

Social networks provide little privacy in this day and age. Either you embrace that fact and make it work, or you sit back and wait for an unpleasant surprise. By embracing the concept of social media, you are accepting the new normal.

The simplest way to promote yourself is by association, which is why politicians hang around people who have better reputations for not lying than they do. Post pictures of you with other people and everyone will immediately associate you with the positive aspects of those other people.

Social media is not about conversation or relationships; **it's all about content.** The content you provide is your biggest selling point. And though it's not the best platform to sell products direct, it is the best platform to move people to where they can buy a product directly. A little celebrity shove can go a long way when it comes to sales.

If you can manage to get your picture taken with a major celebrity like Brad Pitt or Halle Berry, your "coolness" factor will immediately rise. Now you have instant credibility among strangers. By using the credibility of famous people to make you look better, you can now perform all kinds of crimes against humanity and people will still like you. Just look at how positively the world viewed Liberian dictator Charles Taylor when he gave supermodel Naomi Campbell a huge diamond. Later he was accused of committing war crimes while selling "blood diamonds" to buy weapons to kill more of his fellow citizens, but at least he got to hang around a supermodel and look good to the world through his association with Naomi Campbell. See how it works?

If you can't get your picture taken with a famous celebrity, the next best tactic is to get your picture taken with attractive people who are associated with a well-known brand. You may not have a blood diamond to give to a supermodel like Naomi Campbell, but you can still get your picture taken with a Dallas Cowboys cheerleader, a beauty pageant contestant, or a topless dancer from the strip club down the street. The more prestigious the organization, the greater your credibility, even if nobody knows the person you're standing next to.

Besides famous people, get your picture taken in famous or visually appealing locations. Everyone can recognize an icon in a picture like the Eiffel Tower or the Leaning Tower of Pisa, but you can also get your picture taken in front of a beautiful waterfall, a rainbow, or even a car wreck. Nobody necessarily wants to see you, but they will enjoy seeing an interesting person or place in a picture that you just happen to be in.

Social media also allows you to deliver high-value content that is important to the audience. By offering this sought after content, you can also train your audience to do whatever you say, while building them up at the same time. They say the rule of thumb to a successful social media page is posting content multiple times per day. Typically, that would include five to fifteen posts to Twitter, one to three posts and shares on Facebook, and at least one post to a personal blog.

Videos are great for social media too. Especially when trying to sell a product, even if that product is yourself, having a visual demonstration and description can go a long way. One to five minute videos give the audience just enough to get interested. It doesn't always have to be photos either. You could recite quotes from famous people or drop the names of famous people in a humorous way to maximize your exposure. If you are working, and wrote, "Working harder than Ryan Seacrest!" it's already a more exciting statement than just working, and it's forever linked to a Google search for "Ryan Seacrest" at the same time.

If you've ever seen a crowd staring at nothing in particular, but you joined in to see what they were looking at, you already know the appeal of following a crowd for no reason, which is how political parties maintain their followers. (Ok, will try to stop now. It's out of control!) On your social media page, get your friends to link to you so it appears that you're super popular (even if you aren't). As others see how many people are following you, they'll be more inclined to follow you too. The more followers you get, the easier it will be to get even more followers, which is the same technique that propels dictators into power.

Also, don't expect others to find your website, blog, or social media page on their own. Go out and visit other people's sites, especially the people who already have the audience you want to attract. That means if you're a TV evangelist go visit other TV evangelist's websites and blogs and post comments with links directing people back to your site.

As long as you're making interesting comments or offering useful advice, nobody will mind seeing your own social media links advertised on someone else's site. Now if someone is dumb enough to donate money to one TV evangelist, there's a good chance that same person will rush to donate money to you as another TV evangelist. That demonstrates the power of association (and, again, the gullibility of the general public. But we like and need this gullibility. It's the bread and butter of the Fame Game. Just as long as you are wiser.)

Finally, promote yourself as a human being once in a while. Everyone likes to worship celebrities, but they also want to know that celebrities are just ordinary people who happen to make millions of dollars doing nothing in particular all day. When celebrities admit that they're frightened, upset, worried, or just a colossal emotional and psychological wreck from the little things in life like traffic jams, spiders, the criminally shameful lateness of pizza delivery her in LA, or raising kids and not wanting to slap the living daylights out of them every now and then, that brings out their humanity (and sometimes child protective services). People appreciate honesty, so if you talk about being a regular person just like your followers, you can temporarily make them forget that you make more money than they do.

With social media networks, you are now a publisher, TV producer, and radio show host. You can either talk to your fans to engage them, or you can ignore them and let them rally around someone else who doesn't look or smell as nice as you and obviously doesn't deserve all the money that should be rightfully going into your pockets.

When thinking about promoting yourself on social media networks, remember the words of the famous American philosopher Paris Hilton: "The only rule is don't be boring and dress cute wherever you go. Life is too short to blend in."

Take a look at how you can maximize exposure on each of your social media pages below:

Facebook

Create a fan page based on your celebrity personality for your fans-separate from your private account for friends and family. **Private life shouldn't spill into your public brand.** Join groups and fan pages of influencers that you want to be involved with. Grow your network by finding contacts in your address book. Manage privacy settings and make sure posts tagged with your name on it require your approval. Make one to three posts per day.

Twitter

Building up and maintaining your Twitter following can be time con-
suming but the payoff will ultimately be worth it. You already know
people have become "twitter celebrities," and celebrities have started
earning more money for tweets than you make at your desk job. Of all
of the social networks, Twitter is still arguably the most influential. It's
very important to keep up your appearance on the network to keep your
name out there. So what is the best way to begin your Twitter takeover?

1. Secure your name or the closest thing as a Twitter handle.
   Let's face it, you're probably already too late. But securing
   your name, or the closest thing to it is very important.
   HoneyBooBooFan30 was a good time in your life, but your
   name is forever, and way less foolish.

2. Make sure your profile is filled with useful information.
   Treat it like a business card or your resume. Include an
   appealing background that you can design yourself or find
   online. When you become famous, you can sell this background as ad space. It's better to advertise something of
   your own than to leave it blank.

3. Find your niche: everyone has his or her area of expertise.
   Follow accounts pertaining to your specialty, and interact
   with them daily. It's a little like making new friends behind
   the wall of the Internet. But also be sure to show them
   that you are very knowledgeable (or at least pretending to
   be), and make a name for yourself in that circle. Staying
   involved in trending topics can also do this. Since they are
   always changing, you'll be constantly interacting with different groups of people.

4. Only post good, original content. THINK before you
   tweet. This doesn't only pertain to dirty or semi-offensive
   tweets (hey that may even be your angle), but to all tweets.
   Over-posting makes you annoying. Annoying accounts get
   unfollowed.

5. Limit night tweeting. Simply put, people sleep at night. By
   morning, your awesome tweet will be buried under many

more. Don't waste a valuable tweet, just save it as a draft, or get a service like TweetDeck, Buffer, or HootSuite and schedule it for the morning. Reach your maximum audience. Retweets and replies can mean new followers.

6. Put your twitter button on all of your blogs and websites. You want readers to follow you, and you want them to tweet your stories on their own accounts.

7. Get your account verified. Yes it's true, the only way to get your Twitter account verified is to be famous, or have a legion of fake accounts pretending to be you. So by actually achieving this, it means you are often imitated, and never duplicated. Twitter official!

Instagram

Instagram is fairly new on the scene, but made a name for itself as soon as it was purchased by Facebook for one billion dollars (that's billion with a B). The same type of rules apply to Instagram as they do on Twitter, at least as far as securing your name and posting interesting and good quality photos. Utilizing hash tags is a popular way to get likes, followers, and possibly even land yourself on the coveted "popular page." Though Instagram doesn't have any ad revenue streams yet, there are plenty of under the table deals going down on the site if you know where to find them (or better yet, they know where to find you).

Google+

Google is clearly the world's leading search engine (despite what those Bing-it-on challenge commercials have been brainwashing you to think). Google+ is difficult to understand, lacking in users and content, and just doesn't compete with the big three. But it may actually be ahead of its time. One day, it's a safe bet that Google+ will be THE social network (or at least a distant second, third, or fourth option).

Google+ offers an easy way to connect with friends, family, colleagues, and others in separate "circles" choosing what content is available to each. All of this seamlessly connected to your Gmail account, which nearly everyone has already. Just sign up for Google+ to create your profile. Syndicate your content from other social networks for the time being, and engage other users while you can. Remember when Facebook took off, but you were a MySpace hanger-on who claimed you'd never betray Tom and your top eight? Well you did. And you were one of the last ones to the party. Don't be late to the Google+ party. You heard it here.

Pinterest

Men, a disclaimer: Pinterest is technically known as the "girls" social network. Exploring Pinterest will lead you to all kinds of photos of food, crafts, fashion, wedding and engagement ring hints, and abs. Lots of abs. Men who own brands: What are you waiting for?

Pinterest can be a very useful tool in making money. Unlike Facebook, which is a place to build a network of friends and fans, Pinterest is a place to share things that people are passionate about. Tying in products that are for sale on these pin boards has been known to generate a 12 percent pin and buy online, and 16 percent pin and buy offline rate. One of the best things you can do is to target women, and typically those who are money spenders. If that is your demographic, utilize Pinterest to make some sales!

LinkedIn

LinkedIn is more of the "white collar" networking site that's a little less social than the others, but serves a purpose. A lot of industry bigwigs utilize this site, so it's another way of catching their eye. One of the most important things you can do on LinkedIn is to fill in all of the information. Let me repeat: Fill in ALL of it because this is your online sales pitch for yourself that describes all of your talents, hobbies and experiences. When people are searching key words, you want to be on that list of people who pop up. A photo is definitely important to put a face to your name. Empty photo sections on social networking suggest laziness, embarrassment, or lack of openness interest. These are not you–don't be any of those things.

Next, make sure you connect to people that you deal with on a daily basis. They could come in handy at any moment. You never know. Need more people to interact with? Get involved in groups and discussions. One way to grab someone's attention and possibly impress them is to look interested and involved. Don't kid yourselves—looking interested is actually kind of important.

One of the most overlooked and for-your-own-good things you can do on LinkedIn is to **change your visibility settings.** Every time you visit a profile, that person can see that you have paid them a visit. Change your setting to "invisible" unless you want people to know you've been visiting their profile multiple times each day. Then you will just be a LinkedIn stalker. No good. Believe me, I learned the hard way!

Google: The Fame Authority

Google has quickly become the leading search engine on the Internet. "Google it" is the web search phrase even though people have been using search engines since the beginning of the Internet. (Or the beginning of time according to some sources.) In 2008 almost half of Internet users were using search engines on any typical day, which was up from one-third back in 2002. Today that number is probably inching closer and closer to 100%, as search engines are built into cell phones, web browsers and even popular social website search bars that allow you to "search the web."

PageRank has become a standard among websites, which rank sites on a scale from 0–10 and determines where your website will show up in Google search results. Sites who achieve a 5 or higher usually have thousands of sites that link back to them. Like most 0–10 scales, the higher the better. You can check your own page rank at www.prchecker.info.

Also helping that score are the sites that link to you. Google will crawl your site and the sites linking to you and make sure they feature content that are somewhat relevant to yours. Proper SEO (Search Engine Optimization) on your site can help contribute to a higher page rank.

While making your own site fit for a high rank, you can utilize social networks to rely on fans to help make your page even more highly ranked.

SEO: Playing the Fame Game with Google

Have you ever wondered how search engines like Google and Bing decide exactly which sites get placement on the top of the first page? Let us now unlock the mysteries of the Google gods. Here's where you can find out all about how you can land your website a prime piece of Google real estate.

It's definitely no easy task; however, there are a number of tips you should consider while getting into the routine. This will help you maximize your search engine placement.

First? **It's important to match your domain name with your title.** If you've listened at all, you already know that your domain name should be the closest thing to your name that was available. If your name is Lindsay Lohan (hopefully it's not) and your domain is Lindsaylohan. com (it's not), then the title of your site should be "Lindsay Lohan," or "Lindsay Lohan: Used To Be Actress." Or "Lindsay Lohan: Public Train Wreck." (Ok that's enough. Time to give poor Lindsay break. She is just my quintessential example of what not to do should big fame ever come your way.)

Some of the biggest contributors in the SEO game are keywords. Every good post has them in the text, as well as in the tags. When people search the web, they typically just type in a series of keywords that they hope will lead them to what they want.

So how many keywords should you put in a post? Abiding by our American approach of excess in, well, pretty much everything, some think the more keywords, the better the chance of landing on the top of a search. They are wrong. Keyword stuffing is frowned upon and can put you on the Internet's equivalent of the no fly list if you are caught as a repeat offender. When planning the keywords, make sure that you use them in the heading, as well as lightly in the main text of the page. Sometimes more is just more. Sometimes more is less. Sometimes more is a disaster. (Am now going to take my own advice and wrap up this meandering paragraph. But you get the point.)

Proximity and prominence are also important in choosing your keywords. Are your keywords too close to one another, or too far apart? The best bet is to keep them somewhat close together, as if you were trying to create phrases that people might search for. Think of what you would search for if you were interested in the topic that you are writing about. If you'd search for it, someone else probably would too. Search engines also prefer that your keywords are located at the top of your web page, with the most popular locations being the title or headers. This makes it easier to place the title in a search.

Your page content also says a lot about your blog. It is extremely important that the content of your pages should be on topic. Basically,

Lindsay Lohan departing the Beverly Hills courthouse in 2010
(Koi Sojer/PR Photos)

don't have a crummy website. That's one way you'll never make the front page of Google. Remember to add **meta tags** as well. Meta tags are often missed because they are handled backstage. Every time you upload a photo, you can edit the meta tags. This goes for every page you build. It's easy to look past, but important to not miss. It's kind of like writing your name in the tag of your underwear in case it ever gets lost. (I write mine in big block letters.)

Don't forget about links! **Links are the currency of the Internet.** The more sites that link to you, the more your page is worth. As we discussed previously with backlinks and PageRank, the sites with the highest ranks will see the best traffic. Link exchanges are a fair barter of the Internet as well. **Offer sites a link for link partnership and make sure your links are shared on social media.** Get your links out there the good old-fashioned way.

Going Viral

"Great writers arrive among us like new diseases—threatening, powerful, impatient for patients to pick up their virus, irresistible."

—Craig Raine

The scary word VIRUS conjures images of horror in hospitals or terrified corporate executives trying to regain control of the corrupted hard drives of their computers, In the medical and business world, a virus is something to avoid, but in the marketing and business world, a virus is something to embrace, create, and spread until it gains a life of its own. Think of yourselves as benign marketing terrorists spreading a virus around the globe that doesn't hurt anyone but makes everyone magically pay attention to you. (No, that *isn't* the same thing.)

If infecting the world with a virus could always be so lucrative, NBA players would be earning millions by spreading viruses through their sexual activities alone. In the real world, you don't want to catch a virus from an NBA player and need to dope yourself up with medicine to get rid of it before it damages your DNA. However, you may want to spread an Internet virus about your favorite NBA player through pictures and videos. Internet viruses are nothing more than items that people eagerly share with their friends by e-mail, text messaging or grabbing their friend or coworker by the ear and telling them, "You have to see this before I let you finish going to the bathroom!"

While Internet viruses can sometimes be audio or text, the majority of Internet viruses are pictures and video. Think about what makes pornography so appealing to priests and politicians. (Oops, I did it again!) Would you rather see a still picture of a naked woman or a video of a naked woman? Would you rather hear a naked woman talking or read a description of what a naked woman looks like?

Pictures and video reach right into the emotional appeal of people's brains, right past the often-dormant part that in theory should be able to discern the difference between educational television and reality TV. Listening and reading requires time to process information. For many people, any time needed to process information means less time they can be looking at more pictures and videos, so pictures and videos always have a greater chance of going viral than audio or text. It's the ADD of our generation. And it must be factored in for a successful Fame Game.

Definition of Viral Effect

Viral marketing is a strategy that encourages people to pass on a marketing message to others, creating the potential for exponential growth. Like viruses duplicating in the mouth of a Dallas Cowboy's cheerleader, such strategies take advantage of rapid multiplication to explode a single message to reach thousands to millions of people. An Internet virus replicates again and again, doubling with each iteration:

Think of viral marketing as "word-of-mouth" marketing on steroids, which is something Lance Armstrong and Barry Bonds can understand (except for the part about marketing.)

What makes viral marketing so effective is that it relies on other people to spread your message. When someone recommends a restaurant or a movie, that's a simple example of viral marketing. That is what makes viral marketing far more effective than ordinary marketing, because you trust the person giving you the message, or at least you can find the person who delivered that message so you can punch him in the face if you don't like his recommendation.

Because word-of-mouth marketing comes from people you trust, you'll be far more receptive to the message. In comparison, companies often spend millions of dollars for a sixty second commercial that airs on the Super Bowl, only to find that nobody cares. That's an example of wasted marketing or easy money, depending if you're the company paying for the ad or the ad agency that fleeced a company out of millions to create a commercial that people saw as a perfect time to go to the bathroom.

Although word-of-mouth marketing is far more effective than regular advertising, it can only spread slowly, like watching Heidi Montag trying to read a sentence consisting of more than three words. What makes viral marketing especially effective is that unlike ordinary word-of-mouth marketing that often entails getting spittle sprayed in your face while a single person talks to you, viral marketing taps into the limitless social media networks.

Not only do social media networks allow you to socialize with people you may never even know (or care to know), it allows a message to spread rapidly. A single viral message launched in Kentucky can travel to Istanbul, Harare, Innsbruck, and many other cities around the globe that most American high school students have never heard of. Today, word- of-mouth marketing isn't just limited to the water cooler at work, but to everyone on the planet.

Notable Examples of Content Going Viral

One of the biggest advantages of viral content is that appearances matter less than the actual content itself. Yes you heard me right: this is a fancy way of saying that talent is more important than surface appearances, which is the opposite of the way *Sports Illustrated* chooses swimsuit models. That means you could use the fanciest and most expensive video camera in the world, but if you're not capturing something interesting, an ordinary person using a mobile phone can capture a video that will prove far more popular. It's democracy in action!

One of the most-viewed viral videos of all time, known simply as "Charlie Bit My Finger—Again!" is deceptively simple. By December 2012, this video had reached five hundred million views and currently remains the most viewed YouTube item that is not a professional music video. The clip features two English brothers, aged three and one. The younger brother, Charlie, bites the finger of his older brother, Harry.

Babies are inherently interesting, so any time you have something cute (babies, kittens, puppies, nymphomaniac swimsuit models, etc.)

doing anything unusual, it's a key factor in whether the video will go viral or not. Upload a video of one adult biting the finger of another adult and the police will likely pick both adults up for questioning. More importantly, no one will be interested.

Another video that has been viewed over fifty-seven million times also taps into our interest in children. This video, called "David After Dentist," shows seven-year-old David DeVore's backseat trip home from the dentist's office after oral surgery. The medication seems to have put David in an altered state of consciousness as he spouts lines like "You have four eyes," "Is this gonna be forever?" and "Is this real life?"

If you can't capture something cute doing something unusual, you can focus on an adult doing something visually interesting and/or funny, such as comedian Jud Laipply's six-minute video called "The Evolution of Dance." In this video clip, Jud seamlessly demonstrates different dance moves from the robot to the chicken dance to the twist. His video has been viewed more than 138 million times as people laugh at his physical antics while also tapping into the audience's nostalgia for how stupid they must have looked as young adults performing those exact dance steps. Unlike the "Charlie Bit My Finger" video, which emphasized something cute doing something unusual, Jud's video provided humor while showing us something physically interesting.

Oftentimes, viral videos happen by accident and capture something that's not humorous, but interesting in a horrifying manner that makes us want to watch anyway. As our humiliating collective love of reality TV demonstrates, we have a collective fascination for the embarrassing, the dramatic and the morbid. At a September 2007 forum with Senator John Kerry at the University of Florida, student Andrew Meyer loudly questioned Kerry's ties with then President George W. Bush. As the university police attempted to subdue Meyer, he screamed, "What did I do?" and then shouted out, "Don't tase me, bro!" before being tasered by the police anyway, which goes to show you the effectiveness of asking any request of the police. Andrew Meyer's video, recorded by someone else, has now been viewed over four million times.

While videos capturing scary events are inherently interesting, so are bloopers and bizarre situations. A short five-second video clip of a chipmunk dubbed "Dramatic Chipmunk" has been viewed over nineteen million times. What makes this video amusing is that it captured a chipmunk turning towards the camera and looking as if it was caught in the act of something more sinister, such as bailing out a major corporation with billions of taxpayer funds just to get a kickback later.

One of the most popular blooper video clips shows South Carolina's Caitlin Upton during the Miss Teen USA pageant responding to the question of why 20 percent of Americans can't find the United States on a world map. Her nonsensical stream of consciousness babbling shows that the brain is still the most underdeveloped organ used by the human species. (And answered the question by default.)

Caitlin Upton's comment includes, "I believe that our education, like such as in South Africa and the Iraq, everywhere like such as, and I believe that they should, our education over here in the US should help the US . . ." Blooper video clips not only provide humor, but they let us laugh at others who will probably make more money than all of us despite their lack of a single brain cell.

Taking Advantage of Viral Content

Many viral videos occur by chance, for instance a video capturing a cat riding on a robotic vacuum cleaner. Other viral videos are planned, for example placing a cat on a robotic vacuum cleaner until he stays on long enough for you to shoot a video that looks like you captured it by chance. (It's not as easy as it looks I tell you. And I have the scratches to prove it. Maybe I should have tried while wearing my meat dress.)

While such videos are nice, they're unpredictable. Every day, people upload over two hundred thousand videos to YouTube with twenty-four hours of footage getting uploaded every minute. Out of that huge number, some will go viral but the majority will get a handful of views and that's it. While it's nice to create a video that goes viral, **it's even better to create a viral video to promote yourself or your product in some way.**

To demonstrate the power of their blenders, Blendtec regularly released a series of videos showing a Blendtec blender destroying various items from a hockey puck and a chicken to an iPhone and an iPad. The "Will it blend?" videos became viral almost immediately and dramatically increased sales of Blendtec blenders as a result.

Old Spice created a surreal video showing a handsome man, Isaiah Mustafa, urging women to compare him to their man. If they found their man lacking in physical attractiveness, they could at least give him

Old Spice so their man would at least smell like the handsome man in the video.

To emphasize this point and further incorporate the always-successful technique of making people feel inferior (and laugh with you at the same time) so they'll buy your product, the Old Spice commercial showed Isaiah in constantly changing surroundings. First he starts out in a bathroom, then appears in a boat, then on a horse in a seamless display of scenery changes. To further generate excitement, Old Spice had Isaiah Mustafa reply to online comments and questions about Old Spice from websites like Twitter, Facebook, Reddit, Digg, YouTube and others.

While many people try to make money off web pages by selling advertising, Alex Tew went one step further. He offered to sell his entire web page to advertisers for one dollar per pixel. Not only was Alex's idea different, but the novelty attracted advertisers and curious onlookers, which made his web page even more attractive to advertisers. By the time he sold every pixel, Alex made well over a million dollars.

One of the earliest viral video campaigns promoted the movie *The Blair Witch Project*. The movie's producers posted a website that described the legend of the Blair Witch and claimed that children had gone missing in that area for years. The latest news consisted of "found" video footage from three missing teenagers who had gone in search of a witch who didn't live in a gingerbread house.

Since everyone thought the stories of the Blair Witch were true and that people had gone missing in the area haunted by the Blair Witch, the idea of "found" video footage of the three missing teenagers' last days proved irresistible. After all, who couldn't resist watching the demise of another human being just for the entertainment value alone?

To market their new line of shoes, Nike filmed basketball star Kobe Bryant jumping over unusual items, including a pool of snakes and an Aston-Martin driving straight at him. People shared these videos because of the novelty factor and because they weren't sure if the videos were real or created with special effects and wanted to, judge for themselves. (And as aforementioned were bored at work.) Of particular appeal was the desire to see if Kobe Bryant would hurt himself in a graphic display of the frailties of human flesh when colliding with thousands of pounds of metal moving at sixty miles per hour. (Or was that just me??)

The band OK Go specializes in videos of band members doing unusual physical activities from performing a choreographed routine on treadmills to setting off Rube Goldberg-like contraptions while their latest song plays in the background.

Chevrolet decided to create an OK Go music video that featured their Chevy Sonic careening down a two-mile racetrack outfitted with a thousand musical instruments. The car would play the instruments as it drove by as the band members sang while seated comfortably inside. This music video captured over twenty-three million views as a result.

When Felix Baumgartner decided to set the world's record for the longest free fall skydiving jump on the edge of space, Red Bull spotted an opportunity. Since this event would be filmed and people were likely to watch it anyway, Red Bull sponsored Felix Baumgartner's attempt to break the sound barrier in his twenty-three-mile free fall to Earth by plastering the Red Bull logo on his spacesuit.

Most successful viral video campaigns offer something beyond the unusual that people want to see. It's not enough just to show something unusual; it has to be something that people can't wait to see for themselves. It should have several layers of unusual, like me simultaneously turning away the pizza guy and telling you not to bother with fame if you have no talent while complimenting our fearless leaders in Washington.

Seeing a *Playboy* centerfold studying for a physics test or a politician passing a lie detector test may be unusual, but nobody wants to see that. Seeing a *Playboy* centerfold giving a politician a lap dance isn't unusual, but it's still engaging. Now combine a *Playboy* centerfold giving a politician a lap dance (an engaging visual) during the presidential inauguration on national television (an unusual situation) and that suddenly turns the image into a "must see" video, increasing its chances of going viral.

Failed Viral Videos

Most attempts at viral marketing fizzle and go nowhere, like Rush Limbaugh trying to do wind sprints. Occasionally, a viral marketing attempt actually goes viral and generates massive amounts of publicity without relying on someone named Kardashian to promote it. However, sometimes viral marketing campaigns not only fail, but fail horribly. By seeing what didn't work, you can avoid making similar mistakes in your own viral marketing attempts.

To promote the cartoon movie *Aqua Teen Hunger Force Colon Movie Film for Theaters* Cartoon Network paid people to hang sticky LED signs all over Boston. Not knowing what these flashing light devices with exposed wires and batteries were, police assumed they were bombs and shut down bridges and subway stations. The lesson to learn here, boys and girls, is that viral marketing won't work if you scare people unnecessarily. Steer clear of promotional materials that look in any way like bombs, firearms or anthrax. I guarantee you that you will not get the result you wanted.

R&B singer Ashanti learned that lesson when she tried to promote her new album by launching a viral marketing campaign that allowed people to send death threats to their friends. Why anyone thought that threatening someone's life would cause someone to rush out and buy a product remains one of those mysteries of the universe.

To market the Judd Apatow movie *Forgetting Sarah Marshall*, an advertising agency posted signs in various cities, proclaiming their hatred for Sarah Marshall with messages such as "My Mother Always Hated You, Sarah Marshall" and "You Do Look Fat In Those Jeans, Sarah Marshall." What the ad agency didn't realize was that many real people are named Sarah Marshall, and all those real Sarah Marshalls didn't find the random insults amusing. Major league backfire.

To promote the Chevy Tahoe SUV, General Motors posted a website where anyone could create their own Tahoe commercial. While some people created commercials in an attempt to win one of the prizes for the most creative commercials, critics used Chevy's website to mock the car's fuel efficiency and environmental friendliness. One critical commercial promoted this message:

> Hey, 2,325 U.S. kids have died, 16,653 have been injured, and up to $2 trillion will be spent to keep our oil supply safe. If you support the troops you'll get out there and use some of it! Chevy Tahoe: Don't let all that blood go to waste.

Although you can't expect to control whether a message goes viral or not, you can control what that message might be. As a result, you never, ever want to give other people (especially your critics) control over your message. Because as we have established, everyone has critics (even me) and they should never be given a free reign to dump large wads of poop over your marketing efforts.

Creating Your Own Viral Content

You can't predict if a video or picture will go viral, but you can maximize your chances that you'll create something that will at least be interesting enough that people will want to share your message with friends, coworkers, and people they wish were their friends.

But it's unlikely that you'll create something one day, and just haphazardly post it on the Internet, and watch it go viral. Before you post anything, start with a strategy to maximize your chance of success.

First, think about the audience you're trying to reach and the product you're trying to promote. People who enjoy the music of Eminem won't always be the same people interested in learning household tips from Martha Stewart, although they might be interested in shooting someone like Martha Stewart while listening to the music of Eminem.

Once you know your target audience, craft a message that will resonate with them. Your content must:

+ Stand out.

+ Be unusual and original (every viral campaign must be unique like snowflakes or anorexic supermodels.)

+ Contain a message that's both short and simple to understand (remember the universal ADD of the Fame Game targets. It's the First Law of the Online Fame Game.)

For videos, try to keep them between fifteen seconds and five minutes in length. The shorter the better since your video has to grab someone's attention immediately and most people can't hold a logical thought for longer than a few minutes at the most. For pictures, the visual impact needs to be obvious at a glance, such as showing a yeti eating a hamburger or a fisherman holding up the decaying carcass of a mermaid.

Before releasing your viral content, test it on friends and family to get their reaction. If your friends and family members think you're crazy, that could be a good sign or an indication that you're really insane after all. (Or that you might have hit on something. The kicker is you won't know until you put it up. Take a gamble: Bellvue or fame?)

Look at your viral content through the eyes of a total stranger. (Don't kill anyone and rip out their eyes to do this.) Ask yourself if your content is:

★ Funny	Unintended or deliberate, funny content always has a shot at going viral.
★ Unusual	People like weird things, such as cats, dogs, babies, or anyone else doing something unexpected.
★ Visually Interesting	Something eye catching and visually stimulating can become viral. It can also be funny or unusual.
★ A Story	Stories tend to be more interesting than random events. They can be happy, sad, funny, or a mixture. Keep it short.
★ Current	Linking to current events can also increase the odds that more people will find your content with general searches.
★ Relatable	Any topic will likely relate to someone—cats, Star Wars, hits to the groin. Make sure to reach your audience.

Don't upload your content until it's the best you can make it. When it's ready, post it on sites where it will likely gain maximum exposure such as on YouTube or Flickr. Just don't expect people to find your content on their own. **You need to make your content accessible to anyone who stumbles across it, but you also need to promote it to the world at the same time.**

Promoting Your Viral Content

Throwing your content on the Internet is like tossing a bottle of wine into a rehab clinic loaded with washed-up celebrities. You know someone will grab it, but you don't know if they'll share it with anyone else. (I wouldn't.) To get your content shared with others, you must start sharing it first.

Start sending links to your content as part of a press release to media sites such as The Huffington Post, CNN, Fox News, and any other organization that can't do any research or fact-checking themselves, but pretends that they're objective and unbiased anyway. Just get people sharing your content to their audience or their friends as soon as possible. The more people who get your content, the more likely someone will share it with others.

Besides posting links to your content on a website or Facebook page, mention your content on Twitter and other social media networks. Twitter is the second most popular social network in the world, used by over five hundred million people who can't put together any thought longer than one hundred forty characters or less. In fact, people perform more search queries on Twitter per month than Bing and Yahoo combined, but that's probably because Bing and Yahoo suck and all the really cool people just use Google instead.

Trending on Twitter can be a great form of publicity and marketing since tweets cater to the short attention span of the general public. Everyone on Twitter reads the trends, so creating #hashtags that are relevant to an event, story, or product can drive attention to you and your content.

Start by sending a tweet that asks a question regarding your topic and include the hashtag. Ask your followers to retweet this tweet to create a snowball effect that can generate buzz around your content.

If possible, **find a way for your content to benefit a big company and ask if they will tweet your message.** Big companies, such as radio stations, airlines, fashion brands, and beverage companies that make their money selling sugar water, will often have thousands of followers who either support capitalism or enjoy being exploited by corporate interests.

If you can't link your content to a big company, find a way to latch your content to a current hot topic, such as another celebrity going into rehab. Comment on relevant articles on other sites and leave the hashtag in the comment so that others will see and maybe share your content too.

Try to avoid tweeting when a huge news story breaks because everybody will be talking about that news story, unless it's something that involves thinking. It will just let lost in the avalanche.

Also, try to make an emotional connection with strangers you don't know or even care about. Show people that they are not alone when thinking about a particular topic, even if their thought process resembles the Unabomber. Make your hashtag memorable so people will find it easy to share.

Even the best content won't go viral until you start promoting it first among your network of friends, enemies, mistresses, stalkers, fellow addicts, and distant but wealthy family members you hope will die soon and leave you a massive inheritance. Spread the word about your content as much as possible. Once your content goes viral, everyone will comment on how lucky you are, but you'll know that luck is really hard work in disguise.

How to Build a Celebrity Website

When it comes to building your website, there are a few simple steps you can take to getting started. It's okay to start small, because you can always upgrade. By starting small, you can see immediate results, which can keep you motivated:

+ First, register your domain name, such as your own name. However, considering that a lot of name domains are taken by now, and some are unaffordable to obtain, it's okay to come up with something simple and similar.

+ Your site should contain the basic sections for all necessary information, including a homepage, about, press, music/video/photos, blog, social media feeds, contact page, and when necessary, shop and merchandising.

+ SEO can be a game changer. Filling your site with the proper tags and keywords can make your site available by search engines and drive traffic from random visitors who may not have stumbled upon it otherwise.

+ You can obviously hire someone to build a site for you for a price, but sites like WordPress, Wix, and even the GoDaddy site builder offer free or cheap layouts and templates to help get you started, even if you know almost nothing about technology and computers.

When you make it big, your management team will take over this duty for you, and perhaps build you something bigger and better. Until then, do the best you can.

How to Run a Blog

Why Do You Need to Have a Blog?

You may have heard about blogs, but may not know what the benefits might be. Here are some advantages of having a blog:

A blog represents one of the most effective and powerful ways to start building your online brand.

A blog attracts a high position in Google search results for people searching your name.

A blog acts as your recruiting station for your fans and brand ambassadors.

A blog creates an idea incubator and sandbox—easy way to test your creative ideas and see the feedback from your fans and target audience.

A blog lets you express yourself through a variety of media.

A blog defines your domain name as part of your brand.

Here are some tips to help you get your blog set up for success:

Define Your Target Audience

Before you jump on the blogging wagon, ask yourself who you want your blog to reach. Who is the Britney or Bud that will be checking his or her cell phone frantically to see if you posted another update with your words of wisdom? Is Molly a budding teenager torn apart by misunderstanding and love for a vampire or a cheerleader, or a jock who loves sex and beer?

Once you've defined and decided on your target audience, you can answer the questions about how your blog should look and what content it should host. Keep asking yourself, what would Britney or Bud think?

Decide What Kind of Blog You Want to Run

There are at least two different styles of communicating and engaging with your fans and you should decide which style is more appropriate for you, your business model, and your audience.

The first option is to **present yourself as an organization.** Usually this means that the website is written in the third person about you. It has announcement of your performances, projects, main events, and quotes from you personally. Even though it does deliver a sense of a larger-than-life organization running under your glorious name (even if it's really run out of the kitchen in your parent's house), there is a risk of losing personal touch. Even worse, appealing to an audience can come across as inconsistent and even arrogant.

A website like Britney Spears, www.britneyspears.com, is guaranteed traffic. She is on that level of celebrity in which people are searching her site first when they want any information about upcoming projects and tours. The site is clearly run by a management and PR team, however they try to play it off as Britney by linking to her official Twitter in the "news" category, and publishing many personal photos of Britney with her sons.

The second option is to **make your blog more informal and personal to develop a relationship with your fans.** Think of your blog almost like a diary except with fewer references to cute guys/girls you met in high school, and without the more embarrassing confessions like what really happened to your underwear that day. (Sorry, Mom!) Blogs are usually written by you personally and feature details from your everyday life, opinions of other stories, and insights into personal projects.

Many celebrities have jumped on blogging in recent years as another way to reach their fans as quickly and directly as possible. Kim Kardashian launched KimKardashian.com where anyone with nothing better to do with their lives can go to see her family photos, personal photos, and even speak out or correct a story that has landed in traditional press.

Even if Kim Kardashian doesn't write every single post on her blog, she does stay involved with her site. Many celebrities have put out similar product, including Nicole Richie, Khloe Kardashian, Holly Madison, and Snooki. There is no question that they are at least contributing to the blogs, it's just a matter of how much time they are sacrificing.

Research and look at your competition in similar categories targeting a similar audience. Learn from successful celebrity blogs. Look at conversations and comments. Look at what sparks conversations and gets the most views and comments. Learn what aggravates fans and turns them off.

Think how you can improve on what you learned from other successful blogs and make it different. If you look exactly the same as your competition, there will be little reason for someone to visit your blog instead of theirs.

Design Your Website

There are a few particular elements of your website design that you should take into consideration.

+ Make sure that the site's graphics and your name or logo are consistent with your image and brand.

+ Make sure the site is easy to navigate from the front to the back.

+ Include multiple, clear options to contact you or your representatives.

+ Offer a subscription option to notify your fans about new articles and updates to your blog. Email is an additional connection to your fans that along with social networks will strengthen both your relationship and the effectiveness of marketing your projects to your fans (as long as you don't abuse it and turn it into spam).

As surprising as it might sound, the most clicked areas on a website or blog are not the flashy posts, but the Home and About pages, so make sure that both are worth visiting. Ensure that the design and content on both pages catch the audience and give them a sense of credibility and trust. Your About page is your chance to turn random visitors into raving fans because they feel personally connected to you. Spend enough time on your own story and make sure you move your fans with it.

Fancy graphics and logos might grab somebody's attention, much like a Dallas Cowboys cheerleader can grab someone's eye by bouncing up and down on a trampoline, (I know, I've been on a cheerleader fiesta this chapter. But isn't this more fun than my political rants? And see what I mean about ADD ☺?) But unlike a cheerleader, you need actual substance to maintain somebody's interest. That means you need useful information that people will want to see, hear, or read. Just like all forms of media, the cover sells the magazine and the headline sells the article. Now your content has to deliver.

Ideally, plaster your website with photos, graphics, and video, video, video. The more visual, the higher its appeal. The easier on the ear and the more visual your content, the higher the probability that it will engage an audience. However, audio and visual content comes at the expense of search engine optimization effectiveness since search engines can't recognize images or videos. That's why you need to make sure all images are named and tagged using the keywords of your blog.

Stick to 150–300 words per post. If your target audience overlaps with Snooki or any other celebrity on the pages of tabloids, odds are that the sight of long posts will depress them. Anything over three hundred words could make their brains explode, which you obviously don't want to happen prior to them tuning into your online show or buying a ticket to your next event. For precisely the same reason, try to use highlights, bold text, and other eye-catching formatting.

Above all, don't forget to use keywords in your posts. Keywords are one of the triggers that put you higher in the Google search results, when people look for them. We will discuss this at length in the SEO chapter. (Please note that I took the trouble to put this part in both **bold** and *italic*, so you know it must be **important**.)

Keywords can help search engines find your site, but RSS is a technology that can make it easier for people to retrieve your content. Right after Al Gore and George Bush created the "Internets," it became increasingly populated with information posted on millions of blogs and websites. To keep up with this flood of new information would be extremely difficult, since you would have to check each website individually to see if anything new and worthwhile had been posted (only to be let down yet again). It didn't take long for someone to come up with the neat technology called RSS, or Really Simple Syndication.

RSS allows people to receive updates from multiple sites and blogs that they want to follow without actually visiting them. Think Twitter with blog excerpts from your favorite sites. Needless to say this little handy gimmick caught on and became one of the most popular ways to receive the news. Adding the "subscribe to RSS" button to your website or blog is a very useful tool for those who may not otherwise come back on a daily basis.

How to Run a YouTube Channel

Creating a successful YouTube channel is one of the best ways to become famous. YouTube (owned by the mighty Google) is one of the top-paying social networking sites. Once you become a YouTube partner (it's free, fairly simple, and so easy even Kim Kardashian did it), you can start monetizing your videos with ads. There are only a few simple things you need to do to start a successful channel.

Creating meaningful and, most importantly, professional content is a must. Every iPhone out there has an "Upload to YouTube" button on it. Now think of all the useless garbage that people upload to the site every day. If you want to stand out, posting grainy, shaky videos with no substance is what you'll want to avoid. Videos should be shot in the highest quality possible, and most importantly with good sound. Of course, some of the most classic viral YouTube hits are from cell phone videos, but in reality, they are one in a million.

You should try to come across as real in your videos. Encourage viewers to interact with you and one another in the comments section. You should participate in the discussions they are having as well. Beware, the YouTube comments section can get crazy. There are tons of trolls dwelling on the site, and they will find you. They are really, really bored at work and out for blood.

Continuing success relies on the packaging and branding of your channel as well. The name and look of the channel should be relevant to the subject matter. You'll want to attract subscribers who are interested in your content by keeping them engaged. If by chance you reach that elite level, toutside advertisers will want to make sure your page looks presentable. You know the saying "Always dress like you're going to a job interview?" In this case, dress your channel like it.

Finally, make sure to optimize your content for search with good SEO tags. People frequently stumble upon YouTube videos by going to their favorite search engine and typing in "something + video." Either they didn't think to try YouTube first, or they just assumed that typing it in the search bar would skip the process of having to type www.youtube.com but provide them with YouTube results anyways. Did I mention that the ADD audience is also very lazy? The videos that get shown in this instance are the ones with good tags.

Find your identity. On YouTube, there are plenty of different types of videos that get more attention than others. If you have yet to figure out your niche, here are some examples of what you can try. These even require little to no talent! See what catches on.

★ Video Responses	Video responses are becoming more and more popular on YouTube. Start making your own responses to new material by famous YouTubers. If done well, you will be able to gain new followers through it by leveraging other YouTubers with large fanbases.
★ Reviews and Reflections	Rendering your unsolicited opinion about news, people, and products is yet another very effective formula for content generation. It's much easier to be a judge finding flaws in something else, rather that creating something original and being judged. Aside from a nice stroke to your ego, there are quite a few other benefits of passing judgment on others. Companies will even send the popular channels free products to review. Be entertaining and preferably know what you are talking about.
★ "How-To" Videos	If you run out of ideas for your next YouTube video, you can always create a How-To video. It always helps if you actually know how, but if you don't you might end up with a good formula for a comedy sketch.
★ Gimmicks	Create a schtick, and schtick to it. Look at popular channels like Epic Meal Time. Creating impractical meals involving tons of bacon have become a huge hit. Other popular and sometimes funny gimmicks include lip-syncing, dance covers, and voice-overs. Just search for "Single Ladies" on YouTube and you'll see exactly how it works.

Once you've found your way, you have to get people to come to your channel and subscribe. So how exactly do you get in with the crowd? Aside from having quality content to offer, you may have to work your way in by impressing those who are already established, or at least have something to offer. There are a number of ways to get your name out there, some of which include:

★ Commenting	Comment on other channels, blogs, and pages. It may seem a little annoying to some, but it's a very efficient tool for attracting new visitors. You just need to be interesting enough to attract attention.
★ Linking	Linking to other blogs and influencers that have a significant following can get you the introduction to arrange a link exchange with the hopes of increasing traffic.
★ Engaging your viewers	People like to participate. Sometimes the comments section isn't enough. Offer polls, giveaways, and games. There are even quite a few free widgets that will make the task even easier for you.
★ Promote on social media	Encourage your viewers to become your fans on other social media pages. This way your updates will catch their attention, one way or another.

When getting started and developing your brand, you'll want to practically live on YouTube. You've got to make your presence known through comments, likes, shares, and staying involved with others while posting videos of your own. You know how you get to become VIP at a popular nightclub? By going all the time, or knowing someone. So when it comes to YouTube, go all the time, and hopefully you'll become one of the VIPs. No cute halter top will help you once you're here though. You need actual content and strategy.

There are a few common mistakes people make on YouTube that you'll want to avoid. The first is not having a subscription button everywhere possible. If you want viewers to come back, they need to subscribe. If they want to subscribe and can't find the button, you could miss out. Also, don't forget to add hyperlinks in your description when it comes to your social media pages. People are likely to click, but are probably too lazy to copy and paste.

Speaking of copy and paste, don't copy and paste the titles, tags, and descriptions of popular videos into your own, hoping that people will accidentally stumble upon them. YouTube, like Hollywood intellectual property infringement lawyers, doesn't take kindly to stealing and deception. And if sometime took your clever wordplay and jokes about cheerleaders and train wreck reality stars and politicians who can't keep it in their pants and took credit for them, you wouldn't like it much either.

How to Play the Fame Game and Win

"All publicity is good, except an obituary notice."—Brendan Behan

Managing Publicity

Ever since elementary school, people have always been talking about you behind your back. While most of your elementary school classmates have probably stopped talking about you to focus on their own trivial lives, gossip remains a problem. Every time someone says anything negative about you, how can you control what other people say or think about what they read or hear? The million-dollar answer is that you can't stop or control gossip about you, but you can control your responses to any type of publicity. **By redirecting or "spinning" that publicity to another perspective, with a little creativity and imagination you can even turn negative publicity into positive publicity.**

Short of being caught massacring hundreds of innocent people (which is something that only national governments can get away with if they do it overseas or domestically over a long period of time) any publicity can be turned into positive publicity if you handle it correctly. At the same time, negative publicity can tarnish your reputation if you fail to handle it correctly. Some of the typical ways to respond to negative publicity include:

+ Ignore it and hope that it goes away.

+ Redirect and switch attention.

+ Embrace the story, and lead the way to fixing the issue instead of focusing on your personal problem that caused the negative publicity in the first place.

Because the public has such a short attention span, it's often easier to ignore a story and let it die on its own, usually within twenty-four to forty-eight hours. New stories appear all the time and these are much more appealing to a public tired of stale news. In many cases, these new stories will simply bury your negative publicity until nobody even remembers or cares about it anymore.

Anyone remember back in 1997 when actor/comedian Eddie Murphy picked up a transvestite prostitute, claiming he only wanted to help someone who needed a lift home? Everyone remembers Eddie Murphy for voicing the donkey in the *Shrek* movies, but few people remember him picking up a transvestite prostitute late one night in Los Angeles because the story eventually died without any further details to carry it forward. Like many before and after him, Eddie was very thankful to Fame Game ADD.

Negative stories that involve a single incident often won't last long and will soon be forgotten as soon as the public spots a new celebrity or event to get excited about, like a baby fascinated by a balloon. However, ignoring a problem isn't always the answer; otherwise politicians would be doing a great job by ignoring poverty, homelessness, and the declining state of public schools in every major city in America. (What?? I'm right about this stuff!)

Back in the 1990s, Richard Gere was reportedly admitted into the emergency room of Cedars-Sinai hospital in Los Angeles with a foreign object lodged in his rectum. Doctors supposedly took an x-ray and identified that foreign object as a gerbil (either alive or dead, depending on who's telling the story).

Doctors supposedly rushed Richard Gere to surgery and extracted the animal from his behind. Some say the gerbil had been shaven and declawed; others claim the animal had been placed in a plastic pouch. In any case, after finishing the gerbilectomy, the medical team was reportedly sworn to secrecy, but someone on the medical staff supposedly leaked the news anyway.

Despite the fact that this Richard Gere gerbil story has never been verified, even by any of the celebrity tabloids, it soon turned into an urban legend that continues to haunt Richard Gere to this day, and all this occurred before the spread of instant communication over the Internet. By ignoring this negative publicity, Richard Gere allowed the story to spread like wildfire.

When negative publicity threatens to spin out of control, **you need to confront the problem.** That means taking a stand and coming across as open and honest, even if you're lying through your teeth. (See, I held myself back this time from the obvious Washington reference. I can control it!)

When actor Hugh Grant got caught with a prostitute in Los Angeles in 1995, he couldn't ignore the negative publicity. Astutely, he decided to confront the problem by apologizing on *The Tonight Show* soon afterwards. When Jay Leno asked him "What the hell were you thinking?" Hugh Grant responded humbly, "I think you know in life what's a good thing to do and what's a bad thing, and I did a bad thing . . . and there you have it." When Hugh Grant later appeared on *Larry King Live*, he simply told Larry King, "I don't have any excuses."

Despite getting caught with a prostitute, Hugh Grant recovered his reputation and actually increased his fame by admitting he had made a mistake. Such refreshing honesty is something you'll rarely see from anyone involved in politics, which is why it's always so much fun to watch politicians lie and squirm when they get caught doing something wrong. (Sorry. Guess I can't—it's just an overwhelming urge.)

Back in 2001, a twenty-three-year-old Congressional intern named Chandra Levy suddenly disappeared and was later found murdered. When evidence linked Democratic Congressman Gary Condit to an extramarital affair with Chandra Levy before her disappearance, Gary Condit found the problem difficult to ignore (because the murder of anyone isn't easily forgotten unless the victim happens to be a minority).

Yet Gary Condit made a fatal mistake. Although he couldn't ignore the problem, he refused to be open and honest about it. His "pro-family" political stance directly conflicted with his adultery with a woman two years younger than his daughter. Even worse, he consistently attempted to mislead the police about the nature of his relationship with her.

When Gary Condit finally agreed to let investigators search his apartment, he was spotted throwing out a gift box he had received from another woman in a dumpster in one of Washington's Virginia suburbs. It looked like he was trying to destroy incriminating evidence. When Gary Condit tried to clear his name during a televised interview with news anchor Connie Chung, he refused to answer any direct questions about Chandra Levy.

Even though the police later cleared Gary Condit of any involvement in Chandra Levy's death, his suspicious behavior and unwillingness to pretend to be open and honest condemned him even further in the public's eye. All his attempts to distance himself from Chandra Levy only made him look even more suspicious.

Probably the only way he could have killed any negative publicity about his relationship with Chandra Levy would be if he had rushed into Cedars-Sinai hospital in Los Angeles with a gerbil lodged up his butt. If Gary Condit had suddenly held a press conference announcing that he had killed a gerbil in his anus, think how quickly the public would have forgotten about Chandra Levy. As it turns out, the public quickly forgot about Gary Condit because of the 9/11 attacks on the World Trade Center, but you can't always rely on such extreme, outside circumstances to save you from your own stupidity.

While most people think with their groin and squirm away from negative publicity like Gary Condit, sometimes embracing negative publicity can keep you in the spotlight longer. After Kim Kardashian's seventy-two-day marriage to Kris Humphries fizzled faster than the time it takes Stephen King to write another novel (or me to come with yet another political analogy), one might have expected them to put their failed marriage behind them and move on with their lives. Of course, you must have realized by now that Kim Kardashian isn't normal.

Instead of shying away from the negative publicity, Kim Kardashian embraced it. Many accused Kim Kardashian of faking her marriage as a publicity stunt. Whether she did or didn't isn't as important as the fact that she got people talking about her again.

Next, Kim Kardashian dragged out the divorce until Kris Humphries stopped his claims that the marriage was a fraud. Whether this is true or not, it created greater conflict and caused more people with empty lives to speculate on who was right. In the meantime, the focus went back to Kim, giving her even more free publicity to promote her fragrance and clothing lines.

When Kim Kardashian got pregnant with Kanye West's child and still not officially divorced from Kris Humphries, the drama just continued keeping Kim Kardashian in the public eye, enabling her to milk them for even more money. By embracing her failed marriage, Kim Kardashian turned it into a golden marketing opportunity that gave her more coverage than the Super Bowl, and she didn't even have to take any steroids to get there. What do we learn from this? **The next time you face negative publicity, you could really be looking at positive publicity in disguise.**

In 2011 Charlie Sheen was the highest paid television actor, appearing on the hit show *Two and a Half Men*. After multiple stints in rehab (which made rehab look like a Hollywood party but without the cocktails and prostitutes), Charlie Sheen publicly made derogatory comments about the series creator, Chuck Lorre. CBS immediately banned Charlie Sheen from appearing on the studio lot.

Rather than dwell on this negative publicity about being kicked off *Two and a Half Men*, Charlie Sheen chose to redirect the public's attention back to himself. During multiple television interviews, he made bizarre statements, suggesting that he was a "Vatican assassin warlock" with "tiger blood" and "Adonis DNA." He told one TV interviewer, "'I'm tired of pretending I'm not special. I'm tired of pretending I'm not a total bitchin' rock star from Mars."

To further direct attention to himself and away from the potential negative publicity of getting fired from a hit TV show, Charlie Sheen posted videos on YouTube showing himself smoking cigarettes through his nose. Then he launched a nationwide tour dubbed "My Violent Torpedo of Truth/Defeat is Not An Option," which sold out in eighteen minutes, setting a TicketMaster record.

By steering critics away from his firing on a hit TV show and towards his own antics, Charlie Sheen turned his negative publicity into a springboard where he could shamelessly promote himself and milk his followers for money, even though his live show sucked.

How can you use such redirection tactics at work? Suppose you blow a multimillion-dollar deal by sleeping with a client's wife. When the boss comes screaming for your head, what are your options?

A. Ignore the problem and hope it will go away.

B. Deny that you slept with the client's wife despite all photographic evidence that proves otherwise.

C. Admit you screwed up and beg for forgiveness.

D. Give your boss the client's wife's phone number so he can have sex with her too.

If you answered (A) that you can ignore the problem and hope that it will go away, you will likely be mocked by everyone around you as you lose what little respect they may have still associated with you.

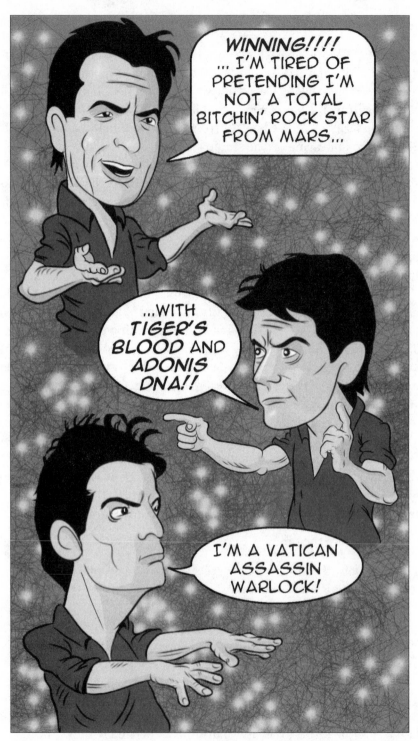

Max Espinoza/Ruben Gerard

If you answered (B) that you can deny the problem ever existed, you'll definitely lose all respect. People will see you as a liar who will likely get elected to political office one day and have all the hookers and power that you want so you can gloat about it to your former coworkers.

If you answered (C) that you can admit you screwed up and beg for forgiveness, you'll at least come across as humble as your boss berates and humiliates you in front of everyone and the security guards escort you out the door. But at least you'll maintain a shred of dignity and self-respect in the process, even as your coworkers giggle and gossip behind your back.

If you answered (D) that you'll give your boss the client's wife's phone number so he can have sex with her too, that's redirecting the problem away from your own negative publicity so people will quickly forget all about it. Even better, by redirecting attention, you can create a more positive outcome. Your boss may even thank and reward you with a raise and a promotion while your coworkers gape in astonishment.

Redirection involves the old cliché that "When life gives you lemons, make lemonade." This cliché is often followed with its lesser known, but equally popular phrase, "After you finish making lemonade, spike it with alcohol and get drunk afterwards to celebrate your accomplishment."

When *Jersey Shore* debuted in 2009, it quickly became a cultural phenomenon. Besides the millions of people watching the show, many advertisers quickly realized the potential of associating their products with *Jersey Shore* by negotiating endorsement deals with the cast members.

NOHO drink, which claims to prevent hangovers, thought they had a perfect spokesperson in the form of Snooki. Snooki's endorsement deal with NOHO represented a lucrative deal, but it hinged on her remaining the hard partying girl that she portrayed on *Jersey Shore*. Of course, anyone could have fun partying like Snooki every night if they were earning millions from appearing on a reality TV show, but that fact often escaped her fans who watched her show week after week.

When Snooki got pregnant, her pregnancy immediately wrecked her NOHO drink deal since the company couldn't associate their anti-hang-over drink with a pregnant woman. However this "problem" turned into an opportunity.

First, Snooki sold an exclusive interview about her pregnancy and engagement to *US Weekly* for $25,000. After giving birth, thereby proving she actually is a human being and not some mutant from another dimension, Snooki sold pictures of her baby to *People Magazine* for $250,000. In her quest to make more money, Snooki used her baby as a prop to promote herself as a positive role model for young mothers, thereby helping her remain in the public spotlight and change her image of a party girl to a respectable mother. By turning her pregnancy into a moneymaking opportunity, Snooki took advantage of it.

Another *Jersey Shore* cast member, Mike "The Situation" Sorrentino, found a different way to turn a negative situation into a positive one. Clothing retailer, Abercrombie & Fitch, publicly declared that they would pay Sorrentino money if he would stop wearing their clothes on *Jersey Shore*. Yet at the time they did this, the company was also selling T-shirts with the phrases "The Fitchuation" and "GTL . . . You Know the Deal."

Mike Sorrentino quickly redirected this negative publicity into a positive direction by suing Abercrombie & Fitch for violating his trademarks on the terms "The Situation" and "GTL." Abercrombie & Fitch claimed they wanted to distance themselves from "The Situation," yet they were selling clothes that specifically referenced that same guy. Sorrentino's lawsuit asks for Abercrombie & Fitch to pay a royalty of $1 million with an additional $3 million for "exemplary and/or punitive damages."

While redirection of the public's limited attention span can often turn negative publicity into a positive spin, a more aggressive tactic is to embrace the problem and advocate for the larger issue to make people forget about your own problems.

After giving birth to two children, Brooke Shields suffered from postpartum depression, which is a mental disorder that affects many new mothers. Symptoms include sadness, fatigue, changes in sleeping and eating patterns, reduced libido, crying episodes, anxiety, and irritability (which sounds an awful lot like the writing process but I know it's a different thing).

Rather than stay out of the public spotlight and let the celebrity tabloids start rumors about her behavior, Brooke Shields went public with her struggles with postpartum depression in 2007. She wrote and promoted a book called *Down Came the Rain: My Journey through Postpartum Depression*. Now if anyone tries to use her experience of postpartum depression to spread negative publicity about her, Brooke Shields can spin that publicity around and use it to sell her book. It's hard to smear someone's reputation if every time you try they make more money as a result and are laughing all the way to the bank.

Many celebrities get addicted to drugs or alcohol, let their professional and personal life spiral out of control, and then appear on daytime talk shows to explain how they've turned their life around. Not only is this tactic designed to gain sympathy from the adoring public, but it's also designed to put the celebrity back in the spotlight.

While the general public ignores the plight of thousands of other addicts sleeping in the streets and urinating on the sidewalks, it can't spend enough money buying books from celebrities detailing their own experiences sleeping in the streets and urinating on the sidewalks. For many celebrities, going to rehab and writing a book about the experience is simply another business strategy that makes their drug and alcohol expenses tax deductible.

Managing Your Own Publicity

There's no one best way to handle negative publicity because every event can be different. Some negative publicity can be spun into a positive opportunity, like Kim Kardashian's seventy-two-day marriage. Other types of negative publicity are much harder to turn into a positive spin, like O. J. Simpson being accused of killing his ex-wife and her boyfriend by slicing their bodies open with a knife. (That could, however, have turned into a positive marketing opportunity for the NRA to prove that guns aren't the only way to kill your ex-wife and her lover.)

The general rule is that when white people get killed, especially attractive white women who are rich, it's a public relations nightmare. If poor minorities get killed, the news media will just shrug and forget about the incident three seconds later. And in most cases, you can't get away with murder unless you're rich.

In your own life, you will always face some form of negative publicity at all times. If you're running a business, there will always be people unhappy with your product or service, and these vocal idiots find meaning in life by screaming about their unhappiness as often as possible to their friends and on the Internet. Since the Internet tends to amplify any voice, you need to deal with all forms of negative publicity immediately.

Here's a quick checklist of responses to consider:

+ Can I ignore the problem and hope that it will go away?

+ Should I admit the problem and hope that it will go away?

+ Can I redirect attention from the problem to a more positive story?

+ Should I embrace and own the story to focus on the bigger issue rather than a personal problem?

If someone makes irrational complaints about your business ("Your waitress didn't bring me a glass of water and then she refused to have sex with me afterwards"), you can often ignore them. Once other people hear the illogical complaints of a moron, they'll dismiss their complaints as pointless.

Now let's say someone has a legitimate complaint about your business ("There was a fly in my soup"). Ignoring the problem will make you look uncaring since the problem is real, or at least perceived to be real and reasonable. In that case, you can quickly admit the problem and offer the customer a refund and even a free meal as compensation. This can stop the negative publicity in its tracks and possibly even win the customer over with your responsiveness and willingness to fix the problem.

If admitting the problem doesn't make the negative publicity go away (he or she is being a pain in the ass), then you can try redirecting the problem to a more positive issue. Tell the irate customer, "Yes, I see that there's a fly in your soup, but that's because our kitchen uses organic ingredients that we purchase from farmers in Third World countries so they can earn a decent living and not be tempted to engage in drug trafficking, terrorism or selling their babies to child slavery rings. We also hire military veterans who have lost a limb so they can work a decent job and gain their self-respect while supporting themselves. Because they may be missing both arms and can't always shoo flies out of the kitchen, that's likely the cause of the fly appearing in your soup. If it would make you happy, I could fire my entire staff of disabled military veterans who sacrificed their lives to protect your freedom and stop supporting Third World farmers trying to make a decent living, or could I give you a free bowl of soup instead?"

If making the complainer feel guilty for bringing up the problem in the first place doesn't work, embrace the story completely to focus on a much bigger issue. Tell the customer, "I see that there's a fly in your soup and that's because the city has cut back on garbage collection services for budgetary reasons. That's why I'm running for mayor of this town to bring back the social services we need without raising taxes. The problem isn't just that there's a fly in your soup, but that there are flies breeding in the garbage that the city refuses to pick up due to striking garbage collectors. As mayor, I promise to negotiate union contracts with city workers in good faith and bring back our social services without raising taxes on hardworking people like you. Why don't we put that bowl of soup aside and let's see how we can work together to make this town as great as it used to be?"

When dealing with negative publicity, you may need to rely on one or more of these techniques. The ultimate goal is to turn attention away from the negative aspect of the publicity and refocus it on something positive. You need to control what people are saying about you, not the other way around.

Publicity, like a fine wine, is best when consumed in small sips rather than gulped down in one shot (and thrown up on yourself hours later). When negative publicity occurs in show business, celebrities typically withhold their comments until the deadlines for the tabloid magazines are past and it's too late to include those comments in the current issue. That means, those comments can only appear in the following issue, which gives the celebrity coverage in two issues instead of one.

Whether you're manipulating negative publicity or trying to generate positive publicity, what grabs people's attention is always something different. To stand out in a room of celebrities, just act humble, stay sober, and don't punch a photographer in the mouth. Since most celebrities can't do that, you'll stand out in no time.

The spotlight will always shine on you as long as you find a way to stand out from the crowd by the way you look, move, speak, or dress. In the words of Oscar Wilde, "Be yourself; everyone else is already taken." Once you know who you are, publicity just makes sure that everyone around you knows that too.

PR Avenues

You can't just sit on the couch and wait for the New York Times to call you, asking you to gift them with your words of wisdom. In order to become a fixture on their speed dial, you must first prove that you have wisdom to offer.

There are many steps to getting your name out there. One of the easiest, though potentially costly, ways to get started is to hire a PR company. Before you decide to go this route, you need to understand what exactly you are buying. By hiring a PR company, you are buying the connections that this person has through their previously established contacts. In choosing a PR company, it's very important to do a little research and see who else they represent. If the company has a significant roster of celebrities already, they can use that as leverage and trade off while pitching you to the media. It's also very important to research who their media connections are, and if placement for you with any of these outlets would be beneficial to your brand.

If you are looking for a cheaper option, DIY PR is also a possibility. The do-it-yourself method requires a bit of knowledge in the industry already, and can produce extensive results if a good amount of hard work and dedication are put into it. Nowadays, a person can reach out and engage any media outlet or influential blogger through social media advertising. However, you must keep in mind that by doing so, you are competing for the attention with other stories and personalities. Therefore, it all comes down to following several principles of online schmoozing that will make you stand out.

Publicity can come from a number of different angles, all with benefits and downsides to each. Some can help clean up the mess of another, and all can aid in making or breaking a career at the same time. Take a look at the different types of media.

Traditional Media

TV: Television is probably the biggest form of media out there, as it has transcended to new levels over the past couple of decades to become a media giant. Hollywood movie stars now flock to TV series instead of movies for the exposure, paycheck, and prestige.

Radio: Though there is a time and a place for radio, it's not a BAD time or place. Millions of people spend hours in the car each week driving to and from work and around town. Radio exposure is not what it once was, but still remains a present day-to-day form of mass media.

Print: Some will argue that print media is dying a slow and painful death. That may be true on some accounts, specifically the newspaper industry, but certain parts of the magazine industry are still alive and kicking with the popularity of the entertainment and celebrity weeklies, even though the Internet provides free, twenty-four-hour coverage of the same stories.

Internet

Website: Websites have become the new 24/7 news source. There are websites pertaining to nearly every topic, from current events, politics, entertainment and sports to celebrity news and gossip. Even though the Internet is a place where many people can provide organized hoaxes, false information, or unconfirmed reports, looking for another confirmation or a conflicting report is at the click of your fingertips. This can be used to either your advantage or disadvantage.

E-commerce: Web stores have become one of the newest go-to places on the web. What originally started as a way for people to purchase goods that they could not get locally has now turned in to the ultimate hunting game, where people will even seek out items they have seen in store for a better deal online. With the arrival of flash sales and sites like Groupon, LivingSocial, and Gilt, e-commerce has become an everyday occurrence in your inbox.

SEO: Search Engine Optimization is very important in creating your web presence. Considering the fact that if someone doesn't know the answer to a question they are bound to "Google it," becoming famous requires you to have a presence on search engines. This can come from making sure names and details are tagged correctly in posts and photos, and press is coming from more notable sources.

Social Networks: The presence of social networks begins as a place for fans to have fun and (hopefully) leads those fans to e-commerce. Many celebrities have benefited since the launch of social media, including Ashton Kutcher, who helped to jump-start Twitter from its inception, and some of the best celebrity newcomers, such as Kim Kardashian, who generates over $3 million per year just from Tweeting.

How to Write a Press Release

The press release is one of the main components in PR. Think of it as your formal announcement or coming-out party. It's a brief statement that provides all of the necessary information for the average person's short attention span, and where they should go should they want to seek more information. Learning how to write one is a huge plus. Reporters tend to pay way more attention to a story that they've read about in a press release. It's also not that hard! Here are the five parts to include.

★ Headline	Headlines sell newspapers and magazines. For press releases, headlines are even more important, because you are trying to persuade journalists to write about it. The headline should be a clear, attention-grabbing description of the subject's main point with obvious news value.

★ Body	The body is where you provide all of the necessary information, starting with the date and location.
	
	Most PR courses will teach you that it is important to include the "5 W's" in the body of your press release to the best of your ability:
	    Who is the press release about?
	    What is the subject matter of the release?
	    When did or will the subject take place?
	    Where did or will the subject take place?
	    Why is this taking place—is there a goal?
	    (H)ow (if applicable) is this made possible?

★ Supporting Materials	Include any additional information about your subject, including anything that adds an interesting angle to the story. A quote from someone involved is always a nice touch, as are photographs, videos, and links.
★ About You	Give a short paragraph about you and your brand. This usually includes background information and previous milestones and accomplishments.
★ Contact Info	Add your contact info, who can be reached, where they can be reached, and where the reader can go to find more information about you or your product.

Where to Release It: There are many places to release a Press Release including some of the more popular newswires. As with everything, you get what you pay for. So if you want your headline scrolling across the marquee in Times Square, head over to a company like PR Newswire, and pay for them to do so. If you just want something quick and free, cross your fingers, hope for the best, and look for sites like PRLog.com.

When to Release it: The best time to release a press release is at the start of any business day, so that you can be one of the first to reach the desk of news editors. When planning a release that does not pertain to breaking news, it's best to hit the wire on Monday mornings, around 8 a.m. EST.

Courting Bloggers and Journalists

Since you already know that bloggers and journalists are the rulers of digital media, who can make or break a career with the stroke of their keyboard, you might want to follow these guidelines to stay in their good graces and make some powerful friends:

★ Compile a target list	Put together a list of the most influential bloggers/journalists that you would like to write about you. You can use media contact databases like Cision or Vocus or do your own search online and find media outlets and journalists that write about your area and will be a good fit for your brand.
★ Do your research	Before approaching journalists, make sure to research their recent articles and projects to make sure their audience, writing style, and media outlets they write for fit your brand.
★ Approach each person individually	Approach each journalist individually and only in the context of what he or she may be passionate about and interested in. Remember the golden rule of Internet PR—first offer what you can do for the journalist and only then discuss how he or she can help you. There's nothing that journalists (or anyone for that matter) hate more than being spammed with mass-mailed email blasts. Don't think the old trick of changing the "Dear _____" to a personalized name is a quick fix either. Any journalist or blogger will see through it in the next sentence. Mentioning the last project or article that journalist did and giving valid feedback is always a good start for a conversation and, potentially, a working relationship.
★ Engage journalists on their blogs, social media sites, and professional networking sites	Additional avenues for engaging journalists are their social media (Facebook, Twitter, Pinterest) or professional networks (LinkedIn). You can start by commenting on their social media feeds or blog articles. At some point, this will get you noticed by the author.

★ **Think twice!**	Think twice before posting anything. Then check your spelling. Then think again before pressing send. Most sites and social media outlets don't come with an undo button. Long gone are the days of AOL 7.0 where you could "unsend" a message before it was read. Gmail still has a similar option, but it's not as easy as it sounds. Better double check your post or comment before posting it, because you don't always get a do-over. Also keep in mind that any conversation with the journalist can become public if they post it online.
★ **Post articles and backlinks**	Post articles mentioning and quoting journalists that you want to engage, and include backlinks to their articles on your blog. Many of them receive Google alerts on mentions of their name and will not resist the temptation to check on what you are saying about them.
★ **Avoid spamming and stalking**	Spamming and stalking can produce the exact opposite results of what you are aiming for. Both are annoying and even illegal, and you definitely don't want to be that person in the eyes of the journalist. We discussed engaging with the journalists through social media and blogs, but you need to know when to stop if the journalist is not responding to you. Keep in mind that there's a difference between being an active contributor and a creepy stalker.

Creating an EPK

An EPK (Electronic Press Kit) can be a useful tool to prepare and deliver to potential management, producers, or anyone who might help to further your career. Basically, an Electronic Press Kit is a portfolio of your work and information. Your website can act as the best version of the EPK, so take that into consideration while you are designing it. Alternatively, there should be a smaller-sized email version of the EPK as some will not take the time to search your entire website for the link.

Your EPK should include:

+ Bio and Headshot: Your latest headshot will create a first impression of you. Since you already know how important a first impression is in show business, don't turn in a poor picture as your headshot, such as one you capture yourself with your mobile phone with a beer in your hand feeding birds. Get photographed by a professional.

✦ Press Clippings: The "P" in EPK stands for PRESS. Show where you have been. Start collecting press clippings, and include them as proof that you have experience and media coverage and are worth the money.

✦ Photos: You already packed the headshot, but it never hurts to add more photos. The headshot helps to decide if you would fit. The rest of the content helps to show your abilities. If you're an actor, include stills from previous projects. If a musician, include stills of previous live performances or studio sessions.

✦ Video/Audio: Including a demo of your work is a no brainer, providing your work doesn't suck. Demo reels, music samples, and any type of short media you can provide can go a long way.

✦ Contact info: Provide multiple ways to reach you. Address, phone number, email, web address, and any social media accounts should be included in the contact info. You want to be present and available in every form of media. Different people prefer different contact methods. Don't be the guy without that point of contact.

Lastly, remember your audience. As with any form of "pitch presentation," you have to know who you are trying to impress and how you can impress them. And remember, a mug shot is not a free headshot (although there are a few occasions—Paris Hilton, Nicole Richie—where the mug shot is pretty good-looking). On the other hand there are the six, YES SIX, mug shots from Lindsay Lohan. (I did promise to get off her back, but I just can't. I think there must be a support group somewhere for this.)

How Would You Like Your Steak? (The Importance of Timing)

"The early bird gets the worm, but the second mouse gets the cheese."
—Willie Nelson

Walk up to a busy nightclub, push your way to the front of the line, and strut past everyone standing behind you and the bouncer will likely throw you out while people scream in protest at your arrogance. Now become a celebrity, walk up to a busy nightclub, push your way to the front of the line, and strut past everyone standing behind you and people will get excited and consider it a highlight of their night to see you cut in front of them.

What's the difference between getting thrown out on your butt and being revered for the exact same obnoxious behavior? Act like an idiot before you become famous and people will just think you're an idiot. Act like an idiot after you become famous and people will love you while they gossip and follow your every move in celebrity tabloids. It's all about timing.

Timing can spell the difference between success and utter, complete, catastrophic failure that taints your family's lineage for decades to come, much like marrying into a family whose last name is Kardashian.

With anything in life, there's always an element of timing. Plan an outdoor wedding and it might rain. Plan an indoor wedding and a falling meteor might crash into the building just as the bride and groom vow to stay together until death do them part. Plan on not getting married at all and you might have to get married anyway when you get your girlfriend pregnant. Or when you get pregnant.

Life is all about the right timing because even the best Valentine's Day gift in the world will be useless if you give it to your girlfriend three days late. Or if you wear your sexiest dress but keep your boyfriend waiting at the restaurant for an hour and a half. Try it sometime and see what happens. You'll be surprised at the results, but probably not in a good way. (Actually the sexy dress can probably get away with it.)

Timing a Promotion

Movie studios understand how timing can affect box office results. At one time, studios thought that the summer was a bad time to release movies because people would be on vacation and wouldn't have time to see a movie. Then *Jaws* dominated the market and defined the "summer blockbuster" that every studio has been trying to duplicate ever since. Now studios save their biggest releases for the summer because people will be on vacation and have more time to see a movie.

If this complete reversal of attitudes reminds you of communist propaganda that changes at the whim of an erratic and unstable dictator, relax. That's just the way Hollywood works, by rationalizing everything to support their beliefs just like irrational people have been doing for centuries. Nobody ever claimed that Hollywood executives were intelligent or rational in any way.

The most predictable way Hollywood times their movie releases involves holidays. Everyone (even Hollywood executives and Kardashians) can see that holidays occur at predictable times during the year. Near Valentine's Day, studios release movies that show people falling in love right before they commit to each other, start fighting over trivial problems, and separate citing irreconcilable differences before coming back together in the last five minutes. It's totally realistic, don't you think?

Before the summer, studios release what they hope will be their blockbuster movies that cost millions of dollars-with most of it going to special effects instead of character development or story structure. Near Halloween, studios release horror films so people can enjoy watching other people suffer and get beheaded and impaled without feeling guilty. Near Christmas, studios release movies showing the joy of togetherness and hope for mankind-with lots of presents and lucrative product placement (aren't we lucky that we get this inspiration and subliminally told what to buy at the same time?) which most people conveniently forget about when January arrives a few days later.

In your own life, how can you tie your publicity to holidays? If you want to promote yourself as a politician who supports traditional family values, create a publicity event tied to Valentine's Day. Now you can pretend you actually care about your wife while you're secretly sleeping with a much younger mistress on the side.

If you want to promote yourself as patriot, create a publicity event for yourself on the Fourth of July. If you want to promote yourself as generous, promote a publicity event near Christmas where you can give poor people all the junk you cleaned out of your garage to paint you as a generous person, even if you live in Florida and donate your old skis and snowshoes to the local homeless. Imagine how grateful they would be.

Holidays are just one event that studios consider to optimize the timing of their movies. Studios also have to consider other major, predictable entertainment events that can suck the attention of potential customers away such as the Super Bowl, the Olympics, and of course, the crème de la crème—the Victoria Secret's lingerie show.

When movies are part of a series, studios often release them on the same month every year. This trains the public when to expect the next movie so they can camp out in line a week in advance and be the first to see it in a theater full of other people who haven't showered for the past seven days. (Remember our Pavlov story?)

Film studios often look at what their competition is doing so they can time their releases away from their competitor's strongest movie releases. When Columbia Pictures set an opening date for *The Amazing Spiderman*, everyone knew that people would flock to see a superhero movie that depicted a fantasy world where the police were actually honest.

To avoid competing against *The Amazing Spiderman*, Warner Brothers Pictures decided to release their own superhero blockbuster, *The Dark Knight Rises*, several weeks later. By avoiding direct competition, both movies could target the same audience and make plenty of money out of the same people before they realized they could have seen both movies at a fraction of the price if they had just waited for the DVD to come out instead.

While studios can plan for events that occur regularly (such as the firing of studio executives when a movie inevitably bombs), they can't plan for the weather (such as blizzards or hurricanes), completely unpredictable events such as terrorist attacks, wars, or Snooki suddenly devoting her life to education so she can become a productive member of society for a change.

Comedic action star Jackie Chan was planning to appear in a movie called *Nosebleed*, where he would play a window washer at the World Trade Center who discovers and defeats a terrorist attack against the Statue of Liberty. When the 9/11 terrorist attack struck the World Trade Center towers, Hollywood decided this script was as unsalvageable as the hope of Kim Kardashian's baby North to turn out normal without intensive therapy later on.

Since movies are products (just like people pursuing fame are products), you can learn about timing publicity for your own brand by watching how movies rise or bomb completely while wiping out the careers of actors, directors, and screenwriters like a nuclear blast. (Dramatic, yes—but true.)

Why Fame Can Be Elusive

When movies like *The Wizard of Oz, Citizen Kane,* and *It's a Wonderful Life* first appeared in the theaters, they flopped. Critics tore the movies apart and audiences shrugged in indifference and went to see more exciting films like *Attack of the 50 Foot Woman* and *Plan 9 from Outer Space.*

Today, *The Wizard of Oz, Citizen Kane,* and *It's a Wonderful Life* are considered film classics while *Attack of the 50 Foot Woman* and *Plan 9 from Outer Space* are considered classically bad. (Remember *Mystery Science Theater?* With the silhouettes of aliens making fun of our corny old movies? Boy, do I miss that show. If it was on today those aliens would have a field day with our favorite reality stars.) How did people fail to recognize the greatness of good movies when they first appeared?

The failure of people to recognize the quality of some of the most popular movies of the century simply highlights the problem of talent. **The public has a hard time recognizing quality,** which is why they worship reality TV stars. Even if you have talent, you still have to promote yourself to get the public to recognize your greatness.

One critically acclaimed movie that didn't win any awards and barely made any money at the time it was released was *The Shawshank Redemption,* a movie based on a Stephen King novel. Despite critical recognition, audiences shrugged their shoulders in indifference and went to see movies based on comic strips and cartoons like *The Flintstones* and *Richie Rich.* We live in a true idiocracy, what can I say? (Another movie I recommend. Not the greatest film but the points made are genius.)

Later, audiences finally recognized *The Shawshank Redemption* as one of the best films ever made. One reason why it took so long for the public to recognize the quality of this film was its obscure name. Because of the movie's title alone, people refused to consider it. Only after they could watch it for free on TV did people finally recognize its quality. (If I dwell for more than one minute on what I just said, I am going to get depressed and eat more pizza. Moving on.)

If a name alone can make that much of a difference, how will a name affect your path to fame? Nobody would have turned Norma Jeane

Mortenson into a movie star and a sex symbol, but when she changed her name to Marilyn Monroe, suddenly opportunities opened up.

Would you want to see a movie starring Chan Kong-Sang or that same movie starring that same person under the stage name Jackie Chan? You could see comedian Jacob Cohen or that same comedian under the stage name Rodney Dangerfield. How memorable would a film be from Allen Konigsberg compared to that same film from Woody Allen?

A name makes all the difference in the world, just ask Eldrick Woods (Tiger Woods), Caryn Johnson (Whoopi Goldberg), Lawrence Harvey Zeiger (Larry King), or Georgios Panayiotou (George Michaels). If you have a name that makes you want to slap your parents, think of something that will be more appealing to the simple-minded public.

At another time, a name like Jonathan Stuart Leibowitz (Jon Stewart) or Walter Willis (Bruce Willis) might have been acceptable, but in today's world of attention-deficit disorder adults and their offspring, you need something short, snappy, and memorable that doesn't involve a four-letter word. Names really can make all the difference in the world.

Although names can make a difference, a good name alone can't save a bad product. *Battlefield Earth* had an interesting title, but even John Travolta couldn't save it with his dreadlocked appearance as an alien based on Scientology's founder L. Ron Hubbard's science fiction novel. Despite the support of Scientologists, the movie bombed anyway, which goes to show that there may be a God after all.

Hollywood tries to reduce the risk by making movies with built-in audiences, such as stories based on comic strips (*Howard the Duck*), novels (*John Carter*), video games (*Final Fantasy*), and cartoons (*Speed Racer*), but a bad product will always be a bad product no matter what you call it.

On the other hand, many movies do poorly at the box office because they were ahead of their time (which is another way of saying that people were too dense to recognize a great movie when they saw it). *Harold and Maude*, a movie about a young man obsessed with death who falls in love with an eighty-year-old woman, flopped at the box office when it was originally released. Now it's considered a cult classic by people smart enough to understand the movie's message.

Other movies flop but suddenly do well when marketed differently. When *The Rocky Horror Picture Show* appeared as just another movie, it bombed. When theaters started showing it at midnight screenings, people appeared dressed as their favorite characters, sang along with the actors, and threw items at the screen. By turning the movie into a participatory event, theaters helped turn *The Rocky Horror Picture Show* into a cult classic.

Blade Runner, a movie starring Harrison Ford as a detective hunting down runaway androids, initially flopped at the box office, but gained an audience with the release of the DVD. Now *Blade Runner* is considered one of the most influential science fiction films of all time along with Stanley Kubrick's *2001: A Space Odyssey*, which also got mixed reviews upon its initial release. This is just more evidence that proves if the public doesn't like something initially, you may need to wait for the right time in the future when people are more sophisticated.

For someone promoting their own fame, don't be discouraged if the public doesn't adore you right from the start like they worship talentless reality TV stars who deserve to be abducted by space aliens and dissected for science. Sometimes developing a fanbase takes time, and sometimes your fanbase may come from unexpected places.

Actor David Hasseloff is far more popular in Germany than in the United States while comedian Jerry Lewis is more popular in France than in the United States, which can help you better understand why Germany, France, and the United States have fought in two World Wars against each other. If you don't seem to be developing a fanbase in your own area, you might need to search for more intelligent people in other places. Your timing might be right, but your target audience may not be ready for you yet.

The hard rock band Cheap Trick started in Illinois in 1974 and released several albums that sold poorly in the United States but proved immensely popular in Japan. When Cheap Trick toured the United States, they played in small nightclubs to a largely indifferent audience concerned about more pressing issues like buying pet rocks. (My pet rock is named Sammy.) When Cheap Trick toured Japan in 1978, frenzied fans mobbed their arrival as the Japanese press dubbed the band "the American Beatles."

The band recorded their live concert in Tokyo for a record called *Cheap Trick at Budokan*, which would later be ranked by Rolling Stones Magazine as one of the greatest five hundred albums of all time.

Originally intended just for the Japanese market, the record proved so popular that import copies started selling in the United States. The record label finally released the album outside of Japan and it quickly became an international sensation, cementing Cheap Trick's fame forever. This is just one of many reasons why the Japanese think people in the rest of the world are inferior.

In the pursuit of fame, some people believe that you need money, yet the amount of money spent on a movie has no correlation to the quality of that movie. Some of the biggest bombs cost millions of dollars, including *Cutthroat Island, Heaven's Gate* , and *Mars Needs Moms*. (Never heard of them? Again, that's my point.) While many people think that you need money to promote yourself, money alone won't buy you lasting fame any more than paying for prostitutes will buy you lasting love. You still need a product that people want.

Many times, studios will blame bad timing on competition. Universal Studios released *Jurassic Park* one week before Columbia Pictures released *Last Action Hero*. When *Last Action Hero* bombed, the studio tried to blame it on competition from *Jurassic Park*, but the truth is that *Last Action Hero* wasn't that good in the first place.

Blaming competition for your failure is like blaming George Clooney for stealing away all the gorgeous women who should be dating you instead. The chances that a pretty young gold digger would be attracted to someone whose greatest accomplishment is working at McDonald's is lower than the chances that Carnival Cruise Lines will manage to provide a ship that doesn't catch on fire or make people sick from contaminated food. Ultimately, nobody is more responsible for the amount (or lack thereof) of your fame than you. Which is good news. You are in charge.

Perhaps the worst type of bad timing involves something that changes the public's perception of who you are. One minute they may love you for something, but the next minute they may hate you for that exact same thing. The only change may be an event that shifts the public's perspective.

When running for president, Mitt Romney joked about the imaginary threats of global warming. When he did this, people thought that extreme weather changes were meaningless fiction, so Mitt Romney came across as intelligent to his supporters. Then Hurricane Sandy struck during the last weeks leading up to the election. Suddenly, Mitt Romney's dismissal that weather changes could hurt people made him look uncaring and ignorant, just like many of his supporters.

Romney's position on global warming didn't change, but the country's perception of global warming did, and Romney suffered from this sudden reversal of opinion. Imagine if the public's taste suddenly changed from light, meaningless entertainment to educational content overnight. Almost every bad reality TV show would immediately find itself cancelled, an event we can only dream about. (Yes! You've discovered my not-so-hidden fantasy world. In it, all monstrously bad reality shows are cancelled, politicians automatically lose their offices and mistresses if they are caught in a lie, the Kardashians are forced to go back to middle school where they left off and volunteer their free time to helping homeless children, and my meat dress looks cute on me—and isn't starting to smell.)

Timing on Social Media Networks

In the old days, magazines appeared weekly or monthly while newspapers appeared daily. Today, anything that appears in a weekly or monthly magazine has probably already appeared on a news website days before the magazine is printed. Even newspapers come out a day too late because most of the news they report has already appeared on the Internet. With printed media becoming as obsolete as chastity belts, the real news appears in real time on social media networks. That means if you want to reach your fans now, you have to know how to time your publicity campaigns on social media networks too.

If you want to be seen and heard, you need to go where the crowd is to reach as many people as possible. If you post your content when fewer people are on a social media network, you might as well be shouting your message to an empty room, which is usually inside any theater showing a Miley Cyrus movie.

Although timing depends on your audience, your product, and your fanbase, here are some general guidelines for the best times to promote yourself on various social networks based on the likelihood that more people will see your information. Keep in mind that depending on your audience, the best times for one audience may be the worst time for another audience:

★ SOCIAL MEDIA NETWORK	★ BEST TIMES TO POST	★ WORST TIMES TO POST
Facebook	1 p.m. to 4 p.m.	8 p.m. to 8 a.m.
Twitter	1 p.m. to 3 p.m.	8 p.m. to 9 a.m.
LinkedIn	7 a.m. to 9 a.m.	10 p.m. to 6 a.m.
Google+	9 a.m. to 11 a.m.	6 p.m. to 8 a.m.
Pinterest	2 p.m. to 4 p.m. or 8 p.m. to 1 a.m.	5 p.m. to 7 p.m.

Weekends and evenings are often the worse times to post on any social media network since those are the times when most people are out partying, getting drunk and getting laid. It's hard to notice someone's Facebook update or Twitter tweet if your face is inside a toilet bowl upchucking the twelve drinks you downed.

Unlike the other social media networks, Twitter can be especially popular during live events such as during the World Cup or Super Bowl, or during major award ceremonies such as the Academy Awards or the Miss America pageant.

Many people tweet using hash tags pertaining to popular events, which taps into the crowd's interest and gets your tweets noticed. If Miss North Carolina appears on TV and you tweeted about Miss North Carolina's breasts being augmented by your uncle plastic surgeon, your tweet will likely catch the interest of everyone currently looking at Miss North Carolina's breasts at that moment. By taking advantage of real-time events, you can maximize the exposure for your tweets (just as long as you can get them to look at your tweets instead of breasts. Tall order I know.)

You've already learned that the most talented person in the world won't get as much fame as the most publicized person in the world.

Likewise, you now know that the best publicity campaign in the world won't get as much fame as the best-timed campaign in the world.

Timing can mean the difference between failure and success, although in the case of promoting Paris Hilton, a successful publicity campaign can make people feel like they lost anyway. If you aren't achieving the measure of fame you want in your own life, check your timing.

Maybe you're ahead of your time, maybe you're targeting the wrong audience, and maybe the general public is too dense to recognize your greatness. Whatever the case, the proper timing can optimize your publicity campaign. Just make sure you have something worthwhile to contribute to society unless you're lucky enough to become a reality TV star.

Media and Media Training

Landing an interview can be difficult enough, but once you do get the opportunity, you want to make the most out of it-and don't take any chances. There's always a chance the reporter is going to throw you for a loop or get off track, so be prepared!

Research, research, and research some more! Never do an interview (especially on camera) without first checking out the show to see how it flows, what types of questions they ask, how they point their cameras, and so on.

Learn your audience. Different networks cater to different viewing audiences. That can be men/women, age differences, political preferences, and local markets. You can't sell an outfit to a customer by telling them they look ugly wearing it, so never put down your audience (even if they look ugly wearing it).

Research the host. Check out his or her bio before sitting down with them. See how long they've been doing the show. You might even find something in common that you can chat about should the conversation change or stall out. See what they tend to wear, and plan your outfit from there. If possible, ask for interview questions ahead of time. Most producers are happy to provide them.

Watch the feedback, and be aware. You could put out the best product on the market, and someone is going to hate it. You could be the funniest guy on the stage, and someone won't laugh. Keep track of the feedback you get so that you can work on it for next time. However, don't take the negativity so hard. There are people out there that can't stand the Beatles, and will bash them every chance they get. (I know: it's positively sacrilegious.)

Maintain a relationship with the producers and others involved. You want to be invited back? Don't act like a fool, and keep in touch with the host and producers as well as you can. And no need to play coy; one of the easiest ways for them to know you want to come back is to tell them you want to come back.

Have a solid message and information to share. One of the main reasons to do a TV interview is to release press releases and information about yourself. Make sure you have rehearsed your point, and make it loud and clear.

Prepare a few funny stories ahead of time. People like a little self-deprecation. It gives them that whole "celebrities are just like us" feeling. Have a few funny, potentially embarrassing stories to tell at all times. (Nothing horrifically embarrassing—just enough to bond.)

Make sure to use the proper personality. TV is about personality. Nobody tunes in for a boring segment. If you have ever wondered why only certain actors and actresses appear on late night talk shows to promote movies with multiple stars, it's because the studios know that this is another chance at getting someone interested. If they sent someone boring with no personality, it wouldn't be a good representation of the product.

Be confident. Act like you've been there before. Remember, you may have to dodge some bullets. No matter what you discussed with the host and producers ahead of time, they are always going to throw out one of those questions they are not supposed to ask. Make sure to prepare and rehearse how you will answer questions like these should they come up.

Networking 101: What You Know vs. Who Knows You

Hollywood's proverb is: It's not about what you know, it's about who you know and who knows you. In Hollywood, it's pretty much good to know anyone and everyone, so if you become gay, Jewish, or a Scientologist with an alcohol and drug addiction problem, you should have something in common with everyone in Hollywood right away. You never know who might hold on to the contact or opportunity that you need at any given moment. Meet everyone you can. Make a memorable and lasting impression so that they remember you. Then take advantage of it.

Family and friends are the single greatest networking circle that you can have. Family is almost automatic, as you can tell by all those Hollywood celebrities who share the same last name with some of the old Hollywood elite, (e.g., Drew Barrymore). Friendships can be equally as valuable, though they have to be earned, just look at Ben Affleck and Matt Damon.

Make conversation with people you bump into. You never know who they may be, who they may know, and what they may have to offer. The question of "what do you do" in Hollywood is quite repetitive and becomes annoying, but has probably been useful more times than you'd imagine.

Be respectful of people you are reaching out to. But also be persistent. Sometimes people just want you to earn their trust or see what you have to offer in return, but that's all part of the game.

How to Work the Party

One of the easiest ways to get people's attention is humor and confidence. Everyone likes a social butterfly, and nobody pays attention to the person standing against the wall in the corner. Make them notice you. (You didn't know I was Dale Carnegie! Google him of you don't know what I'm talking about.) Remember, humor and confidence does not mean loud and obnoxious. If you don't know the difference, you're probably the latter.

After meeting people, always follow up via text and email personally, as well as from your team. A friendly reminder is just what some people need some times. It's not that they have ignored you or didn't like you, but possibly you just slipped their mind. Remind them politely.

As for trading numbers with new people, use your cell phone and call the person on the number he or she gave you while you are standing in front of them. This way you can be certain that they are not brushing you off with a fake number! By pressing send right away, you get to see just how trustworthy they are immediately. Also, it's the easiest way to make sure your number is in their phone.

Ben Affleck and Matt Damon in Hollywood, CA 2004
(Lee Roth/Roth Stock/ PR Photos)

Event Production Know-How:
Before Rolling on the Red Carpet, Learn How to Roll It Out

Before you can roll on the red carpet, you must first learn how to roll out the red carpet. There's a good chance that Hollywood, California, is the event capital of the world. On any given night, a person with the credentials who knows the right person can choose from a handful of star-studded events. So what's the easiest way to get into Hollywood's biggest events? Start producing your own events!

By helping or planning Hollywood events, you will have the chance to generate a lot of content that can potentially go viral on the Internet, but you will also be granted bountiful networking opportunities with some of the industry's biggest names. You never know who might accidentally spill a drink on you and owe you one. Here are some tips on planning a successful event:

Concept: Every event needs a concept. Whether it's a theme, cause, release, or performance, there's always a subject. Think about who you would want there, and how you can get them there.

Guest List: Most exclusive parties will have a guest list. Make sure to send out the invitations to every big name you can think of, and add all of those names to the guest list just in case they do show up, even if they have skipped the RSVP.

Influencers: It's not only celebrities who are good to have at these parties. Some of the industry's top influencers are also important to have on hand. They are the one who can review your event and get it some quality free press as well as introduce you to some of the people you've been dying to meet.

Photographers: What if you threw the most epic party in town, but there was nobody there to document it. (If a tree falls in the forest and no one hears it, did it make any noise? And if I continue to make sarcastic analogies and you get tired of reading them and start tuning them out, do they actually exist? My head is all abuzz with this tangle of logic!)

True, that probably wouldn't happen during the camera phone/Twitter/Instagram-obsessed era, but even if the night was a blur, that doesn't mean the photos should be. **Hire a photographer to shoot your event.** If cost is an issue, look online for photographers looking to shoot for their portfolio. They will usually do it for free as long as they can use a copy of the photos as well.

Media: Invite all of the media you can. They may show up, they may not. They may not show up and regret it when they see the kick-ass photos from your photographer. Chances are, someone in the media will be there. Hint: Treat them like kings even if mentally they may be peasants. (And they are wearing awful clothing and eating all of the foie gras. Who cares? You need them so be nice.)

Sponsors: Sponsors are a key element, because with most events there is a budget cost. Want to have an open bar without spending thousands of dollars? Get an alcohol sponsor. Let another company pay you to set up advertisements and banners at the party. Companies will pay big money and donate product to sponsor the right event. Don't even be afraid to oversell it a bit.

The Witchcraft Celebrity Spell Guide

"The logic behind magic is that we create what we are imagining."
—Mary Faulkner

In the middle of the Iraq War when death squads roamed the streets of Baghdad, blowing up car bombs and shooting at American troops in vicious firefights, the lead story in my local newspaper highlighted Bill Clinton's dog Buddy, who had died after being hit by a car. At that moment, I realized that important facts are irrelevant, and that a single-minded goal to shock the public and arouse a strong emotional response can turn even the most mundane event into headline grabbing stories that beg for everyone's attention.

If you study the best novels and movies, you can dissect them into formulas and recipes. Now apply these same formulas and recipes to any news story and you can create an immediate sensation, which is exactly the same tactics that the news media and tabloids use. When a blogger site named PerezHilton.com can rival CNN.com in Internet traffic and popularity, that's when you start to understand how powerful entertainment can be as a marketing tool (and why so many people believe that Satanic powers must rule over the world after all).

Today, Internet sites and bloggers that rely on sensationalism to attract and retain readers are wiping out serious news programs, newspapers, and magazines. Even the strongest news brands that used to pride themselves on journalistic integrity are falling victims to this trend in a desperate attempt to cater to the growing population of people easily amused by trivia. (It's our old friend ADD again—good to see you!)

Only a few years ago, nobody would have imagined that *The New York Times* or CNN would branch out into celebrity gossip and news to retain their audiences. When people recognize a show on Comedy Central, *The Daily Show*, as more trustworthy in reporting the news than CBS, *The New York Times*, or CNN, that's when you know society isn't what it should be.

This is great news for everyone because it means that you, as a celebrity or a wannabe celebrity, have exactly what media wants, which is a story, no matter how ordinary or insignificant. The trick is to resist the temptation to throw your story out like your tossing a beach ball with no strategy or specific targets in mind. Instead, you need to learn how to turn any story into a big story so that the news media and general public will find you fascinating for no apparent reason at all.

Think of all those tabloid stories involving celebrities such as Lindsay Lohan, Tiger Woods, Kanye West, or Snooki. The basic story follows the same pattern that suckers in the ADD public time and time again.

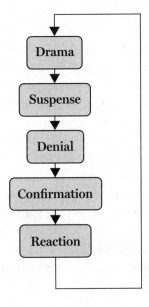

The Pattern of Fame

Let's see how this pattern played out with Kim Kardashian's divorce. First, there was the drama surrounding her marriage. Was she happy? Were they living together? How come they were recently seen in public without each other? Were they still wearing their wedding rings? Each question generated more Drama and fed the curiosity of people seeking clues in their behavior as if prying secrets out of the Rosetta Stone.

Following this media-fueled fiery avalanche came the inevitable Suspense. Eventually we would learn if Kim was happy, if they were still living together, why they weren't seen in public together, and whether they were both still wearing their wedding rings. We just didn't know when we would find the answer to these questions. The longer these questions lingered in the public's mind, the more Suspense they generated in drawing further attention to Kim Kardashian and her marriage. It was like a big, giant tease and the public was just salivating for more.

Just as the Suspense began to die down, the public Denials appeared. Rather than answer the questions that were on everyone's minds, these public Denials simply stoked the public's curiosity even further. Did the Denials mean that the stories were false or did these Denials mean they were trying to hide something that they didn't want the public to know about? No matter what the truth might be, public and frequent Denials served to keep Kim Kardashian in the public spotlight just a little bit longer as people ignored more pressing issues of the day to gossip about someone they had never met in person.

Finally, the Confirmation came (just as the media storm surrounding her had started to fade). Kim Kardashian confirmed that the stories had been true after all. She wasn't happy, they were no longer living together, they had separated and were no longer seen in public, and they were no longer wearing their wedding rings. Rather than end the story, such confirmation only served to stir up interest as people who guessed correctly gloated about their accuracy while those who guessed incorrectly revisited the stories to see what signals and clues they might have missed.

Shortly after Kim Kardashian confirmed the end of her marriage, public reaction set in. People debated whether her whole marriage had been set up as a publicity stunt from the start or if she had actually tried marriage and found that it didn't work out because she could no longer sleep with any guy she met. Whatever the truth may be, the Reaction to her divorce simply defined the end of one cycle and the beginning of a new cycle of drama that kept Kim Kardashian in the public spotlight so she can further profit off her image and her marketing brand-and got her through whatever publicity dry spell she might have experienced before new husband Kanye West and baby North came on the scene.

If you thought only communist governments engaged in disinformation and outright propaganda campaigns to deceive the public, you haven't seen how the Hollywood marketing machine can turn the tiniest detail about a celebrity's life into an all-encompassing story that people feel the need to talk about at work and through forums and chat rooms on the Internet.

The Fame Game simply squeezes the maximum amount of publicity out of a story by gradually releasing tidbits of information to maintain and prolong the media exposure. Even more surprising is how the exact same formula continues to work time after time in the exact same tabloids. Just fill in the blanks with a new celebrity and you magically have the same publicity campaign, whether you're wringing out the last bits of publicity from one of the frequent Kardashian divorces or exploiting Miley Cyrus's latest bizarre behavior.

This "no brainer" approach works for both celebrities and big businesses. Think of McDonald's. Notice how often they update their products from French fries and Big Macs to the McRib sandwich and fish McBites? By providing new information on a constant basis, businesses like McDonald's can maintain the interest of the public because of the "news" they have to share, which is often trivia involving food that will kill you if you eat it more than once a year or so. Celebrity news and gossip is nothing more than fast food for the brain and it's probably just as unhealthy for you as well. But oh so tantalizing for the masses.

Witchcraft Spell Categories

Just as witches use spell books to cast their magic over a terrified populace, publicity seekers concoct similar spells to mesmerize the public with their trivial but well-crafted news stories. The goal of such celebrity news stories is to distract the public's attention away from even more trivial topics like paying their mortgage or rent that month, or raising their children in a responsible and loving manner.

If you want to break a celebrity news story that will catch the eye of the tabloids, and hence every bored person who thinks the lives of celebrities are more interesting than their own, here are the main categories that consistently grab the public's attention:

+ Dating/breaking up

+ Pregnancy

+ Divorce

+ Dramatically gaining or losing weight

+ Arrests/DWIs/Caught with hookers

+ Affairs

+ Celebrity feuds

+ Tell all story/revealing "celebrity secrets"/what "really happened"

+ Personal/human interest stories (my life, my home, my relationship, my career, etc.)

Just pick a category when you need instant publicity or "buzz." You could start a feud with another celebrity over nothing at all. By attacking someone who currently gets more publicity than you, you can ride on that other person's coattails.

Comedian Bill Maher once joked that he would give celebrity tycoon Donald Trump $5 million if Trump could prove that he wasn't the "spawn of his mother having sex with an orangutan." (I personally thought Maher was being kind, you know, not choosing a sub-creature of the underworld instead.) Donald Trump later tried to sue Bill Maher, who in turn criticized Donald Trump for making a mockery of the legal system. Whatever the outcome, this feud winds up promoting both Bill Maher and Donald Trump in the eyes of their followers.

Picking a fight with another celebrity typically only works as long as you're not a has-been celebrity looking to get back in the limelight again. For washed-up celebrities, a better technique is to focus on tell-all stories, such as actress Mackenzie Phillips talking about her incestuous relationship with her father, John Phillips, who was the lead singer of the band The Mamas and the Papas. Committing incest with your father is newsworthy, but committing incest with a father who also happens to be a famous celebrity himself is sure-fire publicity magic.

One separate tabloid category involves train wreck stories that include drunk driving charges, drug and alcohol problems that typically end up with a very public display of attendance at a rehab facility, brushes with the police, and similar problems that would be destructive for most people, but somehow produces more publicity for celebrities (if just for a brief flash of a second).

Think of Mel Gibson's racist rants in front of a police officer or Heather Locklear getting caught and arrested for drunk driving. If anyone unrecognizable did this, people would think the person was just some moron. If a celebrity does this, people still think that person is acting like a moron, but they're fascinated to see it.

While you might be tempted to get instant publicity by crashing a White House party, getting hauled away by the Secret Service, and winding up in the news media, train wreck stories rarely help ordinary people gain instant stardom. Famous celebrities will always get more leeway than the average individual by suffering fewer consequences and are often even rewarded for their problematic behavior. That's one of the benefits of being famous. The rules don't apply to those with money and/or fame.

While the public cheers turnaround and reformed sinner stories, any type of negative publicity is like playing with dynamite. It can help or hurt you, but you will not always be in control, and being in control of all aspects of your public image is what the Fame Game is really all about.

Rather than seek negative publicity by driving yourself straight into the bottom of a ditch just for publicity's sake, find a problem or drama in your own life, expose and conquer it, then make your struggle and victory public. There will always be people who are suffering from the same problem and that will make your story resonate with them so they become your biggest and most loyal fans. Best of all, everybody has a story they can tell.

At one time, Robert Downey Jr. had a promising acting career on TV and in movies. After a series of notable drug-related arrests, his unpredictable behavior soon caused his acting prospects to dry up. This caused Robert Downey Jr. to seek treatment for his drug problems and when he sobered up, his acting career took off once more on the back of his "overcoming addiction" story that now has fans cheering while mostly dismissing and ignoring his notorious past. In the meantime, thousands of other former drug addicts are struggling to put their lives together while nobody cares about them, so you can see how fame can help you get a second chance when most people don't even get a first chance. But no matter, I was cheering along with the rest for an RDJ comeback.

Cast a Spell with a News Story

Once you know the type of category (celebrity feuds, divorce, who's dating who, etc.) that catches attention, the next step is knowing when to start promoting yourself. One method is to steal the spotlight and jump on a train that's already moving. This means spotting developing news and using it to promote yourself or your business.

For example, during Christmas, the news media reported that thousands of American troops would be spending their holidays away from their families while fighting the war in Iraq and Afghanistan. An enterprising greeting card company quickly jumped on this story and introduced a special line of greeting cards geared for military personnel. The media quickly reported this as "news," which garnered free publicity for the greeting card company.

Think of news cycles as customers that are already sold on the issue. Anyone interested in that particular news story will automatically be interested in your related news at the same time. When people criticized singer Beyoncé for lip-syncing during the presidential inauguration, singer Aretha Franklin offered her opinion. Anyone interested in the lip-syncing controversy would likely also be interested in what Aretha Franklin had to say, thereby drawing publicity to Aretha Franklin. **News cycles are the best organic brands you can use to sell yourself, your brand, your message, or your products without paying royalties or licensing fees to anyone.**

In the ordinary world, it's often easier to attach yourself to a local story than a national or international one. For example, if there's another war in the Middle East, there's little you can do to promote yourself as an accountant for a company. However, suppose a local youth center is offering sports programs to keep kids off the streets. If you played sports in school or once belonged to a street gang, you could volunteer your services as an accountant at that youth center. Then you could highlight your past (playing sports or dealing drugs while in a street gang) with your current volunteer work with press releases such as "Former UCLA basketball player helps kids shoot hoops instead of guns" or "Former drug dealer teaches kids that sports can be a legal way to make a lot of money without doing anything important for society."

By attaching your name to a local event that's already attracting publicity, you divert that attention on to yourself. The more ways you can link yourself to a news story, the more credible you'll appear.

Cast a Spell on Existing Customers

In the business world, it's a well-known fact that it's much easier to sell to your existing customers than to acquire new ones, which is why the cashiers at McDonald's always ask if you want to buy French fries with every order, and why stores always have extra trinkets to buy while you are on line waiting to pay for what you actually came in there for. McDonald's isn't interested in making sure you have a balanced meal (or else they would steer you to a better restaurant). Instead, McDonald's knows that if you're already wasting money on bad hamburgers that will kill you, you'll probably be more likely to buy bad French fries that will kill you too.

By satisfying your existing customers, you can turn them into your ambassadors. Word of mouth is the most effective form of advertising, which makes your customers your best salespeople. When your friends tell you how much they love wearing Jennifer Lopez's latest fragrance, you'll be much more likely to try her fragrance too. A friend's recommendation is far more powerful than even the most annoying commercial jingle that gets stuck in your head and feels worse than Chinese water torture.

Besides keeping your customers happy and hoping that they'll tell their friends, you can also turn your fans into walking billboards. Go to any concert and you'll see vendors selling T-shirts advertising the singer or band's name. Now if your customers don't talk about you, their T-shirt silently promotes you at every opportunity.

The next time you buy a Macintosh computer, look for the free Apple stickers inside. Most people paste these stickers on their laptops, in their car windows, or on their dog's butt, which turns that item into a free billboard for Apple. Multiply this a thousand times over and you can see how fans of Apple products have become walking advertisements.

To encourage followers to spread positive word of mouth about you, first deliver a superior product or service. Then encourage them to talk about you. While it's easy for musicians to sell T-shirts with their name on it, the simplest way to spread the word about you is through social media networks.

It's not just about exposure—it's about making people care about you, your story, and your brand. Remember, people are overloaded with information so that their brains have to actively work to filter out boring, useless information (such as a political speech, for example). As the attention span of people grows shorter than that of a goldfish, it's crucial that you appeal to people in a way that they care about. This is the reason why actor Ashton Kutcher manages his fanbase with simple posts about his latest activities on Twitter.

Social media networks such as Twitter and Facebook let you hold a conversation with your followers. The more your followers get to know you, the more likely they'll say something nice about you (hopefully). With more people talking about you, more people on these social media networks will discover you and choose to follow you. Social media networks are the ultimate word-of-mouth network.

For many people in school, social media networks offer the best opportunity to extend their reach beyond their physical location. Say something interesting consistently and no matter what your age, you'll attract followers and groupies who might be willing to have sex with you as a bonus.

David Silverman, an eighth grader from Connecticut, contacts people all the time and asks them five questions. Then he posts each person's answers to those five questions on his blog. Despite his young age and location in a small town, David Silverman has learned how to promote himself by linking his name with famous people.

His customers (his blog readers) keep coming back for more to see who he managed to interview next. Then they spread the word to their friends about this enterprising young boy who has more intelligence than most major CEOs.

Cast a Spell with Pictures and Videos

Here's the seven senses rule: pictures and sound speak louder than a thousand words. Whether it's a post on Facebook or a blog posting, photos and videos grab people's attention much faster than chunks of text. Given a choice between reading or looking at pictures and movies, people will nearly always choose to avoid reading. It's the Second Law of the online Fame Game.

Subliminal influence works the best. Let people draw conclusions and make decisions; don't do it for them. Less is more. Walk someone all the way to drawing a conclusion on how amazing you, your talent and your projects are, but step aside at the end of this journey and let the public reach their own conclusion for themselves. Any forced opinion will be met with resistance and suspicion on a subconscious level. People need to feel like they have control over their decisions even if they're being subtly manipulated by the information they've been given.

The next time you see someone drinking water out of a bottle, that person probably concluded that bottled water is healthier than tap water, even when studies have shown that's not always true. Think of commercials for bottled water, showing a pristine waterfall or glacier to imply that bottled water is cleaner and purer, even if a moose or a duck just used it as a toilet. Yet perception forms their reality, so they'll continue believing bottled water is safer and tastier than tap water, regardless of actual facts.

When promoting yourself, a picture of you next to a celebrity implies that you're important, too. When demonstrating your skill or talent, a video of you cooking a meal or stitching up a gunshot wound implies that you're an authority on cooking or first aid. If you blatantly bragged, "I'm the greatest cook in the world," the first reaction of most people would be to roll their eyes at your claim. However, if you simply provide evidence implying that you know how to cook, people will draw their own favorable conclusions about your cooking abilities, which will likely be higher than their own.

Think of any of your favorite celebrities who actually have talent. Sean Penn never boasts that he's the greatest actor in the world. He simply appears in different roles and gets critical acclaim for his movies while punching paparazzi photographers in the face. Whitney Houston never claimed that she was the greatest singer in the world. She simply sang in concerts and recorded new albums, even while getting punched in the face by her husband, Bobby Brown, behind closed doors. Actions speak louder than words, which means if you're a celebrity, almost anything that draws attention to you can be spun in a positive direction somehow.

In September 2007 Chris Crocker filmed himself crying and urging people to "Leave Britney alone" after Britney Spears spiraled out of control, smacking a paparazzi car with an umbrella, and shaving her head. In less than twenty-four hours, that YouTube video attracted over two million views. The popularity of this video alone got Chris Crocker interviews on CNN, *The Today Show*, *The Howard Stern Show*, Fox News, and MSNBC.

Cast a Spell to Generate Followers

People instinctively repeat—and respond to—the actions of others, which is why dictators and cult leaders have no problem getting masses of people to commit horrendous acts against others and themselves. In other words, as we have established, most people are easily led.

This **mirroring instinct** is the reason why teenagers follow the antics of the latest celebrities, whether it's wearing the same outfits or getting the same haircut. Most people lack clear, distinct goals for themselves so they look to others for a sense of community, belonging, and guidance. This is why Marshall Applewhite could convince men to join his Heaven's Gate UFO cult by cutting off their testicles. If a cover charge that high still couldn't deter men from joining, you can see how easily swayed people can be.

While it's unlikely that you'll use your fame and publicity to castrate men, the best form of publicity encourages followers to imitate you in a visual manner. When Lady Gaga's music video "Bad Romance" used computer-generated effects to give her a doe-eyed look, teenage girls rushed to mimic that look by wearing special circle contact lenses, which incidentally can cause inflammation, pain, and even blindness. (If you thought that girls were smarter than boys, this fact alone should make you question the sanity of both sexes.)

People who admire celebrities often want to look and be like them, which is why gullible people willingly buy anything endorsed by celebrities such as fragrances, clothes, or energy drinks. Even if their fragrances were tested in animal laboratories, their clothes were manufactured in overseas sweatshops, and their energy drinks were loaded with carcinogenic ingredients, fans will continue buying them anyway to express their individuality by imitating someone else. In short, people follow anyone who gives them comfort and empowerment to overcome their everyday fears and anxieties.

Besides acting as a role model for your followers, you also need to provide a strong sense of direction because people like being led, only if they accept the direction you're offering them. In theory, a strong sense of direction should define who a person is but many people have a tendency to borrow their sense of direction and identity from others. Not surprisingly, they usually want to borrow from celebrities, who represent something that people would like to experience in their own lives.

People like Lady Gaga's outrageous costumes because they enjoy her rebellious persona. Similarly, women can relate to Jennifer Aniston's comedic acting roles as the clean-cut girl next door while men may relate to Tiger Woods's athletic ability to put more than a golf ball in a hole on a consistent basis.

A strong sense of direction provides a vehicle for your fans to climb on. This bandwagon typically satisfies a deep emotional need, which turns fans into ardent supporters. For example, angry people often associate themselves with Goth rock and heavy metal bands. Bored people may associate themselves with reality TV stars while angry, conservative people may associate themselves with Ann Coulter.

To further enhance your direction, consider adopting a cause. It might be clean water (no duck poop in MY water!), saving the whales, promoting solar power, helping the homeless, or saving homeless whales that foul clean water with their biological discharges. Pick a Big Idea that you're passionate about and identify yourself with that Big Idea.

Pursuing a Big Idea might make you famous because it's the right thing to do, but it also has very practical implications. If you ever get in trouble, pursuing a charitable cause can insulate you from the public fury and provide a ladder so you can return back to the public's good graces. After all, who can stay mad at someone who supports a cure for cancer or rescuing helpless kittens?

Cast a Spell to Create an Enemy

When your followers know what you stand for, they'll follow you since you represent the ideals they also embrace. That's why you need an enemy, because your worst enemy can be your brand's best friend. (*No*, I'm not smoking crack here. Enemies help give you definition and also give your fans a rallying point.) If you don't have an enemy, create one right away.

One of the best ways to engage your fans is to **get them emotionally involved in protecting you from unjust attacks from your enemies.** Despite their follies, reality TV celebrities like Paris Hilton and Kim Kardashian have numerous fans who actively and vigorously defend them against their critics, such as anyone with an IQ higher than a rock. Such defenders act like an unpaid sales force constantly working to protect your brand and image, even while they let their own lives go down the drain from neglect and disinterest. It's bizarre, but here again, these are the realities of the Fame Game.

Max Espinoza/Ruben Gerard

Fans of conservative celebrities, like Rush Limbaugh and Bill O'Reilly, not only enjoy what their idols say, but how they consistently attack liberals. Likewise, fans of liberal celebrities, like Bill Maher and Jon Stewart, enjoy their attacks on their enemies (often conservative celebrities and their followers). By rallying behind a common enemy, fans feel justified in following and defending their favorite celebrities.

Most people know Donald Trump as a billionaire entrepreneur with an ego the size of the Milky Way. While appearances on his own reality TV show *The Apprentice* keep him in the public spotlight, Donald Trump has no problems attracting additional publicity by constantly feuding with liberals, including comedians Rosie O'Donnell and Bill Maher, along with President Barack Obama.

Fighting always attracts a crowd. However, when fights occur between celebrities, it becomes even more interesting as the feud plays itself out in the public spotlight. Picking a fight with a celebrity only works if you're a celebrity too. If you're just a regular person, you would get more attention picking your nose. But you can attract attention by picking a fight within a cause.

For example, if you want to protest a land development project, pick a fight with the developer and the city that authorized the project. Contact the newspapers and TV stations, and stage a protest involving lots of people shouting and waving signs around. The activity alone will get you attention-or get you arrested, which will also get you attention (and not just from your oversized cell buddy Sven). Protesting an unjust cause is how Martin Luther King went from a minister to an international celebrity, right before somebody shot him.

Cast a Spell (Carefully) with Religion

Nothing stirs up more emotion than religion. That's why many celebrities tie their fame with their religious beliefs. Now if you like their particular religion, you'll be more likely to support that celebrity too.

For example, if you like the Kabbalah, you'll like Madonna. If you like Scientology, you'll like Tom Cruise. If you like anti-Semitism, you'll like Mel Gibson. Celebrities who associate themselves with religion tap into the power, positive emotions, and spirituality associated with that religion.

When Cassius Clay changed his name to Muhammad Ali and embraced Islam, his critics (mostly white people) used this as one more reason to dislike him. Yet his followers (mostly black people and young people rebelling against society) took this as one more sign that Muhammad Ali really was the people's champion, upsetting the status quo and those who still longed for the "good ol days" of racial segregation.

Religion can be a double-edged sword. If you promote your religious values too stridently, you risk alienating people of other faiths (and come across like the Church Lady from Saturday Night Live except not funny). Unless upsetting religious people is part of your brand, such as the comedy of Bill Maher, be careful about attacking religious beliefs. Trying to change someone's beliefs based on two-thousand-year-old traditions will always be doomed to failure, especially if you use logic and reason to deal with faith and tradition. Don't even go there.

You can quickly become a local celebrity just by involving your church somehow in your activities. When you tie yourself to a church or acceptable religion (that wasn't invented by a science fiction writer), you can set up charity programs to feed the homeless or provide kids with after school programs that teach good values but don't involve religious indoctrination that more closely resembles a scene of torture than a humanitarian event.

Remember, not all of these recipes will work for your brand, but the more you try and the more you think about yourself as a brand, the higher the probability of success. Use these techniques alone or in combination to keep the general public interested, although they may be dazed and off balance more than they usually are. Just as a sports playbook lists all possible plays but teams don't use all of them, so can your Celebrity Spell Guide give you options so you can pick and choose the ones you like best.

As you cast your celebrity spells over an unsuspecting public, you may find your fame starting to rise faster than you thought possible. It may appear to be magic, but it's really the power of fame. Given a choice between controlling the public through fame or witchcraft, the spell-binding power of fame would win out every time, except nobody in Salem wants to burn celebrities at the stake. There is too much money to be lost.

Maintaining Appearances: Celebrity Style Guide

Looks can contribute to 60–80 percent of your success in this industry. An actor or actress may not be given many lines in a particular scene, but their look can leave a lasting impression that will make them unforgettable. In most instances, visual memory is much stronger for people than audio memory. Lady Gaga has millions of fans, millions of records sold, and sold-out concerts, but most people talk about what she wore to an event, what she wore on stage, or the visual elements of one of her concerts.

The brain allows thirty seconds for you to make a lasting impression on a new acquaintance. Within just thirty seconds of seeing you, you're newest acquaintance has probably already judged and labeled you, perhaps before you even have had a chance to open your mouth and say hello. This is similar to the shelves at the grocery store, where traditionally the cost of packaging far exceeds the cost of the actual product. This is all for good reason. Packaging is what sells the product. Look at styling as your own personal packaging. Regardless of your immense internal value to humanity, your "packaging" is what will most likely sell you to new acquaintances who have yet to be exposed to your multitude of talents.

Famous Wardrobe Malfunctions

An omnipresent part of celebrity style has become the dreaded (or anticipated) wardrobe malfunction. Most people enjoy a free peep show from their favorite celebs, so some would say that moments like these are probably wished upon daily when young men and women blow out their birthday candles.

Historically, wardrobe malfunctions date back as far as photographers have been snapping photos, but it wasn't until the new age of media came along that the "nip slip" became a "thing."

For the sake of your brain's first memory of the term "wardrobe malfunction," let us travel back in time to the 2004 Super Bowl halftime show, when Justin Timberlake crooned that he was going to have Janet Jackson "naked by the end of this song." He was a man of his word, as with one quick yank of her top, he exposed her nipple to millions of viewers worldwide. This controversy, and the conspiracy theorists who claim that it was a setup, have caused the NFL and network executives airing the big game to take extra precaution when booking the halftime act, even to this day. So the next time you see a lame halftime Super Bowl act, you can thank Janet Jackson and Justin Timberlake.

The nip slip has since become a cultural phenomenon, with many websites and blogs dedicated to that one magic moment caught on film.

Celebrities like Nikki Minaj, Tara Reid, Halle Berry, Rihanna, Taylor Swift, Mischa Barton, Ashlee and Jessica Simpson, and many others, have all had their "oops" moment. There's almost no escaping it for them. Sometimes all they can do is laugh and join in on the fun. It's their "you're not laughing at me, but laughing with me" moment.

During the golden age of Britney Spears, Paris Hilton, and Lindsay Lohan circa 2006, the term "flashed her Britney" was coined after what seemed like an occurrence every weekend where one of the three women named above carelessly got out of a limo sans panties and asked us to salute the bald eagle. It wasn't always a pretty sight, but in the United States, when you see a bald eagle, you salute it and chant USA, USA! (And GET A WAX! GET A WAX!)

In 2012 Sofia Vergara took a different approach when the back of her dress split just before the cast of Modern Family took the stage at the Primetime Emmys. Vergara made light of the image (shown) by tweeting it to her followers with the caption, "Yes!!!! This happened 20 min before we won!!!! Jajajjja. I luv my life!!!!"

Kim Kardashian also took to twitter in 2012 to share a seam split, when the back of her leather dress had enough before a taping of Jimmy Kimmel Live. Kardashian called in reinforcements to sew her up like a ripped doll before hitting the stage, but she also tweeted the entire ordeal, even sharing a photo of the rip. But hey, it's nothing you haven't seen before, and for that matter, it was even a bit disappointing.

From the stage, to the red carpet, to the Atlantic and Pacific oceans and worldwide, the wardrobe malfunction is here to stay. The only question is who will be next.

Best and Worst Dressed Races

With celebrity fashion comes competition. There's only a certain amount of dresses out there, and not enough for each celeb to only wear once, right? So "who wore it best" was born.

The press simply *loves* "who wore it best." (It's a chance to generate controversy with no words at all. Or, actually, four words, which is about the ADD public limit for the page.) On the pages of many magazines and on websites, side-by-side comparisons of celebrities in matching outfits become the centerpiece of opinion commentary. While sometimes the results are obvious, others are up for debate, but there's always a winner in the eyes of the reader and writer.

One thing you can concentrate on is considering this before hitting the red carpet in a famous gown. You can always ask the stylist to try and pick something that has yet to be worn, but that task is getting tougher by the day. All you can do is a little bit of research and wear it better.

In addition to "who wore it best," there's the best and worst dressed lists. Fashion coverage of all major events provides commentary from the fashion elite over the night's best and worst dressed. Naturally you don't want to end up on the worst dressed list, but you know the old saying: "no press is bad press." E! network airs *Fashion Police* weekly and for special events in Hollywood, and Joan Rivers pulls no punches. A lady after my own heart, that one.

Makeup and Hair Tips

Makeup is not always a necessity, and some people flat out refuse to use it. The most important rule to remember when it comes to makeup is not to overdo it or else you'll wind up looking like a person trying to impersonate disgraced TV evangelist Tammy Faye Baker who lathered on her makeup so thick that it looked like she used a bucket and a trowel.

Your face is your "moneymaker." You can wear the hottest dress in town, but if the hair and makeup is not on point, all of the attention is drawn directly to the blemish on your nose or the shiny perspiration on your forehead.

The easiest way to keep up with the trends is to seek advice from professional hair and makeup artists. While celebrities can afford an army of makeup artists to paint their faces before they appear in public, you may not be able to afford to hire a battalion of makeup artists every day. Until you start earning A-list money for doing relatively nothing, start by learning how to apply makeup from a professional. Remember, there are pros out there who can make you the best you.

There are tons of sites and blogs dedicated to hair and makeup tips and tricks along with YouTube tutorials that will show you step by step how to achieve these looks. However, it's best to pay for a session with a professional makeup artist who can help you choose the best look specifically for you. Once you learn what to do from a professional makeup artist, remember those tips and refresh your skills periodically with additional sessions. Your face is literally your billboard to promote yourself (although in Miley Cyrus's case, her billboard is her butt wriggling back and forth while twerking).

Remember, makeup is meant to enhance you while masking your blemishes. You can go out looking flawless, or you can go out looking like the Joker from Batman. Don't try to look like someone you're not. Just take a look at Joan Rivers and ask yourself if you want to go out in public looking like a mutant who survived a twelve round fight with a plastic surgeon, or if you'd rather appear in public looking like a dazzling version of your natural self.

It doesn't matter if you look like a supermodel or a band member from ZZ Top like Duck Dynasty star Phil Robertson, who spits out so many controversial, religious-based comments that he's now considered an honorary member of the Taliban. Whatever look you want to present to the public is what you want your makeup to emphasize. Lady Gaga's makeup emphasizes her borderline schizophrenia instead of trying to enhance her appearance, so think of makeup as another tool you can use to maneuver the perceptions of the general public in your favor.

How to Dress to Kill for the Paparazzi and the Public

Celebrities get photographed doing everyday activities from attending Hollywood premieres to taking out the trash (which can sometimes be more productive than attending a Hollywood premiere). Although few celebrities want to be photographed dumping their garbage, they still want to look good while doing it. If you've ever wondered why there are so many photos of celebrities wearing makeup to the gym or when emptying their waste at the curb while wearing elegant dresses, it's because celebrities know there's always a chance a camera is aimed in their direction. They may have to put in a little extra effort to dress nicely while performing the most mundane activities, but it's better than being plastered on the front of the "worst-dressed" photo essay or the website that reveals what celebrities really look like without their makeup (they look like ordinary people).

How you dress for the paparazzi depends on your celebrity image. Someone who always tries to look glamorous may need to step out in designer fashions even while running on a treadmill at the gym. However, someone whose persona is more of an ordinary guy or gal next door can dress a little less formally. Whatever persona you want to present to the public, make sure you do it even if you're calling the dog or picking up the mail. You never know who might be watching you so you want your image to remain consistent at all times.

In some cases, celebrities may even deliberately dress differently from their persona so they appear more "real" and "natural" as they make their way to another plastic surgery appointment. For some, appearing "natural" can work, but for others, appearing too casual can make them look like a nightmare.

The golden rule is to look presentable at all times. There is no single "best" style out there because each person is different. You want to emphasize your differences from others without appearing like a freak of nature (unless, of course, being a freak is your public persona). There is a time and a place for different outfits. The most important point is to be you, or at least the persona you want others to notice and remember you by.

Fashion Showrooms

Fashion showrooms are hidden treasure chests where stylists are pulling all the looks that you see on the covers of the magazines and red carpets. One of the many perks of being a celebrity is to be able to look like a million dollars without actually spending a dime. Sometimes you can even get paid to wear exclusive designer clothes. If you can rely on your own taste, have extra time, and want to save a lot of money, fashion showrooms are your answer. Most showrooms have in-house stylists that can help you to style yourself for any occasion from the photo shoot for the cover of Vogue to an Oscar after-party.

Find out what showrooms are in your area and establish a relationship with them. Showrooms are interested in the press for the clothing you are wearing, so you better read the chapters about courting the media and be ready before you claim "I am a celebrity and I want you to dress me for free" to the showroom owners. Remember the simple principles of the etiquette we established at the beginning of the book: first you offer what you can do for people and only then ask for what you need. Do some research on the brands that showroom has, prepare a couple of options for media exposure in magazines, on TV, and online that you will arrange for the designer you are wearing and make sure you make an offer that is impossible to refuse. Relationships with showrooms will go a long way for you.

Stylists

If you do have extra cash and feel too busy to drag yourself to fashion showrooms (although I haven't seen a single celebrity that wouldn't like to spend an afternoon in front of the mirror trying on different outfits), then you can hire a stylist that will do all the work for you—pulling clothes, shoes, and accessories out of the showrooms and bring them to you for selection.

Karma Sutra for the Camera

"Madonna is her own Hollywood studio—
a pope-like mogul and divine superstar in one.
She has a laser-like instinct for publicity,
aided by her visual genius for still photography
(which none of her legion of imitators has)."

—Camille Paglia

Before you can even open your mouth and say anything, the camera has already defined who you are by what you look like. You could be the most talented person in the world, but if your hair is a mess, you slouch, you don't wear makeup, and your hand gestures look as lifeless as Tila Tequila trying to read a math book, then your visual appearance will sink you right from the start. In all aspects of life, your visual appearance says who you are long before your mouth can do any talking.

For people who have nothing of value to contribute to society, this can actually be a blessing because it means they can just buy and wear nice clothes to make an instant, positive impression on easily duped people who value surface appearances over substance. For people who actually possess talent, you have to learn to rely less on your talent and more on you good looks, even if you're hideously ugly.

Just remember that once you become famous and have lots of money, nobody will care what you look like. Does anyone really think Mick Jagger would still get all those hot babes if he wasn't a multimillionaire singer with The Rolling Stones? If Mick Jagger worked as a bus driver in North Yorkshire, he would be lucky to have sex with a blow-up sex doll that someone threw in the trash because it no longer stays inflated.

Initially what matters isn't what people think of you, but what people see of you, and the only way most people can see you is through images captured by a camera. If you want to make a good impression, you need to impress the camera first, last, and every time in between.

How to Look Good on Camera

The camera isn't a person, which might explain why Bill Clinton hasn't tried sleeping with one yet. (Haha, good one if I may say so myself!) What looks good in real life can often be far different than what looks good on camera, whether it's captured in photos or film. Cameras tend to mask a person's height while adding to a person's weight, which would be great news for women if it only enhanced their breasts. Essentially, cameras help distort reality even more than the delusional thinking of the general public.

Despite these problems, photos and video remain important because people are visual creatures who don't like to think any more than they have to. Newspaper stories with a photo are much more likely to get read than a better written story that doesn't include an accompanying picture. Even television stories without good eye candy tend to get buried or turned into short two-sentence briefs. If the government really wanted to make all those congressional hearings more exciting, they'd focus on swimsuit models doing all the debating instead of the congressmen.

In general, the fastest way to get someone's attention is through extortion and blackmail. Since that's not always possible, the next fastest way to reach people is through videos followed by pictures. The least effective way to reach people is through text, which is why you rarely see anything exciting happening at the Library of Congress.

Looking good on camera is especially important for televised interviews. Since many people rely solely on getting their news from TV (which explains why so many people can't even identify their own country on a map), if you're not on the TV, you don't exist to a large chunk of the population. (We are back to my existential pondering of the forest and the tree. Very philosophical today.)

When posing before the camera, you need to focus on:

+ Wearing the right clothes
+ Being prepared with extra clothes for any circumstances
+ Acting naturally

Wear solid colors. Stripes, hounds tooth, and other patterns will look strange and cause a moiré pattern that can distract viewers. Keep the focus on your face, not on your clothes. Even *Sports Illustrated* swimsuit models make sure their faces can be seen, even while their string bikinis highlights their breasts and groin.

When appearing in any photo shoot or interview, always bring a change of clothes (especially if you're going to be staring at swimsuit models and might drool or wet your pants out of excitement. That goes for you ladies, too! Ok, that was somewhat uncouth. I haven't gone on a true political rant in several pages. Must be making me punchy.) Make sure that each outfit you bring is a completely different solid color. The reason for this is because you won't know which outfit might look best in that particular studio or location.

If you show up wearing a blue outfit, the background of the studio or location might also be blue. Wearing a blue dress or suit while standing against the blue background of the sky or a wall will make your body seem to disappear so viewers will see nothing but a floating head. (Which I think would look kind of cool but is not the effect you want here.)

Also avoid pure white or black. White tends to suck up light like Charlie Sheen snorting a line of cocaine. Black tends to hide your body, which can be great if you're trying to hide your latest murder victim from the police, but when you're appearing in front of a camera, black makes your body disappear.

When people wear black, they also tend to show generous amounts of skin so their whole body doesn't look like a black blob strolling around. When Angelina Jolie wore a black dress to the Academy Awards, she showed plenty of skin, even sticking out her leg at an odd angle like a streetwalker trying to pick up Hugh Grant. Her white skin contrasted with the black dress, which made her visual appearance more striking.

If, however, Angelina Jolie had showed up wearing a black burqa that covered her from head to toe, she would have looked as indistinguishable as 99 percent of the gorgeous women in Hollywood.

Max Espinoza/Ruben Gerard

Besides wearing solid colors and avoiding white and black, stick with neutral colors or pastels. The camera will boost the contrast and actually make your clothes look better than they really are. Then you can sell them on eBay for a premium and advertise that they were "seen on TV." That alone should artificially inflate the price of your clothes as much as TV exposure can inflate anyone's worth in the public's eye.

Make sure your clothes are comfortable. Don't pick a suit you hate to wear because you think it looks great. If you're uncomfortable, it'll show up in your face and body language. (More importantly, ask yourself why you even own clothes that you hate to wear. Now may be a time to clean out your closet and give the clothes you hate to a homeless shelter. Or ever hear of a yard sale?)

Avoid flashy or dangly jewelry because the jingly motion of earrings and the reflection of jewelry from the lights will be distracting. If you wear contacts or glasses, stick with contacts. Glasses reflect the glare of the lights and make your eyes disappear. While this can create an interesting effect that gives you a vacuous look like Britney Spears trying to actually sing, it can distract from your overall visual appearance.

Wear knee-length socks. If you don't, you risk moving your leg and flashing skin like Angelina Jolie. Unless you are Angelina Jolie, nobody wants to see the bare skin of your leg, especially if it's furry.

Remember, your visual appearance is meant to make you look perfect so viewers will admire your look and think of you as someone special just because you're famous. When people think of celebrities, they don't want to think of them as human beings who clip their toenails, spray snot on their hands when they sneeze, or run out of toilet paper in the bathroom at the most inopportune moments. They want to imagine that people in front of the camera are special, so make those people happy and let them fantasize about anything but reality. For many people, reality is too frightening. That's why people turn to celebrities to escape into a fantasy world instead.

Wear makeup, even if you're a man. Television and staged photo shoots will likely have a makeup person who can touch up the appearance of both men and women so your skin doesn't look glossy and sweaty like you're an actual human being with sweat glands. If you have to put makeup on yourself, get help. Preferably, ask a gay man because they'll know how to make both men and women look their best.

It goes without saying, but I have to say it anyway: don't wear Levi's, shorts, T-shirts, flannel shirts with suspenders, T-shirts, buttons with political messages, or anything trendy. Footage of reporters and public figures wearing leisure suits and giant sideburns in the 1970s are still floating around the Internet. It is not pretty, but it is funny to look at so your kids will feel justified in thinking that their parents must have been complete idiots to dress and look like that.

Treat every photo opportunity like a job interview and dress for it, unless, of course, the photo opportunity is for a porno film. Then you won't have to bother dressing at all.

Besides bringing at least two different sets of clothes to any photo shoot or TV interview, **bring a handkerchief.** Cameramen need lights to eliminate shadows, and those lights are often hot enough to cook a turkey and contribute to global warming. Over time, you'll start sweating and feeling uncomfortable as you gradually bake like a chunk of pot roast in an oven. Bring a comb and whatever hair products you use to freshen up your look as you gradually dehydrate under the lights.

Bring a bag, or a trusted person, who can hold your wallet, cell phone, and car keys. You don't want anything in your pockets that might create a bulge (especially in the wrong places. I know it's tempting but it's not a good idea), be uncomfortable when you sit down, or start jingling in the middle of a shoot. If you're squirming in your seat because your wallet or car keys are jabbing you, you'll look like you're adjusting your underwear in front of everyone. While this can be humorous, it will distract from your appearance. The fewer distractions you have, the more likely you'll hold someone's attention for longer than five seconds.

If you're just going to be photographed like a vapid model standing around in different clothes, then you don't have to worry what you say. Nobody cares if a supermodel even knows how to speak as long as he or she looks fabulous in the right outfit. Just remember that when you're in front of the camera, assume that it's always on so it doesn't catch you picking your nose or giving someone the finger.

If you're going to be speaking, always assume that the camera is on and your microphone is recording everything you say. While running for reelection, Ronald Reagan tested his microphone and joked, "My fellow Americans, I'm pleased to tell you today that I've signed legislation that will outlaw Russia forever. We begin bombing in five minutes." Needless to say, the Russian leaders were not amused.

When Fox News interviewed actor Ernest Borgnine, the reporter asked him about the secret to his longevity. Laughingly Borgnine said, "I don't dare tell you," but then he whispered, "I masturbate a lot," which the microphone picked up. Go Ernest!

Practice Ahead of Time

Before an interview, practice what you're going to say. Nothing looks worse than someone stuttering over his or her words and sounding like an incoherent professional athlete who won a college scholarship but never once stepped inside a classroom. (Or like me when I'm trying to smooth things over after a potentially offensive joke.)

Remember, people first notice what you look like. Then they notice how you move. Finally, they notice how you speak. Rarely will they even remember what you said, so you could babble like a baby the whole time and as long as you look confident doing it, people would still be impressed. This is why celebrities like Britney Spears and Jessica Simpson can get away with being famous while saying almost nothing of significance.

When in front of the camera, act naturally like you normally do when a national audience of several million people is staring at your every move. The two easiest mistakes are to smile all the time (and look like a grinning village idiot) or to freeze (and look like a frozen village idiot). Vary your facial appearance, so you look like the cool village idiot! Smile, look serious, laugh, and look thoughtful. Variety will keep people seeing you as a human being and not as a mannequin, even if you have some stage fright and may feel like one at the moment.

Use small hand gestures because the camera tends to magnify all movements. Watch out for nervous ticks or unconscious habits like stroking your hair, chewing your fingernails, or snorting a line of cocaine to relax. Assume you'll be in close-up the whole time, because you usually will.

Do a practice run the day before. Dress in what you're going to wear and have somebody film while asking questions. The practice run will often show you what works (talking confidently about dropping napalm on other countries as a way to protect our national borders) and what doesn't work (laughing while talking about dropping napalm on other countries as a way to protect our national borders).

Film yourself (not as a sex tape) and see how you appear on camera. Most likely you'll feel so physically and emotionally inadequate after seeing yourself on camera that you'll want to cancel the whole interview altogether. But buck up, be brave, and use the film as a way to improve how you come across to others.

Your message is what you look like and not what you have to say. The camera delivers your message to your audience, so make sure that message is exactly what you want them to see, even if it has no basis in reality. After all, avoiding reality is what the public likes best.

Staying in the Best Combat Shape

Celebrity Diets

"I refuse to spend my life worrying about what I eat. There is no pleasure worth forgoing just for an extra three years in the geriatric ward."

—John Mortimer

Besides getting laid and making money, the other most compelling dream that dominates the collective consciousness of the general public involves losing weight. To give you an idea how schizophrenic people can be about losing weight, nine percent of all *USA Today* best sellers are cookbooks. *The New England Journal of Medicine* even reports that two years after most people go on a diet, they weigh more than before they started the diet. With such a large pool of potential customers like that, it's no wonder that many celebrities flock to the weight-loss industry to further promote themselves and make a few bucks on the side.

Weight loss (and gain) always makes the news among celebrities, even those who aren't trying to profit off their weight loss. Oprah Winfrey's weight tends to fluctuate as drastically as a puffer fish blowing itself up to ward off predators. In Oprah's case, she's such a public figure that every time she gains or loses weight, people can't help but notice, as if her latest weight gain or loss were part of the Dow Jones Industrial Average.

While Oprah doesn't always directly benefit from her weight problems, other celebrities do. That's because celebrities know that a large number of people are interested in weight loss, although not as many are interested in actually doing anything to achieve it. To satisfy the constant desire for weight-loss tips (beyond the obvious like maybe *eating less food*), celebrities often choose the fastest solution by endorsing existing weight-loss products.

Although Weight Watchers is already a well-known and established weight-loss brand, additional publicity can never hurt. That's why Weight Watchers often pays celebrities to endorse their products. Singer Jennifer Hudson endorsed it in 2010 and quickly shed eighty pounds. Such celebrity endorsements imply that if Jennifer Hudson can lose weight following the Weight Watchers program, then you can too. Of course, it would actually be more believable if Weight Watchers implied that if your fat Uncle Fred can lose weight on their program, then you can too. However, few people would be compelled to sign up for Weight Watchers with a marketing campaign like that.

Fellow singers Jessica Simpson and Mariah Carey also endorsed Weight Watchers after being paid millions of dollars (which is an incentive that most Weight Watchers users never receive). Actress and former *Playboy* centerfold Jenny McCarthy chose to endorse Jenny Craig to promote their weight-loss program in return for a fat endorsement check. Like Jenny McCarthy, Melanie Brown, of the Spice Girls, also chose to endorse Jenny Craig because she apparently wanted to be associated with something other than the Spice Girls. By endorsing an existing product, celebrities can make money quickly and easily without having to spend time developing their own product.

Of course, big companies like Weight Watchers and Jenny Craig aren't likely to pay a non-celebrity to endorse their products. However, the principle remains the same. Weight Watchers and Jenny Craig benefit from celebrity endorsements because they get someone who will draw attention to their company. The celebrities benefit because they get paid to associate their name with a company that's paying them.

In your own life, you can apply these same principles if you're trying to lose weight by going on a diet. For example, tell people that you're an accountant or publicity relations manager and nobody will really care (or they'll stifle a yawn in your face while pretending to be interested at a cocktail party). Now let's say you start losing weight successfully using a particular diet or weight-loss program. Suddenly everyone else following that same diet or weight-loss program will see you as a success story.

Within that particular group, you suddenly have credibility. Now if you're looking for a job as an accountant, anyone using the same weight-loss program will be more likely to look at you favorably. By associating your name with a particular weight-loss program, you can promote yourself with other followers within that same program and become a minor celebrity who can exploit fame like a bigger celebrity.

Another way celebrities exploit the strangely fascinating topic of weight loss and dieting is by using it to attract even more publicity to themselves, like pigs attracting flies by rolling around in manure. (Not my best analogy, but I like the image.)

For example, since Kevin Federline's fame basically relies on having had sex with Britney Spears in the past, he needs other ways to stay in the spotlight. One way he did this was by appearing on the seventh season of the weight-loss reality television show *Celebrity Fit Club*.

Since Federline doesn't have much other talent to promote, he later repeated the same formula by appearing on an Australian weight-loss show called *Excess Baggage*. During filming, he suffered a minor heart attack, which actually gave him a bit more publicity.

While the general public may be fascinated if a celebrity gets a hang-nail, nobody cares if a non-celebrity has a heart attack or has an alien burst out of their chest in the middle of dinner, so medical emergencies rarely translate into marketable publicity opportunities if you're not already well known to the apathetic public.

Still, you can apply Kevin Federline's formula for fame by following in his footsteps. While you probably will never get a chance to marry or have sex with Britney Spears, you may still be able to exploit what little fame you do have by something similar.

If you're on a weight-loss program and succeeding, simply promote yourself as a success story. Weight-loss organizations like Jenny Craig and Weight Watchers love promoting success stories to recruit others, so once you start promoting their success with you, they'll be likely to turn around and start promoting you in return, even if it's just as simple as publishing your testimonial on their website or in a brochure.

Now instead of trying to promote yourself alone, you'll have the greater exposure and credibility of a larger organization promoting you. Then if you manage to gain more fame in your own local area, you too can look for ways to have sex with a star and move up to the next level of fame like Kevin Federline.

While many people go on exercise programs to lose weight, only celebrities can turn their efforts into further publicity for themselves. Snooki got pregnant (what are the odds?) and gained weight. After giving birth to a son (I just keep imagining a little *Jersey Shore* Damien child like from *The Omen*.), Snooki hired a personal trainer and promptly lost forty-two pounds, which gave her another chance to appear in the celebrity tabloids to trumpet her results.

Of course, nobody cares about non-celebrities losing weight or exercising, so you'll need to attach yourself to a greater cause. For example, Snooki can lose weight and get in the news because she's already famous. If nobody knows who you are, start losing weight for charity.

For example, promote your cause as losing twenty pounds and for each pound you lose, get sponsors to donate money to a charity such as the Red Cross. Now suddenly people will be interested in you, not because anyone cares about you, but because they care that you're promoting yourself for a charity. The charity will benefit and promote you while you'll get the fame and attention as a result.

You may never get in *People* magazine for losing weight like Snooki, but then again you can hold your head high knowing that you're not anything like Snooki in the first place.

Creating Product Lines

Endorsing existing products is a fast way to associate yourself with a popular brand while making yourself a public spectacle. However, an even more lucrative way to profit from the weight-loss industry is to develop and market your own diet products.

Actress Kirstie Alley tends to lose and gain weight as drastically as a pregnant humpback whale. To take advantage of this, she decided to launch Organic Liaison, which includes Rescue Me, the first USDA-certified organic weight-loss product. Based on her organic weight loss products, she announced that she had lost a hundred pounds.

Of course, once a celebrity loses weight, they can trumpet their successes on talk shows to further promote themselves and their product line at the same time. Even when someone sued Kirstie Alley, claiming that she didn't lose a hundred pounds through her organic weight loss products, that lawsuit simply put the public's attention back on Kirstie Alley. For some people, the lawsuit justified their decisions to stay away from her product, but for many others, it simply made them more curious about the program. And certainly helped them hear about it in the first place.

Developing a product line of your own may be difficult because few companies will want to slap your name on a product if nobody knows who you are. Once again, the answer for non-celebrities is to attach themselves to an existing product and promote that product while touting your own success with that product.

If you join one of many multilevel marketing programs, you can promote yourself and the product while making money selling that product at the same time. If you're truly creative, come up with your own diet program and sell the ingredients to others. If you already work in a diet-related field—for instance, as a personal trainer—you can promote your business like Kirstie Alley promotes her organic weight-loss program. In both cases, you can turn weight loss into profit.

Eating Disorders and Plastic Surgery

When scrutinized under the public eye like bacteria under a microscope, celebrities often feel that they need to appear perfect at all times. For many celebrities, this translates into an unhealthy obsession with their weight, often turning into eating disorders.

While millions of people in other countries starve to death every day, celebrities in pursuit of their perfect body image are busy starving themselves thin or eating perfectly decent meals and then deliberately throwing them up afterwards. It's like ancient Rome only more gruesome—or as our vastly undereducated masses know it as today, the Capital from *The Hunger Games*.

Toss in celebrity magazines that doctor up and Photoshop pictures of celebrities to make them look thinner (and better) than they actually are, and it's easy to see how fame can distort reality to make a healthy body weight and size feel like a giant gurgling monster like Jabba the Hutt from *Star Wars*. (What does it mean to be "the Hutt" anyway? Is that a job description or an alien tribal thing? Anyone know?)

For every celebrity suffering from an eating disorder, there are thousands of fans suffering from similar ones.. While celebrities have the money to deal with their eating disorders, non-celebrities don't. The first step is to realize that a celebrity's image is no more real than Mouseketeer ears on people at Disneyland.

Whenever there's a problem, celebrities can turn that problem into additional fame, whether they're driving drunk or getting caught shop-lifting on Rodeo Drive. Many celebrities use their eating disorders to promote themselves by admitting their problem and then using that problem to get themselves back in the spotlight so others can read about how they struggled.

Lady Gaga has launched a campaign to highlight her own eating disorders and help her followers open up and share their problems with eating disorders as well. By using their fame to help others learn and understand their own eating disorders, celebrities can further strengthen their bond with their fans, actually do something positive for a change, (did I really say something nice about celebrities? Guess so.) and (of course) promote themselves at the same time.

If you have an eating disorder, you can do what celebrities do and admit your problem as a way to publicize yourself. However, celebri-ties publicize their eating disorders on talk shows or celebrity tabloids. Ordinary people have to publicize their eating disorders by associating themselves with a larger organization that's already publicizing the problem of eating disorders.

Whether you're a plumber or a lawyer, you can deal with your eating disorder and then turn around and promote your struggles through an organization like the National Eating Disorder Association. If they use your testimonial to promote themselves, then you can turn around and use your link with that organization to promote yourself. You may never get to appear on a nationally televised talk show to promote yourself through your eating disorders, but you can still publicize yourself locally and help others by sharing your story.

While most celebrities struggle with eating disorders, actors and actresses often embrace dramatic weight losses and gains so they can play certain roles in movies. For his role in *Cast Away* where he played a stranded Federal Express executive, Tom Hanks lost fifty pounds. For her role as a starving factory worker forced into prostitution in *Les*

Miserables, Anne Hathaway lost twenty-five pounds (although she didn't completely go into character by working in a factory and engaging in prostitution. How lazy of her!)

On the other hand, many actors gain weight for certain roles. Robert DeNiro put on sixty pounds to play Jake LaMotta in the movie *Raging Bull.* Renée Zellweger ate doughnuts and pizza to put on twenty-eight pounds for her role in *Bridget Jones's Diary,* which didn't exactly endear her as a spokesperson for doughnut or pizza companies. (But I for one was very jealous that she got paid money to binge on my favorite food.)

Celebrities can hire doctors, nutritionists, and personal trainers to monitor their weight gain or loss, so such drastic weight changes aren't recommended for most people (including celebrities; it's not healthy for anyone, no matter who is supervising. And gives you unsightly stretch marks). Unless you're applying for a job as a fat lady in a circus, you may never need to add weight to get a job (but you may still feel the need to lose weight to get a job since thinner people are often considered more attractive, no matter how awful they might be inside.)

If you plan on losing weight, do so because you want to lose weight, not because of how you think others might perceive you. Remember, there are unhappy fat people and unhappy thin people. If you're not happy with your body, then work to improve it. That will not only boost your self-esteem and improve your overall health, but it will also teach you that what you think of yourself is far more important than what a crowd of random strangers thinks of you. That's a luxury that even celebrities can't enjoy.

Staying the Course

When it comes to success, there's usually a formula—have clear goals and focus on them, know what you're doing, and be prepared. Pursue your dreams with confidence, drive, and energy with the help of your team, network, and resources.

Focus is golden. You want to have a clear objective and stick to it. In order to successfully stay the course, first of all you need to know the course. You should always have a clear intention before you hop on the train, and keep it in your mind at all times. Remembering your goals will help you to stay focused and assist tremendously when you are having doubts or need to make important decisions.

Know what you're doing. Be prepared, and do plenty of research before diving in head first at anything. Whether it's an interview with Oprah, speaking in front of a class, or performing at a dive bar to three locals who are already too intoxicated to understand anyway, make sure you know as much as possible about the audience, the hosts, and everyone around you who is important to the situation. In the case of an interview, always get the questions ahead of time.

Be persistent. The truth is, the universe is a function of statistics. It can take a full day of casting a fishing line before you finally catch a fish. Trying something gives you a chance to succeed at it. Be prepared for failure and to try and try again to increase the probability of success. You should always be thankful for every opportunity you get, because experience is the best schooling you can have. If you get negative feedback, you can always use that feedback to help fix the problem.

Confidence is a key to success, although there is a fine line between confidence and arrogance. This is especially true in the world of power players who can be annoyed or threatened by you and have the power to destroy your career. Even if you have already made it (especially in your own mind), this is a very valuable lesson that you will hate to learn firsthand. Look at poor Charlie Sheen. When he hit the wall a few years back, he butted heads with *Two and a Half Men* creator Chuck Lorre. He was killed off the show, which cost him a salary loss of $90,000 per minute.

You have to start somewhere. Drive and energy are the tools needed when you first are starting out. Hollywood is a world of hustlers, and so too is the world of successful people. You must have the ability to create relationships and teams, be a part of large-scale events, and earn your keep. Whether it's hanging out backstage for Paul McCartney, or running errands for Chelsea Handler (or whoever the Pauls and Chelseas are in your area, you get the drift), in the beginning, it's all about creating opportunities to advance your career.

Staying Sane

Staying sane is also important to your career, or any life path for that matter. Don't let the pain and bad experiences hold you back. There will be plenty of bumps in the road—you can't avoid them. You can let them break you and become just another Hollywood wannabe who got stuck on their way, falling into the abyss of drugs and obscurity. But that's not the fate I want for you, so please stay sane!

Learn how to detox your mind. A clear mind can drive your inspiration and creativeness. Everyone has their "happy place," be it sports, travel, meditation, or even partying. Always make time to do what makes you the most relaxed. Some of the greatest business ideas were thought up on the golf course. You never know when and where you will come up with the next big thing. Find your golf course.

Clean the skeletons out of your closet. The right people can make you, but the bad people can break you. Skeletons always come out, so it's better to set them free from the beginning. It's not even always the pesky media or paparazzi who can cause this type of trouble for you. Sometimes it's the ones closest to you. Just look at the fallout between Paris Hilton and Kim Kardashian over fame.

Do you really think that Tiger Woods would have lost $100 million in endorsements and a nasty divorce had he come out about his indiscretions in a smart way and controlled the situation before his wife took a golf club into her hands and got away with half of his fortune?

Time is the only true asset you have. Value your time! Success, money, power, and fame are only derivatives of time and how you spend it. Spend it wisely. If you are too busy wasting time on the wrong people, relationships, and projects, you're just wasting time. It's very hard to make it alone, in fact almost impossible. Build a strong team of people that are better than you in their own skill areas, and lead them by being a loyal and honest person. Share your success as it comes.

Always give back and help newcomers. Aside from being good karma or mitzvah (one of the words you'll probably want to become familiar with if you plan on working in Hollywood), by helping these newcomers you just may be investing in your own future. You will have to learn how to spot and distinguish between people who are "deserving" and the "users–abusers," of which Hollywood has more than its fair share.

Never take any credit away from yourself. Your past success and achievements are still success and achievements. Remember them. They will be the confidence boosters you need when you want to take on daring new opportunities with an open face. Remember how good you felt after your past success, and never give up hope so that you can feel that way again.

Lastly, confront your demons, whether it's bad habits, insecurities about the way you look, or toxic relationships. These are the type of things that can hold you back severely. Sometimes even being complacent about where you are can be an ultimate setback. Free yourself from anything that holds you back on your journey to success. (Ok, the serious inspirational self-help portion of our discourse is officially over. Take what I said to heart, and we will resume our regular programming. Let's gird our loins, arm our sarcasm, and return to the complex and morally ambiguous land of the Fame Game.)

The Reality of Reality TV

"I play into the perception of me, but it's not really me."

—Kim Kardashian

During an interview, the camera is on you for a few minutes at a time, which gives you a chance to blow your nose or clean out a piece of spinach from your teeth. However, if you're on a reality TV show, the camera is on you twenty-four hours a day, so how do you deal with that kind of pressure without resorting to illicit substances like most celebrities will do?

Reality TV plays a huge role in shaping public opinion, which tells you the sorry state of our educational system. Whether you want to create your own reality TV show or hope to appear on an existing one, you need to know the reality behind reality TV, because what you see is only a fraction of what really happens. By knowing how reality TV really works, you can maximize your own chances for success in playing to the cameras.

Like a fairy tale (but minus the grisly details that adults somehow believe are perfectly acceptable for little kids to handle (evil stepmothers abandoning children in forests, witches shoving kids in ovens to cook them), reality TV is more than cameras recording ordinary people behaving in unusual situations. The reality is that reality TV is as scripted and unreal as your favorite situation comedy or drama. The only thing real about reality TV is that it makes money at much less cost than traditional shows that require actual actors.

The Elements of a Successful Reality TV Show

Every successful reality TV show offers three elements that are crucial in any unscripted show:

* ✦ Larger-than-life characters that can be interesting in any situation.

* ✦ Conflict. Reality TV conflict may make you uncomfortable, but it's like a train wreck that you can't tear your eyes away from, which makes for awesome TV ratings.

* ✦ Access to places most people have never seen before. Think *Pawn Stars, Toddlers and Tiaras, Deadliest Catch*, etc.

The first truth about reality TV is that it has little basis in reality because most reality is pretty boring. Go to any shopping mall in America and watch people walk around. That's reality, and that's boring. Nobody really wants to see that because they get an overdose of overwhelming boredom every day. What people really want is a heightened sense of reality, much like taking LSD but without the danger of getting arrested or suffering brain damage afterwards.

Just like a situation comedy, every reality TV show needs a collection of eccentric characters. Unlike a situation comedy where most of the characters get along, reality TV needs people who will constantly butt heads, fight, scheme, connive, lie, and deceive one another to bring out the worst traits in human beings all in the name of "entertainment." How Roman gladiator of us.

More importantly, reality TV needs characters that can create conflict by fighting in any possible situation whether they're feeding a puppy or building homes for the poor. Reality TV characters must evoke strong emotions in the audience, from sympathy to hatred. If the unique premise of your reality TV show can't turn ordinary people into psychopathic killers, then you won't have an interesting show.

Besides interesting characters and conflict, reality TV shows also need an interesting location that takes the audience out of their drab and ordinary world and puts them in a more exotic environment that few people will ever experience in their lives.

Strand hardened sailors on a boat and give them the job of catching crabs in the Arctic Ocean and you have an interesting reality TV show. Dump ordinary people on an island and force them to eat bugs and rat guts to survive while they plot to eliminate the other contestants and you also have an interesting show. Reality TV is about pushing ordinary people into extremes by making them behave in ways that bring out their raw animal instincts so they'll go after each other's throats like rabid vampires hungry for blood.

The more misery, jealousy, and backstabbing you can create, the happier your audience will be. Watching ordinary people suffer at the hands of their fellow human beings is what makes for a successful reality TV show. If *The Hunger Games* was a realty show where teenagers fought to the death, it would be the number one show on television.

Conflict is the heart of nearly every popular reality TV drama. Think *Jersey Shore*, the *Real Housewives*, *Survivor*, and *X Factor*. Audiences want to see people at their meanest, nastiest moments because watching extremely emotional people is far more interesting than watching a saint inspiring the poor, unless that inspiration includes electric cattle prods, leather whips, and napalm.

The conflict must come from jealousy, anger, insecurity, fear, and other common emotions that everyone experiences. When viewers can identify with the raw emotion you've exposed by exploiting someone, that's when you have a potential hit reality TV show.

Access is the final element of successful reality TV. Remember, most viewers live in Middle America where nothing much exciting happens, which is why so many people find a way to screw up their own lives. Reality TV shows let these people watch emotionally screwed up people in unique locations, from the safety of their living rooms.

Audiences in Middle America want to see situations they might not otherwise experience. *Keeping up with the Kardashians* and *Real Housewives* show wealth, mansions, and high-profile relationships while proving that even rich people can be just as idiotic as poor people. By watching these shows, people in Middle America can see how rich people can be more screwed up than even their craziest relatives when they're off their medication.

Other shows like *American Idol, The Voice*, and other game/talent shows put viewers backstage so they can experience the jitters and fears without actually risking embarrassment before a national audience like the contestants they see on TV. It's all about living these experiences vicariously-and safely.

If you lived in a place like Nebraska or Kansas where the biggest goal of most people is to become assistant manager of the local Jiffy Lube oil change shop, you'd want to escape into another world through reality TV shows too, even if it meant following people like Kourtney Kardashian, who talks in a type of monotone you would expect from someone with a severe head injury and spends her time on TV picking at salads, fighting with her baby daddy Scott Disick (a shamelessly enthusiastic moron who can't believe his luck landing a situation where he will never have to work again) and complaining about her mom who set this multi-million dollar gig up for her in the first place.

Proposing Your Own Reality TV Show

After seeing the dearth of quality entertainment on TV, it should come as no surprise that TV networks are starving for good ideas. Surprisingly, anyone can propose (or as they call it in show business, "pitch") a reality TV show idea. As long as you present yourself as a professional and not a lunatic, you can call any TV network and talk to people who have the power to say "No" to shoot down your ideas, but rarely have the power to say "Yes."

However, these pawns of show business can often direct you to the right people who will listen to your ideas since they have so few ideas of their own. In show business, ideas are the lifeblood of the industry, much like greed, corruption, and deceit are the lifeblood of-can you guess it? Politics of course!

To pitch a reality TV show, you need to define how your show will create conflict and what unusual place it will show viewers so they can pretend to be learning something when they're really just getting fatter sitting on their couch while watching TV and stuffing their face with junk food.

First, briefly describe your reality TV show in a few sentences, called a **logline**. For example, *Survivor* is about putting groups of people in an exotic location and forcing them to compete in games to eliminate each other until only one person is left. *Dancing with the Stars* is about pairing talented dancers with D-list celebrities and humiliating the professional dancers while jump-starting the D-list celebrity's moribund career. *The Amazing Race* is about teams competing to be the first to solve puzzles around the world and not get diarrhea from drinking the local water.

Once you've written a short description of your reality TV show idea, you also need to write a longer description of your concept, called a treatment. A treatment briefly describes how a typical episode of your reality TV show works that doesn't involve anything illegal like killing another contestant (although that would be a ratings bonanza).

Finally, you need to create something called a **sizzle reel**, which shows a mini-episode of how your reality TV show will work by demonstrating the worst human behavior possible. A sizzle reel should show about three to five minutes of your sample reality TV show to demonstrate that you have a great concept.

Don't worry about the visual quality. As long as you have interesting characters put in direct conflict in an unusual location, you can shoot your whole sizzle reel on an iPhone. What's more important is seeing human beings ripping each other to shreds emotionally and psychologically, even if the footage is as blurry and shaky as video footage of Big Foot strolling through a redwood forest.

Make sure your sizzle reel shows real, authentic characters that pop on the screen. If your characters come across as fake or inauthentic, network executives won't believe in it in the same way that nobody believes the Zapruder film shows that only one assassin actually shot John F. Kennedy.

Remember, your sizzle reel must be phenomenal because once you're out of the room, your sizzle reel has to sell your show idea on its own. To make it memorable, include humor. Laughter can be a powerful emotion that will make your sizzle reel memorable, just as long as they're laughing for the right reasons.

Make sure your sizzle reel mentions your show's name. A great title describes the show itself such as *America's Got Talent*, *Toddlers & Tiaras*, and *Teen Mom*. Just don't get too descriptive by naming your show *Losers to Laugh At* or *Pathetic Individuals We Can Shamelessly Exploit for the Easily Amused Who Have No Lives of Their Own*.

After you create your sizzle reel, be careful about sharing it with others, such as on YouTube. While a YouTube video can promote your show idea, it can also attract people who might steal your idea. (Remember, even lawyers don't trust people in Hollywood, so if they're highly suspicious of intellectual property thieves, then you should be too.) If you must share it with others, do it through a private YouTube link or a password-protected site such as Vimeo.

Create an interesting reality TV show concept, write up a logline and treatment, film a sizzle reel, and you'll be ready to pitch your show to various networks who are filled with imagination-deficit executives eager to latch on to your project to boost their own sorry careers in Hollywood.

Once you have a logline, treatment, and sizzle reel, the next step is to get a meeting with actual network executives. When you get such a meeting, you need to know:

1. Who are the people at the network you are seeing and what are their needs?

2. Who is the network's key demographic?

Know as much as you can about the network executives you'll be meeting, what shows they've developed, what shows are most successful for their networks and why, and, of course, any personal information you can learn about them so you can blackmail them later if your meeting doesn't work out. You can often learn a lot about people just by searching Google, Facebook, and websites such as IMDb, which is why stalkers love the Internet so much.

Remember, every network targets different ages and genders, so you have to pitch your idea to the right one. Pitching a reality TV show about guns and explosions to a network that targets older women probably wouldn't make sense, unless that network appeals to bored Minnesota housewives who would love the idea of handling a weapon that could kill their annoying husbands..(I get it and I sympathize. I do.)

To understand the needs of different networks, here are brief descriptions of the type of reality TV shows different networks want and the audiences they target:

The Spike network is predominantly male-oriented (including lesbians who are often more male-oriented than many males). Spike's audience appeals to young males (18–45), but they're interested in broadening their appeal to older males (and lesbians) in the 25–54 age range as well, since older males tend to have more money than younger males still living with their mothers.

Besides seeking shows that appeal to older males, Spike also wants shows that offer diversity, so they aren't forced to show five different shades of white guys all the time. In addition, Spike wants shows that emphasize "infotainment," which is a fancy term that means teaching real life facts through entertainment (since most people are incapable of learning anything after being traumatized from their childhood experiences in school). For example, the reality TV show *The World's Worst Tenants* talks about the legalities of renting while kicking filthy slobs out of their homes and throwing their useless garbage in the streets for neighborhood dogs to urinate on.

Ideally, Spike wants a show that amps up tension while being "horrifying and addicting" at the same time. Spike doesn't want to see people smiling when their audience is far more interested in seeing those same smiling people getting punched in the face or kicked in the groin.

Most importantly, Spike doesn't want shows about "objects" like *Antiques Roadshow*, which emphasizes the latest old piece of trash someone found in an attic that turns out to be worth thousands of dollars more than the person who found it. Spike wants shows that focus on big, obnoxious, over-the-top characters that viewers can't stop watching, whether they love or hate them. After all, what's more exciting to watch? A total stranger getting punched in the face or someone you've grown to hate getting punched in the face?

On the opposite extreme of Spike is WE tv, which targets women who are breadwinners and seeking adventure beyond going on another business trip to random locales around America where everyone is home in bed by 9 p.m. WE tv wants shows that focus on "big, loud, filterless characters" such as the Joan and Melissa Rivers show where the highest-rated episode occurred when Melissa broke up with her boyfriend, which again shows us how people like to feed off other people's crisis and drama like bored, thirsty vampires.

WE tv wants reality TV shows that focus on relationships and over-the-top characters who "bring drama" into their lives through their actions or incredible stupidity. (Often one and the same.) WE tv's key demographic focuses on women (25–54) and especially appeals to 35-year-old women (who are probably really 45 but just lying about their age. But that's ok, I'm not going to touch that one.)

Besides older women, WE tv also attracts many African-American women who are all too willing to demonstrate that black women can often be no smarter than white women when it comes to their choice of what to watch on TV.

Another network that targets women is the Oxygen network, which gets its name because when most men watch it, their first thought is feeling suffocated without enough air to breathe. (Men, no use fighting your woman with the remote on this one. You will lose, so just be graceful about it and buy a second television. And ladies: be realistic. The last thing you want it for your boyfriend to be equally addicted to WE tv or Oxygen. That's a big flashing sign that you probably shouldn't be dating him.) Not surprisingly, the Oxygen network appeals to women (18–49) with their strongest demographics coming from the 24–35 age range.

Women who watch the Oxygen network often come from two-career families, which means they're expected to work full-time and still cook and clean up after the man in the house. The Oxygen network sees itself as "Bravo's younger, sassier sister," which is just a friendlier way of calling the Oxygen network more appealing to women who like to see themselves as bitches.

Oxygen reality TV shows need to be aspirational so it makes people in the middle of the country excited to be doing something that people in New York, Los Angeles, or Miami are doing, no matter how illogical it may be. In other words, Oxygen's audience want to mimic what they see people in bigger cities doing, but without the traffic jams, high cost of living, and rampant crime rate.

Similar to the Oxygen network is the Bravo network, which emphasizes fashion, food, design, beauty, and pop culture. As a result, the Bravo network tends to attract homosexuals along with upscale, educated women. Their typical demographics include adults ranging in age from 25–49, but their prime market falls within the 30–35 age range. Like the Oxygen network, the Bravo network appeals to people in Middle America who actually think people in New York and Los Angeles live more glamorous lives, not realizing that people in New York and Los Angeles often dream they could live in Middle America to escape all the people who live in New York and Los Angeles. (It's a true "grass is greener" conundrum. Anyway, I have my little Wisconsin farm all picked out. It has trees and sky and cows and . . . ok, who am I kidding? I would probably spontaneously implode if I were ever removed from the smog of LA. But it's nice to dream and complain.)

Although the USA Network doesn't focus on reality TV shows as heavily as other networks (who lack the imagination to put on something that actually requires thinking), they are planning two possible shows.

The first new reality TV show is called *The Choir*. Based on a British show (to help give it an air of elitism and cultural significance. Works for me—I for one am impressed!), *The Choir* is about a choirmaster visiting an economically challenged town and asking all kinds of people to become part of a new choir. To make the show interesting, it focuses on people from all walks of life who wouldn't normally socialize with each other.

The show's appeal comes from the choirmaster trying to bring hope to unemployed men and women from diverse fields, such as tough construction workers who you might not expect to sing in a group on a stage. By trying to inspire people, USA Network hopes *The Choir* will buck the trend of most reality TV shows that focus on showing the backstabbing, greedy, selfish side of human nature. For that reason alone, *The Choir* will probably fail.

The other reality TV show coming to the USA Network is about giving people a second chance to follow their dreams (as long as those dreams don't involve taking over the cushy jobs the network executives have for themselves). For example, the show might follow someone who once dreamt about becoming a rock star, excluding the inevitable drug overdose that kills them in the end. The appeal of the show will be seeing ordinary people living dull lives of quiet desperation finally getting a chance to screw up their lives for real by following their dreams that their parents always warned them against.

Although every network has different needs, all of them want reality TV shows that tell a story with passion and integrity, despite much of Hollywood lacking these things. Be an open, collaborative partner because common courtesy and honesty will get you further than lying and deception, although those are the very traits often help Hollywood executives rise to the top.

After pitching a reality TV show to a network, what can you expect in return? In most cases, you can expect to get screwed. However, if a network buys your show idea, you'll get some kind of a producer credit and then be considered a "work for hire" employee, which means you'll probably be fired as soon as possible so other people can take over your project.

Don't expect to make much money off your idea. Hollywood's accountants know how to make money disappear faster than a high-end prostitute buying clothes with a celebrity's credit card. About the only thing you can expect when selling your reality TV show is getting your first big project credit, which you can use to (hopefully) pitch another show where you might actually maintain control over your creation.

Remember, people watch reality TV shows because they want to see authenticity, even though reality TV shows are far from authentic. (It's fascinating. We kind of know it's an illusion, yet we continue to buy into it anyway. Like when I look in the mirror and I see the ripped abs I had at twenty with the sage, commanding presence of Larry King.) You want to create a show with intense characters that audiences will want to watch every week because your show represents an arena far more interesting than one more day of their own lives, an escape from boredom and pressure, and a chance to scorn different characters to feel better about themselves.

Reality TV Survival Guidelines

While some people want to pitch and create their own reality TV show, others just want the instant fifteen-minutes of fame by appearing on one. To get on a reality TV show, become a larger-than-life character. Remember, superficial authenticity is what makes reality TV so appealing, so do your best to appear ordinary but bigger than normal (remember your brand), which is a paradox that makes even quantum physicists scratch their head. (And I'm not talking physically. Giant hats, big puffy hair, platform shoes or other more private enhancements are not what I mean-unless they are part of your brand.)

If you're lucky enough (or unlucky enough, depending on your point of view) to get on a reality TV show, the first rule you need to follow is to keep yourself in front of the camera at all times. The camera won't follow you, so you need to follow the camera by putting yourself in every shot possible. That way when they edit the show, they can't help but keep showing you as often as possible. The more you're seen, the more likely you'll be kept on the show, especially if you can make a spectacle of yourself in every shot.

In every episode of *Jersey Shore*, Mike "The Situation" Sorrentino made sure he appeared in every shot by constantly taking off his shirt and showing off his abs. By doing this, he drew attention away from the other cast members and made himself a constant presence on the show.

Besides throwing yourself in front of the camera at every opportunity, you also need to define a consistent visual look and brand. If one day you wear a Mohawk and the next day you look like a banker, you'll confuse and puzzle the viewer. (Remember your appearance goes back to defining a brand. See how important a brand can be? If you skimmed over that chapter, go back and read it now.)

While you want to be consistent with your visual appearance, you also want to be consistent with the story you tell to the viewer. If you're enemies with someone in one scene, you can't suddenly be friends in another scene (although you can pretend to be friendly before stabbing them emotionally and psychologically in the back).

Being consistent means being authentic with who you are. Don't try to lie because you'll inevitably slip up. Once viewers catch your lie, they'll distrust everything you do, which can be great if you're building your brand as a complete son of a bitch. If you want the villain edit, go right ahead.

When competing on a reality TV show, you want to show extreme emotions. When you lose, you don't just sigh, look at the camera, and declare that you'll learn from the experience. That's boring. What you want to do is make a spectacle of yourself. Scream, yell, and throw easily breakable objects around the room. As long as your outrageous behavior fits your brand, you'll just strengthen your appearance in front of the producers and improve your chances of staying on the show longer.

In shows that involve judges, the judges aren't there to look for the most talented people to keep on the show. The judges are really there to make spectacles of themselves and keep the most interesting people on the show, who as we already know aren't always the most talented ones.

Judges often lower the scores of obviously talented people and artificially inflate the scores of more interesting people. This can outrage viewers who will then call a 900 number to "vote" for their favorites who they see as being unfairly overlooked. Of course, calling such a 900 number only increases the revenue of the telephone company and the reality TV show producers while giving the public the illusion that their vote actually counts, which is no different from most national elections.

As a reality TV show contestant, you can expect plenty of opportunities to get drunk, overload your body with sugar, and deprive yourself of sleep. Nobody wants to see someone sleeping unless they're passed out from a drunken spree or an orgy. People who are awake are always more interesting than people who are asleep, especially since the awake people can often stand around a sleeping person and pose in funny ways in front of the sleeping person, such as sticking their naked butt in the sleeping person's face.

During the first season of *Survivor*, Richard Hatch made a spectacle of himself by strutting around without his clothes on. Whether you liked seeing a naked man roaming around or not, that act alone insured that he would stay on the show since it got the public talking about him. In the world of reality TV, negative news can simply draw more attention to a show to boost its ratings. As long as you're boosting ratings, the producers will find a way to keep you on the show even if they have to fake the judging results. Welcome to reality.

As a reality TV show contestant, your ultimate goal is to increase ratings, whether you are walking around naked, having a drunken crying fit, puking, or swallowing raw rat guts. (I just made myself nauseous with that image. But see how I stopped and gave it extra attention? See how this works?) As long as you realize that talent means little but ratings mean everything, you can maximize your chances for becoming a star on reality TV.

Reality TV is just another way to make money. As a reality TV show creator, you need to provide an attractive arena where audiences can watch ordinary people battle each other like gladiators. The only difference is that gladiators fought to the death while reality TV shows often makes viewers feel like killing themselves after watching a reality TV show for too long.

As a reality TV show contestant, you need to make yourself abnormally interesting (this almost always means abnormal) to draw attention and viewers to the reality TV show. The more you can stir up emotions in viewers, the more they'll want to watch the show, and the longer the producers will keep you on the show. Reality TV is all about shaping perceptions. The sooner you realize that reality is whatever you create, the sooner you can make this work in your favor.

Fame in Politics: Weapons of Mass Distraction

"America is addicted to wars of distraction."—Barbara Ehrenreich

Ah! A whole chapter devoted to my non-so-private obsession. Here we go.

When most people think about fame, they think about movie stars, professional athletes, and musicians. However, the Fame Game also applies to people you might not normally associate with popularity, such as politicians. (As you may have noted, I certainly don't associate them with anything positive like popularity.) Yet politicians have to create, nurture, and fabricate fame just like everyone else. The only difference is that they're smart enough to get supporters to pay for it all while they get the benefit of sleeping with interns and mistresses.

During the American Revolution, people fought for the right to elect their own leaders and determine their own fate. The Founding Fathers deemed political elections so important that they crafted a Constitution and rules for allowing the people to elect their leaders, just as long as they only chose older white men who got rich by exploiting poor male and female minorities.

Of course, the Founding Fathers didn't trust the intelligence of the common people, who likely foresaw the ease at which the masses could be swayed. To avoid placing the nation's democratic future in the hands of complete morons, the Founding Fathers created a bizarre system known as the Electoral College, which allows "electors" to determine who wins, regardless of the actual popular vote. Such an unfair and illogical method for resolving national elections remains in place to this day, and like my new Bluetooth home theater sound system nobody quite seems to know how it works. All they know is that the people don't really elect their leaders, which is what makes American democracy work.

In the old days before mass communication became possible and people could buy cheap Viagra from the comfort of their homes, news travelled slowly and political candidates actually travelled to populated areas to talk directly to the people without the aid of teleprompters, speech writers, or public relations managers.

In those simpler times, debates between candidates actually attracted crowds both for the curiosity factor and the entertainment value it provided. Back then, life moved so slowly that it wasn't uncommon for people to rock on their porches at night to watch the grass grow. (An activity that is widely underrated. Try it and see. And bring your pet rock to join you. Actually bring a large bottle of scotch or some weed to join you, and the grass may start responding when you talk to it.)

In today's world of instant communication through text messaging, Twitter, and mobile phones, life moves at what seems like lightening speed with information bombarding us every second, usually with people tweeting or sending text messages while they're rocking on their porch at night, watching the grass grow. Now, it's not uncommon for people to tune out anything but the most trivial problems that have no relevance or significance whatsoever. This is the reason why so many people wish for the good old days when the public only ignored major problems like racism, slavery, and denying women the right to vote.

As mass communication allowed political candidates to expand their reach to the hoi polloi—first through newspapers, then through radio, and finally through television—the masses of people saw less of political candidates in person and more of their flickering images on their television screen. The more distant politicians and the voting public became, the less people actually knew about the politicians they were entrusting with the role of leading the country, which ironically made people feel emotionally closer to politicians than ever before.

As more politicians arrived to run for more political offices, the inevitable happened. Nobody really knew what was going on, which is what the Founding Fathers foresaw when they created the Byzantine-structure of the Electoral College. The more confusing and complicated elections were, the better American democracy could thrive through inaction, incompetency, and paralysis.

The gradual distancing of politicians from the people meant that the public no longer knew who they were even voting for. In the old days, a politician might be your neighbor. Today, a politician is most often a complete stranger who sleeps with four mistresses on the side (three of them holding the job of "secretary," or "intern," or "publicist," although they can't type, take dictation, or write anything in proper English) and who appear in public only to solicit your vote that will either get lost or "miscounted" in voting machines anyway. (I'm looking right at you, Jeb Bush!)

To make decisions about strangers, people can only rely on what sound bites that politician presents, along with the negative sound bites that his or her opponent presents. As a result, political elections are usually not often resolved by exhaustively examining the merits of each candidate and weighing their experience and abilities with the political office that they seek. Instead, people rely on snap judgments, first impressions, and simple slogans to elect the leaders that will have access to the button capable of activating a nuclear holocaust in less than three minutes. I am losing sleep over this; why aren't more people?

Instead of focusing on political issues and offering their solutions using intelligent reasoning, candidates now focus on shaping their image. What suit they wear, how they speak, where they part their hair and what they say without committing themselves to any particular position is far more important than their actual leadership and problem-solving abilities. Essentially, politicians have become just another reality TV star who we watch from afar, judge, and root for or jeer at depending on the perception others have already shaped for us. By focusing on superficial impressions while ignoring actual substance, American democracy has become the envy and role model of the world.

Showmanship Is Everything

In 1952 Democratic Governor Adlai Stevenson ran for President. Known for his intelligence and eloquence, Adlai Stevenson secured the Democratic nomination with stirring words such as:

> When the tumult and the shouting die, when the bands are gone and the lights are dimmed, there is the stark reality of responsibility in an hour of history haunted with those gaunt, grim specters of strife, dissension, and materialism at home and ruthless, inscrutable, and hostile power abroad. The ordeal of the twentieth century—the bloodiest, most turbulent age of the Christian era—is far from over. Sacrifice, patience, understanding, and implacable purpose may be our lot for years to come . . . Let's talk sense to the American people! Let's tell them the truth, that there are no gains without pains, that we are now on the eve of great decisions.

Needless to say, Adlai Stevenson's opponents ridiculed what they perceived as his intellectual air. Republicans emphasized Adlai Stevenson's differences from the working-class, blue-collar voters and proposed their own candidate instead, a World War Two hero, General Dwight D. Eisenhower. Given the choice between an intellectual delivering a carefully crafted speech and a war hero wearing medals on his chest, guess which candidate made a stronger impression on the voters?

In the 1960 presidential election, John F. Kennedy appeared with Richard Nixon in the first televised presidential debate. Nixon appeared pale, underweight, sickly, and sweaty from a recent hospitalization. On the other hand, Kennedy appeared calm, handsome, and confident.

Those who listened to the debate on the radio overwhelmingly thought Nixon had won. Yet by 1960, 88 percent of American households had televisions with nearly seventy-four million Americans watching the debate. Those who watched the debate on TV thought Kennedy clearly won, not from the strength of his arguments but from his visual appearance. Many even say Kennedy won the election that night, which goes to show, again, that superficial impressions hold more weight than actual thought and reasoning.

Although Nixon performed much better in subsequent debates and greatly improved his visual appearance on television, the damage had already been done. On November 12, 1960, four days after winning the election by a narrow margin, Kennedy himself admitted, "It was the TV more than anything else that turned the tide." Fortunately, we didn't have pseudo-celebrities like Tila Tequila or Kendra Wilkinson on TV back then or else Americans would have elected a brainless bimbo from *Playboy* as president of the United States. (Not that I don't think that's on the horizon, and actually almost happened a few years back. It was a VP spot, and you all know what and whom I am talking about.)

How you look on TV can be crucial, but if both candidates look equally poised, then how they come across on TV can make all the difference in the world. In 1980 President Jimmy Carter provided a lengthy response when asked about health insurance. Ronald Reagan simply turned to him and said, "There you go again!" Nobody remembered what Jimmy Carter said, but everyone remembered that Reagan's four disarming words that effectively discredited Carter—who actually was making some sense at the moment.

More importantly, Ronald Reagan's response hid the fact that he had nothing intelligent to say on the matter and didn't have a plan of his own. Instead, Reagan boosted his own image at the expense of Carter's by saying nothing but coming across as likeable in the process. I have to say it was a brilliant move.

Reagan later won the election in a landslide and uttered his now famous phrase about the environment when he claimed "Trees cause more pollution than automobiles do" and "Facts are stupid things." With quotes like these, you can see why Reagan is revered to this day. You can also see why it's so easy for Nigerians to con Americans by sending them unsolicited e-mail messages offering them millions of dollars in exchange for a few thousand real American dollars first.

If someone says something stupid, most people immediately assume that person must be stupid (or in Ronald Reagan's case, suffering from Alzheimer's disease). That's not how it works in politics. In politics, stupid statements often go ignored by supporters but are vigorously promoted by their critics.

When chosen as John McCain's vice presidential nominee, Sarah Palin (Yes, that's who I was talking about) explained that Alaska's proximity to Russia gave her foreign policy experience. "As Putin rears his head and comes into the air space of the United States of America, where—where do they go? It's Alaska. It's just right over the border."

Despite this questionable statement, Sarah Palin's popularity soared even higher than that of her presidential running mate, John McCain. For people who question Sarah Palin's intelligence, the real focus should be questioning the intelligence of her supporters.

Politics is the only industry where you can say something incredibly wrong and not get run out of town for being an obvious idiot. When former Mayor of New York City Rudy Giuliani ran for President, he emphasized his leadership skills during the 9/11 terrorist attack on the World Trade Center, which occurred when George W. Bush was president. Later, when criticizing President Barack Obama for being weak on terrorists, Giuliani claimed that, "We had no domestic (terrorist) attacks under Bush. We've had one under Obama."

Ignoring facts is easy in politics because most people don't remember the truth after it becomes old news. Nobody remembers the lingerie worn by supermodels during Victoria Secret's fashion show because they're too busy looking at the supermodels. Likewise, nobody cares what politicians say or think just as long as they look good in front of the camera. Political elections are becoming nothing more than beauty pageant popularity contests. The only difference is that unlike political candidates, beauty pageant contestants have to demonstrate that they actually have talent.

As an actor, Ronald Reagan knew how to present himself to the public, so it's no surprise he turned his popularity and skill as an actor into a career in politics. To this day, Republican Party supporters still idolize pictures of Ronald Reagan while pretending other Republican presidents like George H. W. Bush and his less intelligent and more incompetent son, George W. Bush, never really existed.

Following in the footsteps of Ronald Reagan, actor Arnold Schwarzenegger also successfully ran for governor of California. Actors running for political office already have a vast following that they can convert into voters. This is the reason why Mickey Mouse still gets more write-in votes than any living person in America. Given a choice between voting for an actual politician or an imaginary cartoon rodent, it's easy to see which one more people would trust. I go for the cute, perpetually happy mini-rat with red shorts and big yellow shoes every time. Mickey at least never lies.

The "Truth" of News Reporting

In the old days of Walter Cronkite, people actually trusted the news, even if that news only reached them after being filtered through the sanitizing eyes of the network censors. By creating an aura of objectivity, the media could convince people that they were actually getting all the facts about important topics like the Cuban missile crisis (except for the part about how the New York Giants had once offered dictator Fidel Castro a baseball contract to play for them) and the Vietnam War (except for the part about the My Lai Massacre where three US servicemen had tried to stop the slaughter, only to be denounced as traitors by several US congressmen afterward). (Oh am I having fun with this chapter! Hope you are too.)

Of course, the media has never been objective, but it's a pleasant myth that adults like to cling to as much as children like the soothing comfort of believing in the Easter bunny and the tooth fairy. Or of pathetically believing that we will one day rise up en masse and rebel against reality TV programming. Yeah. Not happening, but I can dream.

Max Espinoza/Ruben Gerard

After the American battleship USS *Maine* blew up in a Cuban harbor in 1898 and 268 men were killed, the *New York Journal* made up a story about how the Spanish had planted a torpedo beneath it and detonated it from shore. Follow-up articles contained diagrams and blueprints of the secret torpedoes that Spain could have used, which convinced many Americans that the Spanish had sunk the ship, thereby justifying a reason to go to war with Spain.

Fortunately such distortions of facts to incite the public to support an unjust war could never happen anymore. If any news outlet tried to incite the American people to support an invasion of another country (such as Iraq) based on unverified information (involving weapons of mass destruction), you can be certain the public would demand actual evidence before tolerating an unjustified invasion of another nation's sovereignty. Right? Right?? Who's with me?

In the past, the news media put on an air of objectivity that fooled almost everyone. Today, the news media has thrown off any delusion of objectivity and shifted their focus to deliver only the type of news their particular audience wants to hear. That's because news is less about delivering information and more about ratings. It's no longer important to tell facts. It's more important to maintain an audience, and the easiest way to do that is to make sure you never report any facts that might upset your target audience.

CNN gained popularity during the 1991 Iraq War when they were the only news network to show a live broadcast of the Desert Storm invasion at the beginning of the war. After the war ended, CNN's popularity started to fade without another war for CNN to cover live, twenty-four hours a day. That's when Fox News started reporting the news from a right-wing perspective, under the deceptive tagline of "Fair & Balanced," which would be like Rush Limbaugh calling himself "Slim & Liberal." (Or like me calling myself tolerant of B.S.) In response, MSNBC countered by delivering a left-wing perspective of the news, except with less controversy and lower ratings.

In the old days, news networks presented anchormen to deliver the news. Today, the news networks rely more on personalities to attract an audience and present the news as a way to promote their own political agenda and bias while giving their news celebrities something to say. It's just one big fat "oy" and we keep buying into it.

One of the Fox News conservative commentators is Sean Hannity, who claimed that waterboarding is a fair and necessary interrogation technique for suspected terrorists. Immediately following this statement, Keith Olbermann, MSNBC's liberal commentator, challenged Sean Hannity to undergo waterboarding. In return, Keith Olbermann said he would donate $1,000 for every second Sean Hannity could withstand the waterboarding. Instead of reporting news, the news personalities are busy promoting themselves.

Another popular Fox News commentator is Bill O'Reilly, whose conservative commentary inspired comedian Stephen Colbert's outrageous, conservative parody, *The Colbert Report*. Stephen Colbert says that his parody represents a caricature of a television political pundit who is a "well-intentioned, poorly informed, high-status idiot."

With highly-esteemed commentators on both the left and right wings, the news has become less about informing the public and more about turning news personalities into celebrities to boost ratings on the network. Such news celebrities inevitably cash in on their fame by writing and selling books, further promoting themselves.

The Power of Late Night Talk Shows

In the old days, Johnny Carson and *The Tonight Show* ruled late night television. Like everything else in the news today but not as offensive because of the time slot and more relaxed positioning, such late night talk shows were focused more on entertainment than news reporting, which included obligatory appearances by movie stars, directors, musicians, and authors promoting their latest projects. Late night talk shows used to alternate between silliness and entertainment news with little substance in between, which was no biggie because it was what it was. That all changed when politicians started invading the late night talk shows.

When running for president in 1992, Bill Clinton saw an opportunity to reach the public by appearing on *The Arsenio Hall Show* and playing the saxophone. Not only did this appearance provide free publicity for months afterwards, but it also helped portray Bill Clinton as a candidate that younger voters could relate to. (And when Bill Clinton later got caught having oral sex in the White House, younger voters could really relate to him as a role model.)

After appearing on a late night talk show, Bill Clinton's appearance set the model for other candidates. President George W. Bush appeared on the *Oprah Winfrey Show* while Barack Obama has appeared on *The Tonight Show with Jay Leno*, the *Late Show with David Letterman*, and *Late Night with Jimmy Fallon*. Today, politicians see appearances on talk shows as just one more way to reach the public. After all, nobody really cares about the State of the Union address that puts everyone to sleep, including the people actually attending the event. Politics has gone from pretending to be important and doing what's best for society to becoming just another form of entertainment (while still pretending to do what's best for society).

Nowhere is this more obvious than in Jon Stewart's *The Daily Show*. When Jon Stewart took over the show in 1999, he shaped the focus as a fake, satirical news show. Despite its comical attempts to lampoon political figures and current events, an online poll by *Time* magazine found that Jon Stewart was the most trusted newscaster out of all the television networks.

One reason why so many people trust a satirical news show as a more reliable source for information than CNN, Fox News, and CBS News is that *The Daily Show* often attacks important issues that the mainstream media ignores in pursuit of topics that will attract higher ratings.

After the United States Senate failed to pass (and the mainstream media failed to cover) the James Zadroga 9/11 Health and Compensation Act, which would provide health monitoring and financial aid to first responders of the September 11 attacks who later got sick, *The Daily Show* dedicated the entire December 16, 2010, broadcast to that one issue.

Afterwards, both politicians and 9/11 first responders praised Jon Stewart for helping promote the bill's passage. According to Syracuse University professor of television, radio, and film Robert J. Thompson, "Without him, it's unlikely it would've passed. I don't think Brian Williams, Katie Couric, or Diane Sawyer would've been allowed to do this."

When a comedy show not only covers important issues but has more influence than the mainstream news outlets, it tells you how low the mainstream news outlets have sunk in their quest to focus on pop culture and entertainment rather than report on important information that actually matters. Pandering is fine, but when it's obvious you lose all public trust and credibility, which journalism of all things can certainly not afford.

Political Scandals

Now for the fun part. (For me at least.) When politicians aren't advocating cuts in health care services and authorizing bailouts of failing corporations while they enjoy taxpayer-funded health care as they urge individuals to take responsibility for their own finances without the help of government bailouts, most politicians are pretty boring. They spend most of their time doing nothing, voting for their own pay raises, and taking more breaks so they have more free time than a homeless person.

Despite their insistence that they're sacrificing their lives in public service while banging their taxpayer-funded "interns" in a motel room away from the eyes of their wives (who only appear next to them in events promoting their support for "family values") politicians are only interesting when they create a scandal.

The most popular political scandals involve sex. (Not surprising as the most popular scandals *anywhere* involve sex.) Usually this means a man cheating on his wife with another woman, but it can also involve a man soliciting sex with another man (while advocating against homosexuality) or a man soliciting sex with young boys (while advocating against pedophilia).

Bill Clinton is the most popular figurehead for a politician cheating on his wife with another woman. What makes Bill Clinton particularly newsworthy is that most of the other women he cheated with were uglier than his own wife. Rather than have sex with younger, prettier women, Bill Clinton chose to go backwards instead, which makes him all the more fascinating for his poor choice in loose women. But it also made him more human in the public eye-and a target for every woman who still feels "If he went for that, surely he would go gaga over me." Anyway, it's a new level of public service.)

Naturally, Bill Clinton isn't the only world leader caught in a sex scandal. Italy's prime minister, Silvio Berlusconi, was once charged with paying for sex with an underage Moroccan nightclub dancer named Karima El Mahroug. He was also charged with abusing his political powers to cover up the relationship afterwards by persuading the police to release the girl while she was under arrest for theft. If Berlusconi had only come to America, his sex scandal could have won him the Democratic nomination and his cover-up scandal could have won him the Republican nomination. And a really cool reality show as a nice bonus.

Sex scandals are the fastest way to bring attention to any politician. For six days in June 2009, South Carolina Governor Mark Sanford disappeared. Even his own wife and office staff didn't know where he was. When he was later found, he claimed he had been hiking the Appalachian mountain trails. Later he admitted he had flown to Argentina to have an extramarital affair.

After leaving his job without telling anyone and lying to the public about his whereabouts, Mark Sanford proved more newsworthy for his extramarital affair than for his abandonment of his duties as governor of South Carolina. Apparently governing South Carolina is so easy that you can ignore it for six days and nothing bad will happen in the meantime.

New York Governor Eliot Spitzer created his own sex scandal when he reportedly paid more than $15,000 for prostitutes over a six-month time span. (Where did he get them so cheaply, come to think of it?) Federal agents believe Spitzer paid up to $80,000 for prostitutes over a period of several years when he was first the attorney general (in charge of enforcing laws such as those banning prostitution), and later as governor (in charge of upholding laws such as those banning prostitution). Ah, but at least there is an underlying thematic consistency—prostitution was front and center throughout.

In 2006, Florida Republican Mark Foley resigned from Congress after underage males working as Congressional pages complained that he had sent them suggestive emails and sexually explicit instant messages. Despite a consistent record voting against gay and lesbian rights, Mark Foley later admitted that he was gay as well.

Republican Senator from Idaho Larry Craig was also known for his anti-gay voting record. In 2007 he became involved in his own sex scandal when several men complained that someone tried to solicit sex from them in a men's room stall at the Minneapolis-Saint Paul International Airport.

An undercover police officer investigated by sitting in a restroom stall. First, the officer caught Larry Craig lingering outside the stall and peeking through the crack of the stall door. Next, Larry Craig entered the stall to the left of the officer's stall. In the police officer's own words:

> At 1216 hours, Craig tapped his right foot. I recognized this as a signal used by persons wishing to engage in lewd conduct. Craig tapped his toes several times and moves his foot closer to my foot . . . The presence of others did not seem to deter Craig as he moved his right foot so that it touched the side of my left foot which was within my stall area. Craig then proceeded to swipe his left hand under the stall divider several times, with the palm of his hand facing upward.

After being arrested, Larry Craig showed the police officer a business card identifying himself as a US Senator, but the officer refused to release him.

While sex scandals attract the most attention, any type of crimes committed by people supposedly upholding the law can prove fascinating. In 1990, Washington DC Mayor Marion Barry got caught in an FBI sting operation. During this sting operation, the FBI videotaped Marion Barry smoking crack cocaine as if he were a movie star.

Not surprisingly, Marion Barry spent six months in federal prison. Later he ran for mayor again and actually won, which shows that the voters can be even dumber than the politicians they elect.

The Simplicity of Politics

Nearly every school forces kids to learn how their government works. Usually such lessons are filled with descriptions of the different parts of the government, how they work, how they pass and enforce laws, and how ordinary people can one day aspire to become part of this dull government too. Ultimately, such textbook descriptions on the workings of government are mostly fantasies, much like telling children that storks deliver babies or that Santa Claus builds and hand delivers the latest the Apple gadgets for them at the North Pole. And that they won't get any unless they brush their teeth. (I for one almost never brushed my teeth often and still got my Santa stuff. Ha!)

The truth is much less idealistic. Politicians get paid extremely well, enjoy perks and benefits that ordinary people never get (yet their tax dollars pay for), frequently cross the bounds of ethical and moral behavior and rarely suffer the consequences of their actions as they do as little as possible while taking as much as possible. (It's like the Law of Inverse Karma.) Occasionally, they pass laws.

Instead of demanding accountability and results, the public ignores the entire political process until something interesting occurs like a scandal or a war. If none of those occur, the public busies themselves by watching reruns of *Survivor* or *Teen Mom* while letting the politicians run wild in obscurity.

The few times the public cares about politics is during an election. That's when politicians finally "tell the truth" (by pointing out the flaws of their opponents) while they "spin" the facts (lie or distort the truth) to promote themselves.

Rather than outline detailed solutions to sway the public, politicians have greater success just providing images that represent what they want the public to believe. During the presidential elections of 2000, Al Gore was criticized for being stiff and unemotional. Rather than dispute these claims, Al Gore simply grabbed his wife, Tipper, and gave her a passionate kiss in front of convention attendees and television viewers. That made people think of Al Gore less as being stiff and unemotional and more like a moral version of Bill Clinton because he actually wanted to have sex with his own wife.

During gun control debates, the White House released a picture of Barack Obama shooting a rifle. While this picture was meant to show that Obama supported gun rights, it came across as phony. Critics lampooned this image and hardened their negative perception of Obama as someone who wants to take away their rights to own a gun.

Besides quick images, politicians also have to manage sound bites. Mitt Romney hurt his own image among the poor when he commented that "There are 47 percent of the people who will vote for the president no matter what . . . who are dependent upon government, who believe that they are victims . . . These are people who pay no income tax . . . and so my job is not to worry about those people. I'll never convince them that they should take personal responsibility and care for their lives."

Missouri senatorial candidate Todd Akin wrecked his election chances by alienating women and pro-choice supporters when he stated, "If it's a legitimate rape, the female body has ways to try to shut that whole thing down." Such a comment about human reproduction made

Todd Akin look out of touch and ignorant, which no amount of arguing could ever change.

When President George W. Bush visited the wreckage of the World Trade Center following the 9/11 attacks, he gave a speech. When a rescue worker shouted, "I can't hear you!" thinking quickly, Bush responded, "I can hear you! I can hear you! The rest of the world hears you! And the people—and the people who knocked these buildings down will hear all of us soon!" Such a statement made Bush appear in control and committed to avenging terrorism, which greatly improved his public image (until he stumbled over his own words at another event).

Sarah Palin also improved her public image among her supporters when she described herself as a "mama grizzly," which was far more flattering than the words most people used to describe her intellectual capabilities.

With public perception dependent on photo ops and sound bites, the world of politics has sunk to the level of celebrity gossip tabloids where superficiality trumps substance. The next time you worry about the state of the economy or the threat of thermonuclear war, just remember that the people in positions of power are probably the least qualified to be there.

In 1973 dictator Augusto Pinochet took over Chile in a military coup. During his reign as leader of Chile, Pinochet reportedly killed 1,200–3,200 people, imprisoned 80,000 people, and tortured up to 30,000 of his own citizens, including women and children. When faced with declining support and the threat of a civil war, Pinochet offered an election so people could choose whether to let him stay in power for another eight years or whether he should step down.

For twenty-seven days leading up to the election, Pinochet only allowed the opposition fifteen minutes of free national airtime late every night to convince people that he should leave. Initially, Pinochet's critics wanted to use these fifteen minutes of airtime to highlight the thousands of people who "disappeared" during Pinochet's reign along with showing graphic photographs of dismembered bodies and tortured victims.

René Saavedra, an advertising executive, argued that telling people the truth would only instill fear in them and make them afraid to vote. Instead, René orchestrated a feel-good TV campaign, branded with a cheerful rainbow logo. Instead of showing pictures or videos of torture victims, René's fifteen-minute video featured happy people riding horses, running through pastures, and singing songs that closely mimicked a typical advertising campaign for anti-depression medication, shampoo, or luxury cars. It was like watching the Pied Piper.

By not focusing on the brutal truth, but painting a picture of a happier, cheerful future without Pinochet, René's campaign promoted the idea of democracy as a product. It worked. People actually voted Pinochet out of office, which may have been the first time an advertising campaign helped overthrow a dictator.

Political winners simply managed their public image better than their opponents. This important but limited skill makes them highly qualified to manipulate public perception, but highly unqualified to actually get anything done with any intelligence or foresight.

Fortunately, the rest of the world elects their political leaders with just as little logic and reason. That means the world will likely continue in much the same way as it has done for thousands of years, where pressing issues get ignored while trivial topics garner the public's attention.

Once you realize that politics is no different than show business (including the liberal use of illicit drugs and pursuit of sexual affairs), you'll realize that the fate of the world lies in the hands of people no smarter than reality TV stars like Snooki. When you realize this truth, you too may feel the urge to build an underground bunker and prepare for the end of the world. In many cases, the end of the world has already come, but we're just waiting for everyone else to catch up. Ok, thank you for indulging me. This was a wonderfully cathartic political binge and I feel much better now. Let us now return to the chief subject at hand: How you can do this too.

Let's Play!

"Kids don't even read comic books anymore. They've got more important things to do—like video games."—Ang Lee

In Hollywood, a blockbuster movie typically earns $100 million after several months in the theaters. On the other hand, a blockbuster video game, like *Call of Duty*, often earns $100 million in the first few days after its release. (Drug cartels often earn $100 million within the first few minutes of releasing a new shipment of cocaine to Hollywood celebrities, so that's the most profitable business of all.) Ignoring the profit potential of illegal activities, video games are now more profitable than the movie industry (not including pornography). So it's no surprise that video games have become a new force in reaching the general public in ways that, again, don't entail too much thinking or reading.

Video games started as bulky arcade machines that swallowed quarters like Hollywood swallows aspiring actors and actresses and spits them out as emotionally and psychologically broken shells. (I know, my flair for the dramatic. But I could have said "empty rotting carcasses that lie dismally by the side of the road," but I held myself back. Your welcome.) Back then, video games only had a limited influence on teenagers who used video games as a way to socialize with their friends without getting drunk and hanging out in bars like their parents would do.

Then video games migrated to the home as separate game consoles and on personal computers. Now video games could be played all the time, which meant that they wound up collecting dust when kids got bored with them three seconds later and found something better to do.

Much later on, video games shifted to smartphones and tablets, making them available anywhere you went, which meant that people often played video games in the middle of corporate meetings, while watching movies in a darkened theater, or during dates when the conversation suddenly turned awkward and uncomfortable. (What can I say? I for one pay homage to the heavens on a daily basis that I am alive during the smartphone era. Just imagine what it would be like to sit through tedium without Candy Crush at your fingertips. Oh, the horror!)

Since video games are more profitable than movies, Hollywood now looks to popular video game franchises that are making a ton of money so they can turn them into bad movies that lose a ton of money. How we continue to reap the fruits of real ambition.

Yet the appeal of video games continues to influence the film industry, social networks, and new age media. Video games have proven so popular because they keep us engaged through play and competition against ourselves and others who are inferior to us. In addition, playing video games often teaches us something other than the emotional joy of ramming a chainsaw in the middle of a zombie's forehead and watching blood gush out like a geyser.

Besides killing imaginary characters, video games can also teach physical dexterity skills, strategy and decision-making skills, and information about historical events (that involve killing real characters who usually don't speak English). Because video games can often teach players something new without any conscious effort on their part, they've proven popular with advertisers to reach lethargic people and convince them to buy a different brand of soap. Teaching through game playing has spawned an entirely new field known as "gamification."

The University of Washington found an unusual use for gamification when they created a protein folding game called FoldIt. The object of the game was to find the optimal way to fold a protein related to HIV, a problem that had gone unsolved for fifteen years. After forty-six thousand people played the game online, someone discovered the optimal solution in only ten days, which shows that scientists either aren't as smart as they think they are, or are lazier than they pretend to be. Whatever. This was very ingenious of them.

Since scientific breakthroughs rarely attract the attention of anyone, most people are more impressed when gamification affects trivial issues instead. When rapper Jay-Z launched his memoir *Decoded*, he had pages of his memoir printed on various surfaces, such as food wrappers and the silk lining of a Gucci jacket, which were hidden around the world. Each clue correlated with a specific detail from his memoir. In total, over three hundred pages in six hundred placements in fifteen locations worldwide were hidden as a challenge for players to find, assemble, and decode together online. The result created a groundswell of activity and buzz, landing *Decoded* on the best-seller list for nineteen weeks, despite having far less social significance than unlocking the mysteries of HIV.

To promote their Optima sedan, Korean carmaker Kia launched a gamified ad campaign, targeting adults between the ages of twenty-five and forty-nine. The results of the campaign showed:

+ Average "plays" per user: 1.27
+ Average time spent per user: 129 seconds
+ Click-through rates to the Kia Optima site: 19 percent

Kia also discovered that their gamification ads increased a consumers' likelihood of purchasing an Optima by eleven points, and also increased product awareness by seven points. Now if Kia didn't have a name that resembled the acronym K.I.A. (Killed In Action), they might actually have a chance at selling more cars in the United States, especially to military veterans.

As someone who craves fame, you need to appeal to the public by using the same techniques of video games, which include:

+ Attracting people because your message looks like fun

+ Holding the attention of people because they're having fun

+ Letting people compete so they'll be motivated to share your message with others

When people are having fun, they tend to be more receptive to learning new information (even if it's just an ad) and sharing your message with others. When people aren't having fun, they're usually at work, but that's beside the point. They don't engage with your message, and quickly move on to something else.

Gamification Through Polls

Gamification turns marketing and promotion into a game that actively engages the target audience. One of the more common examples of gamification appears on websites that offer polls or surveys asking questions such as "Would you rather fall in love with a vampire or a werewolf?" or "Which makes a worse husband: a vampire who can suck out your blood or an alcoholic who can throw up on you and make your life suck?"

Polls and surveys encourage people to vote and express their opinion. Even better, people enjoy seeing how others may have voted and if they don't like the results, they can vote over and over again. By getting people to interact through a poll, websites can attract people, get them to come back, and keep visitors amused so they (hopefully) tell others about the site.

ESPN Sports Nation hosts a number of daily polls on their website. Again, like Pavlov's dogs that learned to drool at the sound of a bell or mere sight of the person who feeds them, sports fanatics have also learned to visit the ESPN Sports Nation website to take a new poll every day, and they don't even need to hear a bell to do it.

While fans can vote on the ESPN Sports Nation website, they must tune into the ESPN Sports Nation TV show to see the results. This helps drive viewers to the TV show while letting fans interact with a website that doesn't host pornography.

Rottentomatoes.com has turned polls into its main attraction. On Rotten Tomatoes, fans can vote and rank any movie from the latest insipid blockbuster to an older movie that people once thought might be great until they realized it was just another insipid blockbuster. The new standard for movies is "what percent" approval rating it got on Rotten Tomatoes.

School children have long understood the appeal of polls. Kids often ask each other, "Who do you think is hotter, Jennifer or Katy?" or "Which girl do you think will get disillusioned with life first, become an alcoholic, turn to prostitution, and die from a drug overdose in a seedy motel room in the inner city, Jennifer or Katy?"

Polls can be a great way to attract people interested in giving their opinions. Many websites not only offer polls to engage visitors, but display the results of past polls so people can either cheer or gnash their teeth at the results. The more emotional you can make your website to visitors, the more they'll be entertained and likely buy something they don't need, thereby earning you some cash from their lack of self-control.

In-Game Advertising

In the past, advertisers had to compete with prying people away from video games long enough to look at commercials they didn't want to see. That's all changed with in-game advertising where real ads appear in the middle of the fake world of the video game.

For example, we see that many sporting events display real advertisements on racecars or on the walls of a stadium. In the past, video games used to display fake ads to create the illusion of a real stadium, but today, video games are selling fake ad space to real companies to generate cash from checks that might ultimately be fake. (Did you follow that bit of irony? I'm not sure I did, and I just wrote it. Read it again and if it still makes no sense please let me know.)

When running for reelection, President Barack Obama purchased ad space in video games including *Guitar Hero* and *Madden NFL*. Now as people played the game while connected to the Internet, the ads would pop up in the background, urging players to get out and vote for Obama, even if they were too young to vote, unable to vote, or simply sick of politics to the point where they felt that voting was a meaningless charade to create the illusion of democracy. (I never said I was done, even after my cathartic chapter.)

Because the ads would appear through the Internet, video game companies could even target voters in certain states. After the election, the game would stop displaying Obama's reelection ads and replace them with ads for other products that people probably didn't want to see either.

While companies can use advertisements in games to promote themselves, celebrities simply appear in video games as themselves. Guitar Hero, a game that glamorizes rock music (but not the drug-induced, orgy-filled lifestyle typically associated with guitarists), displays the actual musicians. As players hear and play their favorite songs, they see the animated versions of their favorite bands such as Aerosmith or Van Halen, or individual singers like Taylor Swift or Jimi Hendrix.

Mark Hamill, who played Luke Skywalker (in the only three *Star Wars* movies worth seeing) has appeared as a character in the video game *Wing Commander*. In other video games, Mark Hamill simply supplied the voice for a character, but the company used his celebrity status to market the video game anyway. Now people who want to hear the authentic Mark Hamill voice for a character that has no relationship to Mark Hamill can be assured of its true authenticity.

While Mike Tyson, Usain Bolt, and Michael Jackson have appeared as themselves in video games, other celebrities may only appear as part of a promotion. To promote the *Call of Duty: Modern Warfare* game, Activision released a live-action trailer featuring Sam Worthington, Jonah Hill, and Dwight Howard. Even though these actors didn't actually appear in the video game, their faces popped up in the promotional trailer, giving them additional exposure to the public while helping promote a game that glamorizes violence at the same time. So many benefits at once.

Until you're a big company (or a celebrity with a big ego and a wallet to match), paying for in-game advertising probably won't make sense to promote your fame. Likewise, appearing in a video game or supplying the voice for a cartoon character won't likely be an option until you're an over-the-hill celebrity like Mark Hamill.

However, you can use these techniques on a smaller scale. **Find what people are looking at and put your ad there.** Make your ad offer a poll or survey to get people engaged since they probably have too much time on their hands anyway. Through the magic of online advertising like Google AdSense, you can even buy online ads that only appear in front of people in a specific area or fit within a certain demographic.

To tap into the gamification trend, Coke introduced a big game ad campaign that's a variation on the Choose Your Own Adventure books kids used to read in lieu of picking up an actual book. In the ad, a man and a camel in the desert see a giant Coke bottle shimmering in the distance. As they start off towards the Coke bottle, a busload of show-girls, a group of cowboys, and a group of Mad Max characters overtake them. Then the giant Coke bottle turns out to be a sign that reads "50 miles ahead."

The question posed by the ad is "Who will get there first?" To choose, people have to visit the Coke website and vote. This drives visitors to Coke's site while getting them engaged and increasing the chance that they'll tell their friends about the campaign. The more people getting excited about Coke, the more likely they'll increase their chances of getting diabetes from drinking too much Coke.

Video Games as Political Tools

When John McCain ran for president, his website featured a video game called *Pork Invaders*. Rather than explain in boring detail how John McCain would balance the budget, the video game let visitors play a game so they could see how McCain's plan to balance the $900 trillion budget deficit would have worked by cutting hundreds of millions of dollars in spending (and, of course, providing kickbacks to his supporters at the same time.)

Al Gore often speaks on global warming and even helped create a documentary warning people about the threat of climate change. Of course, talking about something scientific like climate change typically evokes yawns from people who associate science with devil worshipping. To reach people who are often intimidated by words, numbers, and logic (again, most of our country), Al Gore plans to create an interactive video game so players can learn the effects and causes of climate change.

Trying to understand the weather is actually much easier than trying to understand international affairs. To help people understand the ramifications of dealing with Iran, the Truman National Security Project created a video game called *Tell Me How This Ends*. In the game, people take on the role of the president (minus the temptation to have an affair with an intern) so they can weigh the costs and risks of taking military action against Iran, which is yet another country that most American high school students could never find on a map.

To mock the entire American election process, Comedy Central released a mobile app called *Comedy Central's Indecision Game*. The game attempts to figure out who is really smarter, Democrats, Republicans, or Independents. Players attempt to outwit their friends and family by correctly answering political questions and earning votes to score an Election Day victory without having to rig the election to do it.

The military has also turned to video games, in this case to recruit volunteers. The US Army created *America's Army*, while the Army National Guard developed and published *Guard Force*. *America's Army* lets players go through basic training complete with barbed-wire obstacle courses and target practice, but without the obnoxious drill sergeant screaming in your face and waking you up after four hours of sleep.

Guard Force lets players rescue flood victims from rooftops and deploy helicopters and tanks to rescue skiers trapped in an avalanche. By playing *Guard Force*, players can learn what it's like to be in the National Guard (besides avoiding the Vietnam War and pretending to be patriotic in the process).

In the old days, organizations tried to use speeches, pamphlets, and rallies to sway people's opinions. Nowadays, it's easier, cheaper, and smarter just to create a video game that promotes a certain agenda and let people "play their way" to your point of view instead.

Game Shows Meet Reality TV

Game shows have always been popular with bored housewives and children pretending to be sick so they could stay home and watch TV instead of going to school. Reality TV, however, has adopted the game show format by pitting contestants against each other in vicious battles designed to traumatize contestants and hosts alike in bloodthirsty interpersonal conflicts that makes everyone feel there is no hope for the human race.

Survivor put contestants in near starvation conditions and forced them to brave the elements while competing in games that even primitive tribes don't understand. *The Voice* and *American Idol* challenge singers to compete. Of course, *The Voice* emphasizes actual singing talent, which means—again—that someone like Britney Spears would have gone down in flames

While you can get on a game show or even create your own, it's more likely that you can apply the game show format to attract publicity for yourself. Suppose you're a politician trying to create a positive impression among voters despite being a politician. Rather than running another series of negative ads telling the truth about your opponent, run a contest instead.

Invite voters to dig up the most embarrassing fact about your rival and offer a reward for the best revelation that totally derails your opponent's political campaign. Now you'll have incorporated gamification into your campaign and given people a reason to follow you as a candidate.

Sales people typically run contests to see who can make the most sales, regardless of the ethics involved in the product they're pushing. If you're part of a church or school, raise money by offering a game to challenge the lethargic public. Let people donate money and then vote for how their money should be spent so they can have the thrill of seeing if their favorite method wins or not. When you engage people to act in your behalf, they become invested and often continue to follow you.

Turning your publicity campaign into a game can grab the public's attention and keep them focused on you. When people have fun promoting you, you'll reap the rewards of the fame, and that can be more fun than playing any game by itself.

CHAPTER 5

Money, Money, Money:
How to Build and Run a Fame Business

"Don't confuse fame with success.
Madonna is one; Helen Keller is the other."—Erma Bombeck

The Business of Fame

Most people think that time is money, although having all the time in the world never seems to bring any money to homeless people sleeping in tents under freeway overpasses. Time isn't money. Fame is money, but only when exploited properly through the lens of a brand, a following, and multiple methods for extracting cash from the bank accounts of those followers.

Every celebrity must first gain fame on their own, which forms the core of their brand. Oprah Winfrey gained fame through her talk show and later expanded into magazines and her own television network. Venus and Serena Williams gained fame by playing tennis and later expanded into their own fashion line. John Wayne Bobbitt gained fame when his wife, Lorena, cut off his penis and later tried to extend his fifteen minutes of fame by appearing in porn films.

Celebrities expand into areas beyond what made them famous because fame can be fleeting. Professional athletes eventually get old and retire from their sport. Actors eventually get old and pushed aside for a newer generation of actors. Reality TV stars quickly realize they have no talent and no fame once their reality show gets cancelled. That's why reality TV stars need to find another way to make money or risk returning to normal life with the stigma of being that "loser who was once famous on TV for no reason."

Fame is a business. Failure to capitalize on your fame is no better than failure to cash in a winning lottery ticket. When harnessed properly, fame can change your life faster and better than any amount of education could ever do. When fame isn't harnessed correctly, fame can turn into a millstone around your neck.

Just ask child actor Gary Coleman, who achieved fame early in life and spent the rest of his life never achieving the same level of fame or fortune ever again. Struggling financially in his later years, Gary Coleman even declared bankruptcy and worked as a shopping mall security guard to make money. If you think your life sucks, just be glad you didn't experience your greatest achievements in life before you could reach puberty.

How Much Do Celebrities Earn?

Look at your current paycheck after you get a raise and you might be pleased at what you see. Now realize that many celebrities earn your entire paycheck in a few minutes of work, and that's how much more celebrities make than you do just for being famous. (Now don't get depressed like I just did writing that. We are here to try to put you on a path where you have a shot at changing this. Go down a shot of your favorite libation and let's move on.)

The size of your income has nothing to do with your talent; it has everything to do with what you do with your talent. Think quantity, not quality. Nobody would mistake McDonald's for serving gourmet food, yet McDonald's earns millions of dollars every day from their restaurants all over the world. A five-star restaurant in New York or Los Angeles might serve tastier meals, yet they only make a fraction of the money that McDonald's makes. The more you can touch others (without being accused of pedophilia like Michael Jackson), the greater your income.

That's why celebrities endorse products and start their own product lines. Each branch of the celebrity's brand acts like a minibusiness that generates income even while the celebrity is sleeping, overdosing, or committing felonies.

Every year, *Forbes* magazine releases their annual Forbes Celebrity 100 list of the highest-paid celebrities in the world so ordinary people like you and I can feel inferior about ourselves. To further diminish whatever feelings of the importance you thought you had, just realize that the top 100 celebrity earners were worth over $4.5 billion alone. If slavery were still legal, all of us would be working for Oprah Winfrey.

Forbes consistently ranks Oprah Winfrey as one of the top earners, making over $290 million in a year. Her total estimated net worth is $2.7 billion, which is enough money to buy Portugal, Spain, and Greece and turn them into parking lots for the rest of the European Union that actually have jobs. (I just poked fun of countries outside of the USA. Refreshing, right?)

Oprah earns the bulk of her fortune through television and radio, but she's also involved in film, magazines, books, and motivational speaking. By the time Oprah dies, experts believe her vast empire will equal the gross national product of China. Experts also probably believe that if Oprah continues gaining weight, she could one day have the gravitational pull of Rhode Island.

Another woman with a fortune that nearly equals Oprah's is everybody's favorite inventive housewife, Martha Stewart. With her reputation for turning everything from used dental floss to rusted tin cans into beautiful works of art that are suitable for chopping vegetables in the kitchen or brightening the walls of a penitentiary, Martha Stewart has an estimated net worth of $638 million, which she intends to spend on additional crafts supplies in an effort to create her own space shuttle capable of orbiting Venus.

Like Oprah, Martha Stewart also earns the bulk of her income through radio and television, but her conglomerate, Martha Stewart Living Omnimedia, has also branched out into television production, magazines, cookbooks, household cooking products, publishing, books, retail merchandising, an, of course, insider stock trading.

Rapper Jay-Z earned his vast fortune by making music that young people play at annoyingly high volumes from their car radios with their windows rolled down. Jay-Z's fortune, estimated at over $450 million, comes mainly from music. Like other celebrities, he too has branched out beyond his core competence into bars and nightclubs, books, a clothing line, real estate development, publishing, casinos, advertising, and even a stake in the Brooklyn Nets basketball team.

Probably the only business Jay-Z hasn't found any success in involves getting older white Americans, especially in the Midwest, to recognize him as a positive example of a black entrepreneur. You know who doesn't care? Jay-Z. He focuses on his core groups of younger followers with cash to burn. As he should.

Continuing the theme that women and minorities represent some of the richest people in America (while most women and minorities continue to believe that their opportunities are limited by white men) many professional athletes (often minorities) have found success in the business world after their sporting careers have ended.

Magic Johnson is estimated to be worth over $500 million. Most of his income comes from television and sports, but Magic Johnson also holds investments in movie theaters and studios, food services, and sports teams (with a minority stake in the LA Dodgers). He benefits from these investments while giving motivational speeches that usually center around the theme of "HIV & Aids Awareness."

Another athlete who struck it rich is Arnold Schwarzenegger, estimated to be worth between $100 and $800 million, depending on how many more housekeepers come forth with illegitimate children he fathered. After making a name for himself as a bodybuilder, Arnold branched out into acting (if you can call it that) along with the purchase of some minor holdings in real estate and restaurants like Planet Hollywood (which is one of the few restaurants where even movie stars feel they paid too much for a hamburger).

Lady Gaga reportedly earns over $90 million through her albums and concert tours, and recently launched her own fragrance. Now women all over the world can smell like a sweaty singer after she's been performing for two hours.

Golfer Tiger Woods earns over $85 million a year with a total net worth of $500 million, not counting the money he has to pay to his ex-wife for his fooling around with other women behind her back. Tiger Woods makes money through endorsements for Gillette razors, Gatorade sports drinks, and Nike shoes. (Strangely enough, Tiger Woods has yet to endorse the dating site AshleyMadison.com, which encourages married people to cheat on their spouses. I'm just saying.)

While most people can understand how talent could propel someone like Oprah Winfrey, Jay-Z, and Tiger Woods to a lucrative and well-deserved lifestyle, it's much harder to justify the outrageous salaries that reality TV stars make. Because reality TV stars are no different than anyone else, their lucrative payout often makes people question the existence of a higher being.

The entire cast of the reality show *Jersey Shore* reportedly earned $100,000 per episode for acting obnoxious, getting drunk, and demonstrating to the world that there's no correlation between being rich and being smart. Kim Kardashian even earns $40,000 an episode to appear on her reality show, *Keeping Up with the Kardashians*. This fact alone has convinced millions of people that either an absence of higher power and any true objective morality—or society's allegiance to demonic forces determined to watch us destroy ourselves for their own amusement-might be the only possible explanations for Kim Kardashian's success. (I'm personally going with option #3.)

Beyond the money celebrities get for singing, acting, or just being their normal, useless selves (reality TV stars), most celebrities rely on endorsements and other businesses ventures to insure that their income doesn't evaporate the moment their fame fades away. When you're famous, endorsements will come to you because everyone likes being associated with a winner (or at least someone more famous than they are).

While it's tempting to endorse any product just for the paycheck, celebrities (or their smarter business managers) choose endorsements and separate business ventures carefully. Every endorsement or business venture has to enhance and reinforce the celebrity's brand. That's why you'll never see Lady Gaga endorse a product associated with conformity or Donald Trump endorse a product associated with either humility or natural-looking hair pieces.

Besides being known for her music, Beyoncé is also well known for her House of Dereon clothing line, which matches her brand as a sexy performer. On the other hand, LeBron James has endorsement contracts with Nike, Sprite, Glacéau, Bubblicious, Upper Deck, McDonald's, and State Farm. Of course, if LeBron James is eating food from McDonald's, he's more likely to throw up his lunch than throw up the ball for two points.

Of course, not all celebrities are successful at running a business. Many celebrities have gone broke or filed for bankruptcy by dabbling in businesses they know nothing about. On the other hand, celebrities often do much better in areas that they do know something about, which means most celebrities would excel as drug dealers, bartenders, or pimps.

Because of their fame, celebrity-run businesses can often capture a significant amount of market share right before the celebrity fouls up the whole operation and flushes another million dollars down the drain. Given the choice between losing money in a business or losing money by snorting it up their nose as lines of cocaine, you can see why so many celebrities prefer the happier route of losing money through drug addiction instead.

Alternate Ways Celebrities Make Money

The top three ways celebrities make money (other than suing each other for alimony) are performing, endorsements, and outside business ventures. However, celebrities also make plenty of money in a multitude of other ways, some of which are entirely legal and ethical.

For years, singers, comedians, supermodels, and athletes had no problems endorsing products from cars and exercise equipment to food and drinks. However, actors often shied away from endorsements for fear it might overexpose them to the public or that their "artistic image" (If there was a way to do shouty capital quote marks I would use them here, but just imagine that I did) might be tarnished from being associated with salespeople. For that reason, actors typically only endorsed products overseas in Asian or European markets where their commercials would never be seen in America.

Now with nearly nonstop celebrity coverage through tabloids and celebrity gossip websites, the barriers between actors and the public is breaking down like Rush Limbaugh's arteries after he wolfs down a dozen chocolate doughnuts. For that reason, A-list actors are now venturing into product endorsements for the first time.

Actress Jennifer Aniston endorsed SmartWater through a series of supposedly "leaked" video ads that prove she uses SmartWater in her ordinary life (as opposed to her non-ordinary life dealing with Angelina Jolie at movie award ceremonies). Just as Jennifer Aniston has broken the barrier for actors endorsing products, so has her ex-husband, Brad Pitt, done the same by endorsing Chanel 5 fragrances.

Endorsements do have their limits. Besides making sure a product endorsement fits in with the celebrity's brand, celebrities are also banned by law to endorse drugs or nutritional supplements. The government believes that: "A celebrity appearing in drug advertising is more likely to mislead consumers," but it's perfectly okay for celebrities to mislead consumers when choosing perfumes, clothing, cars, or soft drinks. Fortunately, despite their deep knowledge of the facts and issues at hand, most celebrities don't endorse political candidates to avoid misleading the public into voting for the wrong person during an election. (My dripping sarcasm here is reaching acid levels. Whenever I see this I am tempted to reach for the jar of hemlock I keep on hand for such an occasion or stick my head in an oven. Whichever will be faster.)

Outside of endorsements, the second most popular way celebrities cash in on their fame is through appearances. Since people like being associated with celebrities, they're more than willing to pay them outrageous fees to do the most trivial task, such as show up.

Paris Hilton can make anywhere between $100,000 and $250,000 to show up at any event, although many people would pay even more than that for her to go away. Her path-to-fame student, reality TV star Kim Kardashian, generally earns $50,000 to show up at events such as nightclub openings. Though, during her thirtieth birthday week, she made $500,000 from a string of nightclub appearances. That's because promoters know that having a celebrity appear at an event can get individuals excited about showing up at that same location.

Even reality TV star Jon Gosselin of *Jon and Kate Plus 8* fame, once got paid $10,000 to appear at nightclubs and other events. Now that nobody cares who he is, people ask him to pay them for the indignity of being seen with a faded reality star like Jon Gosselin.

Sometimes promoters want celebrities to do more than just show up and stand around like a waste of a human life. In those cases, celebrities get paid for actually doing something useful. Business gurus Jack Welch and Richard Branson charge $100,000 to give a speech. Jay-Z was paid $1 million to perform at a Las Vegas New Year's Eve party while Beyoncé was paid $2 million to perform at a private St. Barth party on New Year's Eve.

Christina Aguilera was paid $1 million to appear at a private Halloween party for an hour while Justin Bieber was also paid $1 million for an hour-long performance at a private party. Rihanna once got paid $8 million to turn on Christmas lights in a shopping mall and perform a concert there afterwards. (I got paid $10 and got free doughnuts to speak at an "I'm too attached to my pet rock" support group. Not too shabby.)

Strangely, Rutgers University paid *Jersey Shore* reality TV star Snooki $32,000 to speak. That was $2,000 more than they paid Nobel Prize and Pulitzer Prize winning author Toni Morrison to speak, which shows you how seriously Rutgers University believes in higher education. Their students will likely graduate with crushing student loan debts that they'll never be able to pay off for the rest of their lives, but at least they can say they heard words of wisdom straight from the mouth of Snooki.

People will pay just to be around celebrities. In fact, more people spend money for celebrities to appear at their events than they spend to help end world hunger and poverty. (I'm not going to say it again. Ok I will: which goes to show you where the world's priorities really lie.)

The basic idea is that somebody with too much money on their hands (and not a strong enough addictive habit to soak up their excess cash) wants to impress people. For example, a rich, corporate executive might throw a Christmas party for employees and hire someone like Katy Perry or Justin Bieber to sing for an hour. Now that corporate executive will have bragging rights for the rest of the year on how they wasted shareholder money on entertainment instead of on research and development or marketing while the company slowly goes bankrupt and the corporate executive retires with a golden parachute as everyone else gets laid off.

In many cases, an ordinary housecat can perform the same functions as a celebrity at any event. (Sorry, I do not mean to insult housecats.) However, people often feel so in awe of being close to a celebrity that they're willing to pay big bucks just to see someone in real life who is on TV (and not on *America's Most Wanted*).

Charity events often hire celebrities to show up and make people so happy at being near a celebrity that they'll be willing to donate more money in the throes of giddiness. According to *USA Today*: "Having a star at a fundraising event will almost guarantee more money for a charity's coffers, sometimes boosting the take by fivefold or more."

Rather than appeal to people's sense of compassion and morality, it's apparently far more lucrative to appeal to people's sense of egotism and irrationality. If human beings really did evolve from apes, those apes must be scratching their heads and wondering how humans could possibly think they've evolved in any way, shape, or form beyond a single-celled amoeba.

The band, Creed, which had hit songs like "Take Me Higher" and "Arms Wide Open," hasn't had a big hit since the early 2000s. Yet they still charge $150,000 for an appearance, even if most of the people seeing this band will ask, "Who's Creed and how come the band's name rhymes with 'greed'?"

Just for sleeping with Britney Spears, Kevin Federline expects more than $300,000 per appearance. Typical questions that Kevin has to answer on a regular basis include "What's it like to have sex with Britney Spears?" and "How much can we pay Kevin Federline to go away forever?"

The boy band New Kids on the Block sold millions of records in the 1980s and 1990s. After virtually disappearing from the music scene, the band still charges $500,000 per appearance, which is enough money to feed the entire nation of Malawi for twenty years. (Don't know what or where Malawi is? Google it. And GET OFF OF FACEBOOK FOR TWO SECONDS AND PICK UP A NEWSPAPER!!)

Singers and bands typically earn more than actors and reality TV stars because they can actually perform and do something besides stand around like human mannequins. Plus musicians often need more money to support their multiple addictive drug habits from the days when they were famous. So there you have it.

Appearance fees might be outlandish, but they also have a drawback. The celebrity actually has to show up somewhere on time and sober. For many celebrities, meeting these criteria can be challenging.

As an alternative, celebrities also branch out into endorsements and licensing. Endorsements involve a celebrity promoting a brand, whereas licensing involves creating a "celebrity's version" of a brand. Many professional athletes, who most people never hear about, sign endorsements to wear Nike, Reebok, or Adidas shoes. Now if they get knocked unconscious and sprawl facedown on the ground as the cameras zoom in, sponsors want everyone to see which shoes they were wearing when they got a concussion.

However, big-name players like LeBron James, Kobe Bryant, and Tiger Woods don't just endorse a product; they sign licensing deals worth hundreds of millions of dollars to put their name on Nike, Reebok, or Adidas shoes. Now if Tiger Woods gets knocked unconscious by one of his angry mistresses, the camera will show that they weren't just wearing ordinary Nike or Adidas shoes, but that they were wearing Kobe Bryant Adidas or Tiger Woods Nikes.

Endorsements typically use a celebrity to highlight an existing product. That's why Serena Williams endorses Gatorade rather than coming out with her own Serena Williams energy drink for black women who like smashing tennis balls at people's heads.

Licensing deals typically occur with high-profile celebrities to create new products. For example, Donald Trump sells Donald Trump steaks and Donald Trump ties (for hanging yourself with after you realize you just gave more money to a billionaire who doesn't need any of it).

Licensing isn't about Lindsay Lohan getting caught driving drunk without a driver's license (a rare occurrence that happens only during weeks with seven days in them, somewhere on Planet Earth). Instead, licensing is about slapping a celebrity's name or face on an item and making money through the sale of that merchandise. Sports teams license their team logo for T-shirts and caps while singers (and people who lip sync while pretending to sing like Britney Spears) license their face and name to sell merchandise at concerts.

The advantage of licensing is that celebrities get a cut of the profits, often 30 percent, while doing nothing but agree not to sue the retailer. The retailer takes all the risk and expense of manufacturing and distributing products. By slapping a celebrity's face or name on the product, the retailer hopes to sell more products than without that celebrity's name or image. After all, how many people would buy a plain, white T-shirt at a concert instead of a T-shirt describing the 2014 concert tour of The Rolling Stones?

Singer Katy Perry sells her own perfume and nail polish so you can look like someone who John Mayer might want to nail one day. Instead of creating her own licensed perfumes, actress Natalie Portman simply endorses an existing product, Miss Dior. While Katy Perry has a distinctive personality as a singer, Natalie Portman has a less distinctive personality as the other girl from *Black Swan*, as well as a preachy vegan. (Vegans are ok in my book, just not the preachy ones. If I want to snack on my meat dress, don't yell at me.)

Both endorsements and licensing are meant to sell products through the positive association people have with celebrities (which isn't always justified, if they only knew the truth). Celebrities help give products higher exposure.

Since there are so many different types of perfumes on the market (and most of them basically consist of nothing more than water and whale vomit) fragrance companies often need a celebrity's face to make their brand of color-treated mystery fluid stand out. Given a choice between perfume that has a fancy name on it or a perfume that has a fancy name on it along with a celebrity's name and face on it, most people will gravitate towards the celebrity-endorsed perfume every time, even if it costs more and smells worse. This shows us that spending power and common sense have nothing to do with each other.

A second reason to pay celebrities obscene amounts of cash to do nothing more than stand next to a product is to enhance a brand's value. Gatorade already has an image of boosting performance during physical activity, such as playing baseball or banging a hooker. Now show a bottle of Gatorade next to Michael Jordan and people will fantasize that Michael Jordan owes his basketball playing skills to drinking Gatorade. That almost everyone you know buys into this incredible leap of logic helps us better understand why SAT test scores have been steadily declining among high school students over the past decade.

The best endorsements and licensing involves combining a celebrity's actual talent (if they have any) with a related product. Rapper Dr. Dre is already known for his music, so he parlayed his musical credibility by creating his own licensed audio products called Beats by Dr. Dre. People assume Dr. Dre must understand audio equipment so they trust that he won't sell them a piece of junk just to make quick cash off gullible fans. (You know thing they say about assume. It makes something I can't quite remember out of "u" and "me." Oh well, maybe it will come to me.)

Even if a product is a piece of junk, a celebrity's name on the label can often magically make people feel that the product's shortcomings must be due to their own failings as a human being rather than a fault with the product or the celebrity itself. And by reducing the chance of returns, companies can increase their profit margin just as much as by selling more products.

Perhaps one of the oddest ways celebrities are cashing in on their fame combines endorsements with appearances to give celebrities titles at major corporations. After losing their lead in the smartphone market, BlackBerry launched a new version of their phones and announced they had made Alicia Keys their creative director. After cashing in BlackBerry's check for making her creative director, Alicia Keys' first task was to use that money to buy herself a better phone than a BlackBerry.

Giving a celebrity an empty title is often a strategy that desperate companies use to draw more attention to themselves, short of lighting their CEO and all their board of directors on fire. Polaroid hired Lady Gaga as their creative director to be the "new face" of the company, because every company wants to be associated with a face that wears hats that look like lobsters. Singer will.i.am took a similar position as creative director at Intel, because singing and microprocessor chip design are so closely related.

Land Rover even hired former Spice Girl Victoria Beckham to be their creative director. Most likely the people who were young enough to remember the Spice Girls have forgotten everything they hated about them. Like the very elderly with dementia who reminisce about the joys of fighting in World War II, such people will likely retain the positive memories of the Spice Girls that they can then transfer to the Land Rover brand.

Becoming creative director of a major corporation can be a windfall, but not every celebrity can be lucky enough to have a flailing company hire them as creative director. To take matters into their own hands, many celebrities have taken endorsements directly to the consumer.

Most celebrity endorsements involve the celebrity posing with a product, cashing a check, and walking away. Since products can still fail despite celebrity endorsements, many celebrities are not only endorsing products, but actively selling them too through the Home Shopping Network or QVC.

Suzanne Somers, who gained fame by acting like a dumb blonde on the popular 1970s sitcom *Three's Company*, has turned celebrity endorsing and selling into an art form. In the 1980s, Suzanne became one of the first celebrities to appear on an infomercial when she promoted the ThighMaster. Thanks to Suzanne's endorsement and her constant presence on TV hawking the product, many people bought the ThighMaster in hopes that Suzanne Somers would go away.

After successfully promoting the ThighMaster, Suzanne Somers promoted other fitness equipment that most people will never use like the FaceMaster and the Torso Track. Suzanne soon branched out into clothing and jewelry lines along with various skin and hair care products. By buying Suzanne's products, women all over America can pretend to be a washed-up actress, too.

George Foreman, the two-time former World Heavyweight Boxing Champion and Olympic gold medalist, marketed his George Foreman lean-mean-grilling-machine to the tune of $375 million worldwide sales. Now people associate George Foreman with eating hamburgers instead of getting punched in the head by Muhammad Ali.

Martial artist Billy Blanks used his fighting skills to create a new form of exercise called Tae Bo, which sounds a whole lot better than calling it "another way to fleece the public." After opening a fitness studio in Los Angeles, Billy Blanks started attracting celebrity followers like Paula Abdul and Carmen Electra. When Blanks joined the infomercial circuit selling Tae Bo DVDs through DRTV, Tae Bo became a pop culture phenomenon that still makes people question "why?" to this day.

An even more direct, but less publicized way, celebrities sell directly to the consumer involves sex tapes. Supposedly filmed and "leaked" to the public (while the affected celebrity mounts a massive publicity campaign to recover the sex tape to keep it from being exposed to the public) the sex tape industry is actually orchestrated by the celebrities themselves.

First, celebrities film themselves having sex. Next, they hire someone to "leak" the sex tape. While they publicly claim to sue the person who supposedly leaked the sex tape, they're secretly giving written permission to an adult film distributor to sell the sex tape to the public while they collect royalties. Sex tapes not only earn celebrities extra money, but they're also good for a giant leap in publicity at the same time.

We covered the Paris Hilton and Kim Kardashian sex tapes earlier in the book, but a slew of other Hollywood celebrities jumped on the bandwagon. In an attempt to jump-start her career, Montana Fishburne, the daughter of actor Lawrence Fishburne, filmed her own sex tape. To boost his sagging career, actor Dustin Diamond, who appeared on the show *Saved by the Bell*, released his own sex tape. With so many celebrities releasing sex tapes, probably the only people not having sex in Hollywood these days are the people married to these celebrities.

After her fame from reality TV created financial hardship, Octomom Nadya Suleman filmed a porn video of herself masturbating. Using the profits from this porn film, she purchased a five-bedroom, three-bath, three-car garage home with a fourteen thousand square foot backyard with a gated pool, spa, slide, and gazebo. If you thought life wasn't fair when supermodels got rich winning the genetic lottery, then you'll likely weep and gnash your teeth upon hearing how Octomom earned so much money for doing so little.

The Fame Business for You

Fame can mean international recognition like Madonna or George Clooney have, or it can just mean local recognition in your hometown, school, or office. Whatever measure of fame you have, you can always find a way to capitalize on your notoriety while shamelessly promoting yourself even further.

First, start with a positive attribute about yourself. Once you know your main attribute or brand, look for ways to expand your brand into other areas. Suppose you love food like Paula Deen. After she divorced her husband, Paula had $200 and two kids to raise. Since she suffered from panic attacks, she wanted a job where she wouldn't have to leave the house. By combining her love of cooking with staying at home, she started her own catering service making sandwiches.

She quickly outgrew her catering business and started a restaurant that offered a cuisine high in fat, sugar, and salt, just like what you might get at McDonald's, only tastier. Then she self-published two cookbooks, which further expanded her reach to the public. Word of her restaurant spread to The Food Network, which showcased her restaurant on several shows. The Food Network later invited her to create her own show. And that's how Paula Deen grew her love of cooking from a hobby to a multi-faceted mini-empire.

You may not get your own TV show (although you can create your own TV show on YouTube), but you can expand your reach to others by focusing on your core competency (if you have one). Kate Gosselin's only core competency was giving birth to eight children, yet she managed to parlay this one accomplishment in her life into a reality TV show. To further expand her presence into the lives of those who wish to ignore her, she wrote several nonfiction books that became *New York Times* best sellers, which tells you (Can you guess where am I going with this? Just making sure you are paying attention—my train of thought should be fairly predictable by now. Anyway, say it with me: *just how low The New York Times has sunk.* (It's like a Greek chorus.)

The point is that Kate Gosselin, who has as little actual talent as her ex-husband, wrote books as a way to extend her presence because there was precious little else she could do without being exposed as the meaningless woman that she is. She tried appearing on other reality TV shows to boost her popularity, but that was like promoting spinach on Saturday morning cartoons to make it more appealing to children. It didn't work.

In your own world, there are multiple ways to extend your fame throughout your life:

+ Apply your brand in other similar activities. Suppose you're known as the "tech gadget guy" at work. Now if you get a second job as a night cashier in a gas station, you can be known as the "gas station tech gadget guy who gets robbed every weekend for gas money and his tech gadgets."

+ Branch out into alternative activities. If you're the guy that everyone goes to when they have a technical question, publish your own book like Kate Gosselin did to branch out. Just don't rely on your current way of earning money by itself because that could disappear as quickly as Danica Patrick losing another lead in a NASCAR race.

Fame by itself can be nice, but it's a lot better when coupled with boatloads of cash thrown in your direction just because you happen to exist. No matter how much or how little fame you have, you can grow it, extend it, and apply it outside your field of expertise.

Fame is fleeting, so take advantage of your fame in any way you can that doesn't break any legal or ethical codes, unless that's the kind of fame you want to pursue. When you become famous, you can either bask in the glory of recognition from others as a way to boost your self-esteem, or you can bask in the glory of recognition while earning thousands or even millions of dollars for the exact same activity.

Fame is a business. Just like a business, you have to nurture it, improve it, and constantly maintain it. The moment you stop, fame dissipates as quickly as the restraint that Tiger Woods demonstrates around women who aren't his wife. **Fame isn't money, but potential money.** It's up to you to turn whatever fame you have into cold, hard cash.

Monetizing Your Fame

"Money, if it does not bring you happiness, will at least help you be miserable in comfort."—Helen Burley Brown

Fame is power, but fame is pointless if you can't turn it into cold, hard cash or at least turn it into the power to waterboard someone you don't like with impunity. Nobody wants to become famous just for the sake of having total strangers annoy them in public when they ask for an autograph and talk to them as if they've known them all their lives. The whole point of becoming famous is so you can have greater opportunities to enjoy life, and that typically means having more money.

The biggest mistake people make with fame is thinking that it will last forever. The second biggest mistake people make is failing to monetize their fame as soon as possible before their fame falls apart faster than Lindsay Lohan has run-ins with the law.

The most common way to make money off fame is to do more of whatever made you famous in the first place. If you're a musician who suddenly has a hit single or album, that's the time to start touring and taking money from your fans' wallets by selling them concert tickets and memorabilia.

If you're an actor who suddenly appears in a hit movie, start getting yourself in other movie projects as soon as possible before people forget about you and a new star takes your place and kicks you to the curb like yesterday's garbage. If you're a reality TV star who suddenly appears in a hit reality TV show by acting like a human train wreck, keep acting like a human train wreck because that's probably the only talent you have, so you might as well milk it for all it's worth.

Whatever makes you famous is your main money-making activity, but don't rely on this forever, or even for the next five minutes. That's because you have no idea how long your main money-making activity will last. Many reality TV stars go bankrupt the moment their reality TV show gets cancelled (and everyone cheers as they come back down to Earth and actually have to work in a real job for a change).

Many singers or bands release a string of album flops that essentially ends their popularity and forces them to sing their handful of hits over and over again for the rest of their lives as though trapped in the seventh circle of hell. Many actors appear in a string of movie bombs and suddenly find that the only way they can stay on TV is to sell a household appliance on the Home Shopping Network or get roaring drunk and crash their car into a tree.

Fame is fickle. One second it's with you and the next second it's flirting with someone newer, younger, and prettier than you. Every second, you're getting one step closer to being a washed-up has-been with no future, so you better take advantage of your moment in the spotlight now while you have the chance.

Making an Appearance If You're Not a Celebrity (Yet)

If musicians and reality TV stars from the ancient past can still convert their long-forgotten fame into five- and six-figure incomes, there's nothing stopping you from getting a dollop of fame and turning it into lucrative appearance fees for the rest of your life. The only difference is that until you can appear on TV, your appearance fees will be far less, despite having far more to offer. That's just the nature of the Fame Game—repeat our mantra with me one more time, boys and girls: the people with talent get paid the least and the people with the fame get paid the most.

For ordinary people, the best way to duplicate appearance fees is to give speeches. Every industry has conferences and seminars, and they always need speakers to entertain, inform, or amuse guests before the guests rebel and steal all the furniture from the hotel where the seminar is taking place.

Public speaking requires having actual talent, but as you gain a reputation for either speaking or entertaining in some way (performing magic tricks or singing, for instance), you can use your public speaking engagements to gradually build up your fame and promote yourself to others who should be paying you a lot more for showing up.

Endorsements for the Celebrity-in-Waiting

Until you're a recognized celebrity, you probably can't parlay your miniscule level of fame into national and international endorsements or licensing. However, as a humble human being who has yet to be tainted by the Hollywood marketing and celebrity creation machine, you can always start locally. As the Chinese say, "The longest journey begins with a single step," which explains why China is still trying to catch up to the West after their disastrous flirtation with communism.

Watch your local TV news or listen to your local radio stations and you'll often see or hear local celebrities in your town advertising products. An ex-mayor (whose scandals haven't yet been exposed) might endorse a law firm or a car dealer. A popular local news anchor might appear in a commercial promoting reading at the public library or adopting a pet at a local animal shelter. The principle is the same: slap a celebrity's face on a product or organization and use his or her popularity to make something else popular by association.

As a local celebrity or even a nobody, you could even create your own products as a form of licensing. A popular barbecue restaurant might market their own line of barbecue sauces under the owner's name such as "Wild Bob's Barbecue Sauce: So good it can make human flesh taste edible!" (Yuck. I just made myself a little sick there.)

As someone with little or no local fame, you can promote yourself by linking your face to higher profile organizations. Want to promote yourself as caring and concerned? Get your name and face associated with charities that help orphans or homeless single mothers (just as long as you aren't known for creating single mothers in your spare time.)

While companies use celebrities to boost their own profile, you can do the reverse by associating the higher profile of an organization with your face. If you want to be known as the best real estate agent in town, get your face associated with an organization that works with developing affordable housing. For ordinary people, **linking your name to a higher profile organization is one sure way to boost your own fame** in the eyes of a confused and inattentive public that still believes reality TV shows are based on truth.

Problems with Endorsements and Licenses

Endorsements and licenses are like marriages; they don't always work. Unlike marriages, at least nobody has to worry about taking care of children afterwards, unless you count the emotional level of most celebrities as being that of a child. When a celebrity associates his or her face with a product, the linked association works both ways.

One celebrity who screwed up a perfectly good endorsement deal was Lance Armstrong. Nike had been perfectly happy with Lance Armstrong's endorsement, right up until he admitted he doped his way to his seven Tour de France victories. One moment, Lance Armstrong's name created the positive association of a fierce competitor, the next moment, Lance Armstrong's name created an association of lying and cheating. Nike wasn't interested in being associated with the latter (which is why they never asked for an endorsement from Bill Clinton).

Hertz Rental Car had an even bigger problem when they paid O. J. Simpson to endorse their company. Unfortunately, O. J. Simpson then got accused of murdering his ex-wife and her friend, and Hertz smartly decided that associating themselves with an accused killer wasn't good publicity any more, especially with a corporate name that already sounds like an expression of pain.

Weight Watchers promotes themselves as a weight loss program, so they were initially thrilled when actress Kirstie Alley became their spokesperson when she lost seventy-five pounds. Later, when Kirstie gained back those seventy-five pounds and ballooned in size like a python trying to swallow Rush Limbaugh whole, suddenly her body no longer looked right endorsing Weight Watchers, and Weight Watchers had little choice but to refuse to renew her contract.

Besides meltdowns, drug busts, temper tantrums, and other problems normally associated with celebrities or spoiled babies growing up in Beverly Hills, endorsement and licensing deals involve more than just signing a contract and writing a check. It's important to match the right celebrity with the right product.

At one time, the band KISS sold a KISS Kasket, a coffin adorned with the KISS logo and pictures. While associating death with rock musicians makes sense, given how many of them find their way to an early grave, it does represent a strange product for any celebrity to endorse and expect to get their fans excited to buy it.

Actor Sylvester Stallone, better known for the *Rocky* and *Rambo* movie franchises, once sold pudding packed with protein. Although Sylvester Stallone's image as an action figure makes sense for promoting health and muscle products, protein puddings seem like an odd combination, like watching a Chihuahua try to mate with a Rottweiler.

Sylvester Stallone, *Rocky Balboa* Premiere, Hollywood, CA, 2007
(Insidefoto/PR Photos)

Following a similar twist of questionable choices, Hip-hop artist Nelly sold energy drinks under the name Pimp Juice after his hit song of the same name. People immediately protested that the drink (and song) glorified prostitution, but the energy drink can still be found in Australia. Apparently Australians don't find the idea of drinking Pimp Juice (or prostitution for that matter) objectionable . Then again, Australia probably doesn't have too many black pimps who might get offended either.

Rocker Ozzie Osbourne, famous for biting the head off a bat during a concert, once promoted the butter substitute "I Can't Believe It's Not Butter!" If Ozzie Osbourne had held a decapitated bat in one hand while cradling a container of "I Can't Believe It's Not Butter!" in the other, it might have made sense in a twisted sort of way. Why any ad agency thought that a heavy metal rocker would be a perfect spokesman for a healthy alternative to butter remains one of those eternal mysteries like Stonehenge that will never be solved.

Not every celebrity can endorse or license every type of product. Seeing Sylvester Stallone endorsing a muscle-building product makes sense. Seeing Sylvester Stallone endorsing lip gloss and makeup does not, unless you're going for funny or targeting hardcore lesbians.

Perhaps the biggest potential problem with any endorsement or licensing deal comes down to the all-important question of money. Who gets what, how much do they get, and what do they have to do to get it?

Usually the answer that everyone gives is "I get a cut, I want it all, and I don't want to do anything to get it." When everyone starts from this position, the lawyers jump in, take as much as they can for themselves, and eventually negotiate an agreement.

The simplest arrangement pays the celebrity a flat fee for the celebrity to endorse the product for a fixed amount of time. The company wants to pay as little as possible and keep the celebrity tied to them for as long as possible. The celebrity wants to get paid as much as possible while staying tied to the product as little as possible. They all hopefully meet somewhere in between.

The problem with a flat-fee arrangement is that once the celebrity gets paid, he or she has little interest in continuing to promote the product or company. To give celebrities an incentive, companies often offer a royalty arrangement such as 8 to 30 percent in addition to an upfront payment. Once a celebrity sees a way to earn more money, he or she will likely promote the product or company more vigorously and remain on their best behavior.

Although a high royalty rate can be enticing, it's not the only criterion by which to judge an endorsement or licensing deal. After all, a 20 percent royalty rate on nothing is still nothing, which I have no doubt is a math problem that well over half of all high school students can't solve. What's more important than a royalty rate in any deal is the product distribution and marketing plan.

Distribution means: how will the product be delivered to gullible consumers? Will big-box retailers like Wal-Mart sell it after they drive all the local mom and pop shops out of business? A large distribution network increases the chance of selling more units than just selling a product by mail order.

Of course, distribution means little if nobody knows that the product even exists. Every product needs a marketing plan to alert consumers that there's a new product that they need to buy right away because their favorite celebrity is getting paid to stand next to it, so therefore it must be exactly what they need. Makes perfect sense.

Despite not being a household name in the United States, Filipino and global boxing icon Manny Pacquiao earned enough to rank sixteenth in *Forbes'* list of the twenty highest-paid celebrities, with $67 million in earnings (which isn't a bad payday for letting someone else try to punch you in the face. I would take it, happily. No shortage of plastic surgeons here in LA to fix my face afterwards.)

Manny Pacquiao's global endorsements include Nike, Technomarine, Hewlett-Packard, and Hennessy, placing him ahead of earnings by TV psychiatrist Dr. Phil McGraw ($64 million), business mogul Donald Trump ($63 million), pointless TV host Ryan Seacrest ($59 million), manufactured singer Britney Spears, and philanderer Tiger Woods (both with $58 million).

Even reality TV stars, such as Snooki, JWoww, and the Situation from *Jersey Shore* have come out with their own line of tanning lotions and sprays due to their famous tans. Mike "The Situation" Sorrentino has even gone one step further and licensed a deal with Wizard World comics to produce a comic book about his life.

With so many celebrities endorsing or licensing products, pretty soon everyone can express their individuality by wearing the same clothes, eating the same food, and using the same products as everyone else. Although most products involve beauty, fashion, beverages, and home goods, many celebrities are now branching out into technology and gadgets. Snooki even has an iPhone and Android app. Just take a picture of yourself and you can make yourself look like you're wearing sunglasses and animal print clothing, just like Snooki would. How very exciting for all of us—I just can't handle the thrill.

The more famous you get, the more money you can make just for the mere act of existing. While millions of people toil away in manual labor that actually produces something tangible for society, celebrities promote products that are no different from any others except for the celebrity's endorsement or licensed name slapped across the front of it.

For many people, choosing to buy a product because a celebrity tells them to is all the convincing that they ever need. In the near future, expect for celebrities to start endorsing national leaders including dictators and other oppressive governments. As long as a celebrity endorses a brutal regime, that endorsement will likely go a long way to keeping people happy. If a celebrity says it's okay, then who are we to think otherwise?

Product Development

"If advertisers spent the same amount of money on improving their products as they do on advertising, then they wouldn't have to advertise them."—Will Rogers

As a famous person, you are a product, but it's hard to monetize your physical body as a product unless you're a prostitute. Even then, prostitutes can only service one customer at a time, which means you can't make any real money unless you raise your prices and service only rich clients like corporate executives and politicians. But again, that's for another time and book.

When creating any product, you have to follow certain rules to maximize success. First, **you should be extremely passionate about that particular product.** If you don't care about a product, you'll have a hard time selling it to others. Think how successful Megan Fox would be trying to sell acting lessons. She obviously doesn't care about acting, so any attempt to sell them to others would come across as phony and unrealistic as her performances in the few movies she's made that haven't bombed at the box office.

Besides enthusiasm for a product, a second criteria involves making sure that your **fanbase significantly overlaps the product's target market.** Nicole Richie's fanbase will likely care about fashion, makeup, clothes, whining, and weight-loss programs that don't involve anorexia. Even if Nicole Richie suddenly developed a passionate interest in studying quantum physics, it's still unlikely that any of her fans would care about a quantum physics product. Thus such a product would likely have the same success as her short-lived acting career.

Third, any product needs to fit within the brand of that celebrity. Just as a quantum physics product wouldn't be appropriate for Nicole Richie's brand as an airhead, so would lipstick and perfume be difficult to sell for Jean-Claude Van Damme, unless the perfume smelled like sweat, gunpowder, and shell casings,

More importantly, **any product needs to appear consistent with any existing products that the celebrity may be hawking.** Notice that when Jennifer Lopez endorses a skincare product, the colors and graphics emphasize her face and body. Now if Jennifer Lopez were to endorse a hair care product, the ads would appear visually jarring if they displayed Jennifer Lopez as a cartoon character or crawling around in the mud while wearing a camouflage military uniform and cradling an AK-47 under her armpit.

Since celebrity products are all about money, it's important that **both the celebrity and the company making the product have a financial stake in the deal.** That way both will be motivated to make as much as possible so everyone (except the public) comes out ahead. Some terms of celebrity deals include:

+ Territory

+ Length of the deal

+ Minimal guarantee

+ Promotional plan that celebrity is supposed to execute (number of appearances, ad campaigns, interviews, etc.)

Territory refers to the country or region that the product manufacturer and celebrity will target for their advertising barrage, which is often followed by an actual landing by the celebrity him- or herself, storming the targeted area like a commando to make as many sales as possible before fleeing the scene.

The length of the deal refers to how long the celebrity and the product manufacturer will remain trapped together as though married. The product manufacturer often wants to keep the celebrity tied to their product for as long as possible while the celebrity often just wants to make a quick buck and get on with whatever it is they do when they are not pimping themselves out to the highest bidder in corporate America. Whatever that is.

A minimal guarantee often means a cash advance for the celebrity to guarantee that even if the product bombs as badly as everyone fears, the celebrity still makes a certain amount of money. This is also why celebrities want short time periods in the deal because if a product bombs, no one wants to be linked to a failure for any longer than necessary.

To market a product, the celebrities must use their unholy influence over the masses to push the product as much as possible. The product manufacturer wants a fixed number of TV and radio interviews along with personal appearances, such as having the celebrity appear at press conferences to pretend that he or she actually uses the product and that it's the secret to the celebrity's looks (instead of genetics, surgery and makeup from a competing manufacturer).

Obviously, celebrities want to do as little as possible while product manufacturers need them to keep promoting the product a guaranteed number of times in a guaranteed number of ways. As long as the celebrity does the minimum required by the contract, everyone should profit and be happy, except for the public who buys and uses the product only to find that they don't look like a celebrity after all. But they will buy the very next item that the next celebrity endorses. It's positively mystifying, but that is precisely what makes the Fame Game the beautiful money-making machine that it is.

Merchandising Products

As someone who's actually normal and doesn't get your face splashed across the tabloids every other week, you're probably not going to have a

cosmetics company or a beverage company ask you to create an international product line. However, you can still jump on the merchandising
gravy train to separate more money from the pockets of your fans by
selling your own line of merchandise yourself.

Such products are commonly referred to as "white labeling," not
for any possible racist overtones, but because the products are generic
enough to be useful, but still able to be customized with your logo,
face, or any other item that you think people will buy out of impulse.
For example, many white label products include coffee mugs, T-shirts,
mouse pads, pens, posters, carrying bags, and water bottles.

Such white label products offer three advantages. First, the products themselves are easily manufactured and popular among all types of
consumers (except for the really cheap ones). Second, the products can
be easily customized just by throwing a picture on the front of the item.
Third, the product can be manufactured or printed on demand.

That means you never keep an inventory of merchandise. Instead,
people order a product from your website, your website pays a print-
on-demand manufacturer to create, customize, and ship that product,
and you and the print-on-demand manufacturer each take a cut of
the profits while the customer gets a customized product. Doesn't that
sound nice?

The major advantages of print-on-demand products include:

+ No inventory cost—you don't need to make anything until someone
  orders a product

+ No production and development cost—everything is already made
  and ready to be customized

+ Just like companies do when they give away stuff to their customers, you turn your fanbase into walking billboards advertising you
  and your brand so your fans are essentially paying you to promote
  your brand

+ Immediate receipt of cash—typical licensing deals can take from
  three months to a year before you receive any money from the deal

+ Creative control over product design and messages—you're in
  control 100 percent of the product design, but that also means you
  have to do 100 percent of the work too, or at least farm it out to
  Third World countries that can do the work for you cheaper

✦ Ability to monetize social media following and web-traffic with much higher profit margins than advertising

To get people to buy customized generic products, you need a catchy logo or graphic of some kind that you can trademark or copyright. What people are buying isn't the product itself (who really needs another coffee mug or mouse pad?), but the positive association that person has with your brand.

Your product logo simply needs to be fun, memorable and something that people can show off to others.

Common Product Categories

Since women tend to spend the most money buying stuff (except for prostitutes and porno videos), it's no surprise that the best-selling product categories cater to women, or at least men who would like to be women. So it's no surprise that the most popular product categories involve fashion and lifestyle items such as apparel, accessories, and jewelry.

Even though Jessica Simpson first became famous for singing, her fashion line topped $1 billion in sales, which is probably $999 million more than her album sales ever generated for her. In addition to shoes, apparel, accessories, and fragrances, her line also includes diamond jewelry. Simpson's niche focuses on a simple yet fashionable look that allows women to feel like they'll never have a hit single for the rest of their lives, just like Jessica Simpson. Just sharing the dream I guess.

Nicole Richie is another celebrity who has built a successful fashion empire off the backs of impressionable young women. Richie has jewelry line called House of Harlow 1960 (named after her three-year-old daughter Harlow), which also includes sunglasses and shoes. That way if somebody robs you for your jewelry, the robbers will be tempted to take your eyewear and footwear along with it.

Besides fashion products, the second most popular product category involves beauty products such as skin care, makeup, and fragrances. After divorcing Tom Cruise, actress Katie Holmes has become co-owner and creative director of Alterna Haircare, which includes products spiked with caviar so that more of your body can smell like criminally expensive fish.

Another actress who doesn't want her income to depend on the whims of movies is Drew Barrymore. Her Flower Cosmetics line includes lipsticks, glosses, eye shadows, mascaras, and nail polishes. Best of all, these products are reasonably priced so struggling actresses can look good at a low cost when they have sex on the casting couch to get their first big role in the movies.

Kat Von D, the tattoo artist and reality star, plays up her bad girl image with a makeup collection that promotes her "bad girl" image. Her cosmetic line includes everything from electric glosses and lipsticks to pro brushes and look-at-me liner.

Former supermodel Cindy Crawford sells her anti-aging, glow-inducing skin care line called Meaningful Beauty, which can help all those cougars on the prowl look good while hunting for younger men. Her seven-product Advanced Aging System promises to make you look younger after only a month. (I have a cheaper way. Just act really, really immature).

Just as Elizabeth Taylor came out with her White Diamonds perfume, Sarah Jessica Parker also offers her own fragrances dubbed the Lovely Collection. Madonna markets her Truth or Dare line of perfume for women who want to feel like a Material Girl, or just a tramp. Lady Gaga markets her Lady Gaga Fame perfume, which actually doesn't smell like raw meat (and therefore I refuse to buy it). Christina Aguilera sells her Signature by Christina Aguilera perfume to women who don't want to be associated with Madonna or Lady Gaga. Even Britney Spears sells her Britney Spears Fantasy perfume for women who want to fantasize whatever the public is associating with Brittany Spears at this moment. She has certainly kept branding consultants very busy over the years trying to redefine her.

While female celebrities often gravitate toward fashion or fragrances to milk their fanbase for money, male celebrities often target alcohol and beverages, correctly assuming that most men just want to drink their way to fun and health instead looking or smelling good. And for some reason, we keep thinking it will work. (Oh well, something to look forward to in Heaven one day).

Hanson, the boy band of brothers that last had a hit in the 1990s, have their own brand of beer, an India pale ale named "MMMHop." Now when you drink Hanson's beer, you too can get a little queasy like I always have listening to their music.

Inspired by his song "Old Whiskey River," Willie Nelson has his own Old Whiskey River Bourbon, the drink of choice for old men who spend their weekends getting drunk when they realize how much back taxes they still owe the IRS. (BTW I find extensive quantities of alcohol a good remedy for anything IRS-related. For some crazy reason they make people cranky.)

Justin Timberlake has released a tequila called 901 (although 911 would be a more appropriate name after drunk girls start attracting the unwanted attention of a large group of horny fraternity members). The name 901 comes from the saying, "9:01 is when the evening ends and the night begins," which sounds a whole lot better than saying, "9:01 is when the evening ends and the drunken idiocy begins."

Even Danny DeVito, an actor who looks like an overgrown gnome, has his own lemon liquor called Limoncello. Now when you're alone in a singles bar late at night with no prospects for getting laid, you can think about how Danny DeVito, with all his millions, is probably getting laid that night while you aren't. That should make you want to ingest enough Limoncello to black out.

Most people believe celebrities must be authorities on alcohol given how many of them become alcoholics and end up in rehab. Maybe one day, celebrities can bring their expertise to endorsing high-end hookers too. (Which they actually do now but it's just called private recommendations). However, not many people believe that celebrities are also authorities on consumer electronics, though most people would pay good money to see a celebrity electrocuted once in a while. Despite this, celebrities are spreading their fame to consumer electronic devices such as headphones.

Dr. Dre and Monster offer Beats by Dr. Dre headphones. Monster has not only teamed up with Dr. Dre, but has also released Sean "Diddy" Combs's Diddybeats in-ear headphones featuring ControlTalk noise isolation. Of course, noise isolation is something people rarely practice when playing rap music while driving, but it sounds sufficiently important to justify a celebrity endorsement.

Shawn "Jay-Z" Carter has teamed up with Skullcandy to release the Roc Nation Aviator headphones while Lady Gaga has her Heartbeats earphones.

By studying what celebrities are currently marketing, you can see what types of products you should focus on at your level of fame. For women, you can't go wrong with fashion and beauty products to give women all over the world a false sense of hope that they might actually have a chance with George Clooney. For men, focus on products that enhance a man's image, such as alcohol, to give men all over the world a false sense of hope that they could actually compete with George Clooney for a beautiful woman in a bar.

There's a reason these product categories are popular with celebrities—because they make money. If you want to make money too, follow the celebrities, but don't make the same mistakes they do.

Mistakes and Failures

Not all products succeed. Here, I am going to say it again with my shouty capitals just in case you missed it: NOT ALL PRODUCTS SUCCEED. Sometimes a product just sucks and makes you realize that without a major celebrity backing it, it would never have seen the light of day in the first place.

Donald Trump once tried launching his own brand of alcohol called Trump Vodka under the slogan "Success Distilled." Combining Donald Trump's billionaire image with luxurious vodka seemed like a good idea, until you realize that most billionaires' choice of unaffordable stimulant is cocaine, not vodka. (Plus, Donald Trump just doesn't conjure up images of tasty vodka or of tasty anything for that matter, at least for me. I keep imaging little hairs from his toupee falling into my vodka.) As a result, Donald Trump couldn't even unload his vodka on Alcoholics Anonymous meetings.

Actor Dan Aykroyd had his own failure with vodka when he tried marketing Crystal Head Vodka. As the name implies, the vodka came in a bottle shaped like a skull, because associating a celebratory alcoholic drink with the Grim Reaper's image is always a surefire way to drum up sales. When people collect a product for the packaging instead of the product itself, that's when you know your product isn't a winner.

For some odd reason, vodka seems to be the common denominator for failure among celebrity products. Mike "The Situation" Sorrentino once promoted Devotion Vodka, a low calorie, sugar- and gluten-free vodka infused with casein to provide protein while you get drunk. This odd combination may have contributed to the product's failure—no one in their right mind wants to mix their vodka with daily nutritional guidelines in their head—but whatever, was worth a shot I guess.

The Situation also took an equity stake in the product. Not only did he get a fee to promote it, but he should have made extra money through shares of the company. Now The Situation and Devotion Vodka are suing each other, claiming breach of contract. Any time there's money involved in show business, get as much guaranteed cash up front as possible because lawyers can always twist contracts around so nobody but the law firms make any money from the deal.

Generally, products fail for a variety of reasons:

+ They don't match the celebrity's brand and public image (how many people associate Dan Aykroyd with alcohol?)

+ They're too strange and bizarre (protein-laced alcohol?)

+ They suck in the first place (anything promoted by Donald Trump)

If bimbos on shows like *The Bachelorette* and *The Real Housewives of Orange County* can successfully promote products, then anyone can do it. Stick to popular categories that the unwashed masses can easily understand, and link your name to a decent product. The product needs to deliver on its promises, but the celebrity posing next to it also needs to market that product to their ravenous fans. When you can combine a decent product with the high-profile status of even the dumbest celebrity, you'll have a winner, no matter how useless that celebrity might really be.

Celebrity MBA

Celebrity Business Plan and Budget

First and foremost for building a business is always having a plan and a back-up plan. Running out of money and having to quit on your dream right before the finish line is the most disappointing feeling and will haunt you for a long time. You don't always have to "plan for the worst," but you should at least prepare for the worst. This could mean having a second option should things not go your way, having another plan on deck and ready to go, and the guts to try again.

To put it in terms you might understand better, starting a business is like taking a trip to Vegas. You go hoping to make a lot of money, but you're also aware of the possibility of losing everything. Business is also a gamble. Just don't sell your plane ticket home (or your home).

Celebrities are thought of as the "rich and famous," but sometimes they're just "famous" because celebrities seem to go bankrupt pretty often. So just how does this happen? How exactly does one blow millions of dollars in a short period of time and have to file for bankruptcy? Simple. They blow their money as fast as they get it. Expensive homes and cars are just that. Think of it like making a couple extra hundred dollars and immediately having enough for that new handbag you've been wanting. You spend it right away, and it's gone.

Before Larry King was LARRY KING, he was just Larry King. He hosted a radio show in Miami back in the 60s and was arrested in 1971 after being accused of stealing $5,000 from his business partner. The charges were eventually dropped, but poor money management and the stain on his career left him out of a job for nearly four years, causing him to file for bankruptcy. It wasn't until 1978 that he landed a talk show in Washington, DC that would later turn into *Larry King Live* and earn him his fortune and empire.

Boxer Mike Tyson hit it big from a young age. From his debut as an eighteen year old in 1985 to his retirement around 2005, he earned an estimated $350 million for his fights, earning upwards of $30 million per fight in his prime. So what led him to being $23 million in debt and filing for bankruptcy? Tyson bought mansions, cars, and, yes, Bengal tigers. (You really are no one until you own your own human-eating carnivore). There was even one time that Tyson dropped $174,000 for a gold chain with eighty carats in diamonds at a Las Vegas jeweler. In a shocking turn of events, just eight months later he filed for bankruptcy. An article in the *New York Times* reported that he owed the U.S. and British governments $17 million in back taxes, $750,000 split among seven law firms for his legal troubles, and $300,000 for personal limo services. In the present day, Tyson is earning a paycheck through cameos in *The Hangover* and his own television show where he plays with pigeons.

But just when you thought it could only happen to washed-up wrestlers, you're forced to take a closer look at Walt Disney. Yes THE Walt Disney. He too once filed bankruptcy. Before he was sticking you for $100 admission to his parks from beyond the grave, Disney owned

Laugh-O-Gram Studios in Kansas City. Laugh-O-Grams created animated fairy tales that were shown in local theaters and eventually became popular, causing him to seek financial backing to support the company. When the backing firm went belly up, Laugh-O-Grams went under as well. Walt even tried to save the venture by living in his office and eating beans from a can before saving up enough money for a bus ticket to Hollywood and closing the studio. And you know how that turned out.

In sports, some athletes earn more money per season than most people make in a lifetime, so how do they fall victim to their own riches? Poor money management. Typically, 60 percent of NBA players will file for bankruptcy within five years of retirement. The 40 percent includes names like Michael Jordan, Shaquille O'Neal, LeBron James, and Kobe Bryant, who make the majority of their riches from endorsement deals. Baseball players are said to be four times more likely to file for bankruptcy than the national average. In the NFL, 78 percent of their athletes file for the big B within five years following retirement. Career ending injuries and non-guaranteed money that's already been spent plays a big role in this.

Financial advisors can be the best "investment" for illustrious people, or anyone looking to save responsibly. That is unless you have a financial advisor named Daryl McCauley, who was arrested for stealing more than $3 million from his brother, Dane Cook. My advice here? Be advised, when being advised.

Market Analysis

Market analysis is a very important process for any business. The business of fame is no exception. In order to grow your audience and strengthen your influence, you need to have a very clear understanding of who your fans (and potential buyers) are and what makes them tick. Here is the short list of questions that you will want to know about your current and potential fans:

★ Age	What is the age range of your target audience? As tempting as it is to grab everybody from toddler to retiree to claim as your potential fan, the more focused your selection is, the easier it is to craft your product, presentation, and marketing campaign.

★ Education	What is their education level and highest degree? Not only will this give you an additional insight into their ambitions, financial situation, and likes and dislikes, but it will also give you an insight into their future and how their preferences (and hence relationship with your brand), can evolve.
★ Income	What is the average income of your target audience? By knowing this, you can price your products to satisfy their desire to buy something that they probably don't need.
★ Hobbies and pastimes	What does your target audience enjoy doing in their spare time that's legal? If your target audience lives in a retirement community in Boca Raton, you probably aren't going to be successful selling them hip-hop music regardless of your talents.
★ Likes, dislikes, and system of beliefs	If you are trying to establish a relationship with someone, you better know what makes them purr and what makes them growl. Do they believe in ultimate justice and true love? Or in total destruction and the apocalypse? Are they more into *Twilight*, *The Hunger Games* or *Fifty Shades of Grey*? (And have they realized that all three are the same story, different day?) Needless to say, Justin Bieber wouldn't be able to replace Marilyn Manson at his concerts and vice versa.
★ Geography	Know where your fans usually are concentrated and in what geographic locations.
★ How they communicate	How does your target audience talk to each other (just as long as they're not just talking to themselves)? If your target audience prefers e-mail and Facebook, then you need to reach those people there.
★ How they discover new products, artists, and performers	How does your target audience find new celebrities to follow? By watching YouTube? By watching TV? By listening to podcasts? By talking to their pet rock and listening for a response like I do?

Keep in mind that nowadays fashions, trends, and people's preferences are changing every day. It is crucial to stay in touch with your fans and know what they like and what gets them going, before the wind changes and your celebrity becomes as obsolete as Ed Hardy T-shirts and the Paris Hilton haircut.

Competitive Analysis

Now that you know who your potential fans are, you need to find out who is currently ravaging your fields of fame and hunts in your divine forests of stardom. Before claiming your place on Olympus, find out who is currently occupying it and what it would take for you to squeeze your tush in and carve a piece of the fan pie:

★ Who is your competition in your target audience?	Are you competing against Justin Bieber or Lady Gaga or against a street band from next block? Are you competing for attention with Donald Trump or a loud bully from your school?
★ What they are selling to your target audience?	What are the products, talents, expertise, experiences, and capabilities that they are selling?
★ At what price point?	How and how much they are getting paid?
★ How are they communicating to the fans?	How is their fanbase organized? Is it a fan club, blog, or social media page? How do they receive their information and what are the ways you can reach them?
★ What kind of resources do they have behind them?	Finances, media, connections, and relationships.
★ How strong is their influence over their fanbase?	How loyal are their fans? Would they easily consider another product or personality or will they aggressively deny it? Will they follow your competitors and support them through media turmoil or downtime- or scatter and turn to competition?

★ What makes them successful and popular?	What is so appealing to their fans? What is the sales point in their product? Is it the image, the story, the presentation? Or is it actual talent or unique skills?
★ How often do they generate news and release new projects? When is their quiet time between news cycles and announcements of new projects?	Quiet time in your competition's news cycle is the time to attack and introduce yourself and your projects. This is the time when connection between your competition and your target audience is the weakest and given the chronic ADD of both the media and the public you can shift their attention to yourself while your competition is media hibernating.

SWOT Analysis

SWOT Analysis stands for Strengths, Weaknesses, Opportunities, and Threats. Try to assess objectively where you stand and where you can improve by answering the questions in the left column and filling the answers for each of the Strengths and Weaknesses columns.

	★ STRENGTHS	★ WEAKNESSES
Your talents and creative skills		
Your personality		
Your connections and resources		
Your relationships with the media		
Your capital backing		

	★ OPPORTUNITIES	★ THREATS
New projects or products		
Capturing fan base		
Media exposure		
Resources and production capabilities		
Sales and marketing		

Planning World Domination:
Project Management and Execution

One of the most important rules of business 101 is project execution. Sure, some projects are difficult, and some are nearly impossible, but you'd be surprised by the amount of great ideas that never come to fruition because they are never executed.

Not surprisingly, most wannabes in the entertainment industry stay wannabes because notwithstanding an abundance of creative ideas, they have close to no discipline or project execution skills. Some are lucky enough to understand this and either acquire this essential skill set or attract a strong management team that can cover for their shortcomings. Others end up bitter and broken in the ditch on the side of the road to stardom. (We have tossed a lot of people in that ditch in this book. Getting crowded in there. But just trying to motivate you, in case you need any more.)

To avoid this sad fate, you need to learn how to plan and execute. If you haven't fainted at the sight of the tables you had to fill out in previous chapters, by now you should know almost everything necessary to take over the world with your celebrity and raise your stardom in the sky of pop culture, bright enough to make Elton John look like a "candle in the wind."

Now you need a plan of action including creative projects, your Internet and social media presence, PR plan, and budget and business plans.

Here is how a very simplified version of such a plan can look:

1. Register social media accounts

2. Create an EPK

3. Launch a website and a blog

Working with Your Fanbase

Your personal brand works in the same way as a business. As you attract a bigger fanbase, more opportunity will open up to you. Think: "If you build it, they will come." If you build your business properly, the success will follow.

Audience analysis is a key in this step. You must look at your audience and figure out their wants and needs. If you keep the audience coming back for more, you will keep the advertisers coming back for more. It's no wonder why you see some of the most elaborate and biggest advertisements for upcoming TV shows and movies on some of the leading entertainment websites. Advertisers love sites with heavy traffic. If a blog gets a million unique visitors per day, and an advertiser can get just 10 percent of those viewers to tune in or purchase their product, that's a hundred thousand people who they might not have reached otherwise. If a purchase is involved-as little as ten dollars, the average price of a movie ticket-that's a million dollars! Yippeeee!!

Building your fanbase is one thing, but you must also make sure to keep your fanbase. This starts with keeping things interesting for them and keeping them involved. Getting fans, entertaining them, and then getting some more is sort of a "wash, rinse, repeat" cycle, but it's the only way to be sure that your fame is constant and expanding.

Here are some tips for keeping fans engaged on your social media page:

Reply and answer questions from fans

1. Post personal/ behind the scenes photos and video

2. Host contests and giveaways

3. Share exclusive new material first as a way to say thanks.

Some of the biggest celebrities out there engage their fans on a daily basis through their social media networks. Sharing first-look material, personal photos from behind the scenes, and giving away prizes aid in broadening a fanbase, bringing them together, and making them feel like a family (or a cult. Looking at you, Beliebers!)

In some ways, fans have gotten so hardcore that they have created little groups or communities online and will often go to battle with fans of other celebrities. There's Lady Gaga's "little monsters," Justin Bieber's "Beliebers," and Nicki Minaj's "Barbz." Then there's the "Twi-Hards," the "Directioners," the "Rihanna Navy," and so on. You get the point. Yes, a normal person can be a fan of all of those mentioned acts, and a few of those acts might even be BFFs in real life. But there are always the crazed fans out there who put all of their focus into one group. As ridiculous as it sounds, it's not necessarily a bad thing. Without fans, there are no celebrities. Please your fans! They will determine your success.

Justin Bieber at "Justin Bieber: Never Say Never," UK Premiere O2 Arena, 2011

(Solarpix/PR Photos)

The Cost of Fame

Although people like fantasizing about becoming famous, be aware that there's always a price for everything and that includes promoting yourself. As with any business, you'll need to have a budget and a plan. You've got to know where to spend, and where not to spend money to maximize your budget. Yes, there are celebrities who make it out of nowhere, but they still must endure a cost, even if they are earning from the get-go. Much of the time this is seen with reality stars who skyrocket into the spotlight. For regular folks with hopes and dreams, it's a long, expensive road traveled. These expenses can range from headshots, web design, advertising, PR, and merchandising. Can it be worth every penny? You bet! Bill Gates once said, "If I was down to my last dollar I would spend it on PR." That speaks volumes to the importance of the PR industry, and how it is really worth the money you spend on it for the good of your career.

Here's where you need to start.

Assembling your kit can be an initial expense. Getting headshots, creating demo reels and developing your website or blog all require costs. Mailing or hand delivering these items to studios, executives and agents can take time and money as well. Stuffing envelopes with photos and resumes may not seem like the glamorous life of a Hollywood celebrity, but you have to crawl before you can walk. Not very original but never truer than here.

When it comes to advertising, there's always a cost. Not to say there won't be a reward, but paying for a ten-second spot on a TV or radio station may not be as resourceful as purchasing space on Facebook or within Google AdWords. You want to be sure to choose the option that best suits your brand and will most effectively reach your target audience. Since the Dawn of the Internet Age, an entirely new element has entered the advertising game. Considering that people spend hours upon hours each day surfing the net, on social media sites and writing emails there are tons of places you can land your ad to be seen by the masses.

For setting up your blog or website, you will have to pay for the domain name and hosting service as well as the graphic design, web development, and maintenance that will make your online presence attractive to your viewers.

A wise man once said, "You have to spend money to make money." This, too, is true in the Fame Game. Only once you reach that level will you be making a lot more than you spend.

Merchandising can range from cheap to very expensive, depending on what you'd like to sell. If you want to become a famous fashion designer for your original designs, you are going to endure the costs of creating patterns, samples, and paying those who assist you in product development. To get your T-shirt designs out there, there is a competitive market for wholesale at low prices, and even a few e-commerce shops that will do all of the legwork for you, but take the bulk of the profits for themselves.

When cost becomes an issue or matter of priority, it's best to put together a plan of the most effective ways of spending your money. For certain elements of this process, there's always the good old-fashioned DIY (do-it-yourself) approach. DIY can save you a lot of money, but will cost you in time and sometimes even quality. Yes, it's simple to set up your own social media pages, and they can be managed with little time or effort, but sometimes it's best to consult with an expert on as much as possible. More important than telling you what you should do, or are doing right, they can tell you what you are doing wrong, and what is wasting your valuable time. Economy and strategy of your words and presentation and how you position them are your Internet marketing lifelines.

If you do choose to utilize experts, make sure you do some research and look at their track record in the exact area where you need them. If somebody designed a brilliant website for a car dealership, it doesn't mean he or she would be able to design a website for a musician. Keep in mind that as far as brilliance goes, you very often get what you pay for. And try to form a relationship or partnership with these experts so that they are invested in your projects and take it personally rather than as another hired gun.

1. **Plan your budget ahead of time and stick to it.** Of course leave a little wiggle room in either direction, but don't let yourself go overboard.

2. **Remember the 80-20 rule.** It's the little things that make the most difference. Focus your budget and spending on 20 percent of activities that generates 80 percent of the result and revenue. You'd be surprised how much you'll be rewarded.

Here is a table estimating some costs that you may occur for hiring help and doing it yourself.

ITEM	HIRED GUN COST RANGE	DO-IT-YOURSELF COST RANGE
★ Website Design	$500–$5,000	$30–$200 Through automatic site builders or site templates like GoDaddy.
★ Photo Shoot, Head Shots	$100–$1,000	$10 Doing it yourself or hiring your nephew in exchange for skipping a beating or some runs to the liquor store are feasible options, but not recommended unless your nephew is David LaChapelle.
★ Graphic Design	$250–1,500	$0 You might be able to get away with doing it yourself with some basic graphic skills, maximum taste, and decent graphic editing software like Adobe Photoshop—especially if you can complete it before the trial period expires.
★ Web Video Recording	Professionally produced video can run from $500 to thousands depending on the level of the production and the crew.	A decent webcam and mic will run you anywhere from $50 to $300 and might let you get away with a basic talking video.
★ Social Media Ads	$100 and up	You can run social media ads on virtually any budget starting from just a $1 per day or even less.

ITEM	HIRED GUN COST RANGE	DO-IT-YOURSELF COST RANGE
★ PR	Personal publicist will set your wallet back $500–$3,000 per month but can put you forward in terms of your fame and recognition. See the following tips in this chapter on how to select a right publicist. Make sure you get the right publicists with the right connections in the media where you want to be on their roster already.	If you follow instructions in this book you will be more effective and produce more results for yourself than 90 percent of the publicists that you would meet. And keep in mind that unless you can afford to hire a publicist in-house, your publicist will likely be juggling several other clients and rotating his or her attention, often giving bigger ones with higher retainers priority.
★ Merchandising	Merchandising development can run you thousands to tens of thousands of dollars if you are hiring a product design and development company.	With basic graphic design skills and direct-to-product printing technology widely available, you can launch your line of T-shirts, cell phone covers, jewelry, posters, canvas, etc. at virtually no cost. You can find more information on how to build your own merchandising lines in the Developing Products chapter and the resources at the end of this book.

Celebrity Team

"The main ingredient of stardom is the rest of the team."—John Wooden

In the beginning while you're still considered a nobody (by everyone except for the delusions in your own mind) you'll have to do everything yourself. As someone with no proven track record, you'll have to prove yourself as a marketable commodity. Some people give up at this stage and just turn to prostitution, pornography or law school, but for everyone else, the first step is to start demonstrating your talent, however feeble it may be.

Start by working for free. Initially, you need experience so you can (hopefully) keep improving, but what you really want is exposure and money. Exposure means that the more people that know about you, the more famous you'll be. The more fame you have, the more power you'll have over others, and that's attractive to everyone who wants to exploit you for their own purposes.

Besides massive exposure, the second commodity you want is money. Once you reach a certain level of fame, you can start earning some. The moment someone sees your potential for earning money, that's when he or she will be willing to exploit you for his or her own purposes. For most people, the first team member they'll need is a manager or an agent.

But as much as celebrities would like you to believe otherwise, nobody becomes a star completely on their own. To succeed, every celebrity has a team of people helping to promote that celebrity behind the scenes. In other words, other people do the work and the celebrity gets to bask in the glory while often doing relatively little to deserve any of it. But the successful ones do pick the right people.

Managers and Agents

The number one biggest fallacy in show business is that a manager or an agent will get you work. The reality? The manager or agent won't do anything for you until you start earning money so you can pay their commission, which usually ranges from 10 to 15 percent of whatever you make. That means you have to find your own work and let your agent negotiate the contract. The more you make, the more they make, so you can see that managers and agents only have a financial interest in working with people who are already making money through their fame. Our handy dandy catch-22 again.

Managers get their name because they manage a client's career by recommending the best career choices, which often proves to be completely wrong (like the Jennifer Grey career-murdering nose job) but they still get paid anyway. Agents typically negotiate contracts, which managers cannot do legally and because most managers are probably illiterate and couldn't read if their life depended on it.

Both agents and managers can find work for their clients, but they have no financial incentive to find work for anyone except for the clients who are likely to bring them the highest amount of cash with the greatest chance of success for the least amount of effort.

If you're a struggling actor in Hollywood, this explains why it's so hard for you to get an agent. If you finally do get an agent, that's why you probably never hear from them until you start earning money. Agents and managers simply spend most of their time on the clients who can earn them the most money. Until you can do that, agents and managers may take you on as a client, but they'll rarely waste time doing anything for you until you start doing something for them first, such as earning money for their commission.

There are different levels of managers and agents. The top Hollywood management firms deal with big-name celebrities who can earn them hundreds of thousands of dollars in commissions for a single project, so that's in short why top Hollywood managers ignore most of the world (including their own families).

Management firms tend to specialize in representing certain types of talent, since it's nearly impossible to understand all the legalities (unethical tricks) in every field of show business. One management firm might specialize in musical talent like Kelly Clarkson, Ice Cube, Snoop Dogg, and the Dixie Chicks. Another management firm might specialize in actors and comedians like Robin Williams, Woody Allen, and Billy Crystal. **The key is finding the right management firm that you want to give 10 to 15 percent of your future earnings to.**

Many actors start with smaller agencies or managers until they find their "big break." Then they get swooped up by the power players who can make money off them without having had to nurture them while they were poor. Bigger agencies and managers can make stars even bigger (or at least give them bigger egos).

While some actors will keep their original management out of loyalty, they'll land bigger deals through the larger agencies, which have first choice on the most lucrative projects because they can blackmail the big shots in Hollywood.

One of the largest and oldest global talent agencies is the **William Morris Agency**, which represents artists from all facets of the entertainment industry, including motion pictures, television, music, theatre, digital, publishing, lifestyle, and physical production. Despite their delusional beliefs to the contrary, however, William Morris isn't the only important big agency around.

On a night in 1975, talent agents employed by the William Morris Agency—Mike Rosenfeld, Michael Ovitz, Ron Meyer, William Haber, and Rowland Perkins—met over dinner and brainstormed about creating an agency of their own. Before they could obtain adequate financing for their new venture, the top people at the William Morris Agency heard about their scheming and fired them all because there's no such thing as job security in Hollywood unless you're a drug dealer.

With nothing but a $35,000 line of credit and a $21,000 bank loan, the fired agents started the **Creative Artists Agency** in a small Century City rented office outfitted with card tables and folding chairs. The five agents only had two cars among them, and their wives took turns working as the agency receptionist. Now the Creative Artists Agency is a powerhouse comparable to the William Morris Agency, but the agents still make it a habit of sleeping with the receptionist after work out of nostalgia.

ICM Partners (formerly International Creative Management) is another talent and literary agency that doesn't have time to deal with aspiring actors, writers, singers, or anyone else who isn't already making bucket loads of cash. ICM Partners represents creative and technical talent in the fields of motion pictures, television, music, publishing, live performance, branded entertainment, and new media.

As soon as you can demonstrate that you're either earning lots of cash or have a ton of fame through self-generated means such as releasing videos on YouTube, that's when you'll attract the attention of one of these larger agencies or management companies. Until then, you may need to start out with a much smaller agency or manager, like a chain-smoking, washed-up actor named Phil who smells like he hasn't showered in a week. But it's ok. Put on nose plugs and don't look around his office too carefully and make your start there. It's a beginning.

Publicists and Marketing

Once you're steadily making money with an agent and/or manager helping you find better paying work that furthers your career (or at least provides more money for everyone), you can start thinking about paying someone to market you. The whole purpose of marketing is to extend your fame so you can earn more money and get your face plastered across billboards and magazine covers all over the world.

The role of a publicist is to let everyone know that you exist and how wonderful you are so they'll spend more money to see you or buy your products. Since publicists can't accurately measure the amount of publicity they generate for you (nor can they accurately measure the effectiveness of their activities), they don't get paid a percentage of the money you earn. Instead, you pay them a retainer for services and hope that they actually do something constructive with that money instead of running off to Las Vegas to gamble with it. But until you've reached a certain level of fame, you don't need a publicist (unless you have a lot of spare cash lying around that you have nothing better to spend it on).

Eventually, a publicist can help promote you so you can spend your time nurturing your talent or just partying hard every night until you drop from exhaustion. With a publicist on your side, you can let someone else get your name out there and field all the unpleasant questions you don't want to answer yourself.

Creative Team

An agent and manager can help you make money and a publicist can help you increase your fame, but you still need a creative team to create videos, music, or graphics that your publicist can use to carpet bomb the media and announce your virtues to as many people as possible. (I know. This may be more involved than you thought, but if this were easy everyone on Planet Earth would be a winner of the Fame Game. Like we mentioned early on, in most cases the "overnight success" is a product of plenty of hard work. Stick with it.)

You'll likely need a graphics designer who can create logos and drawings, along with a video producer to create videos (even sex tapes, if that's a marketing tool you decide to use), and possibly an audio producer to create music.

You'll also need a website designer, who can create and maintain your website, plus a social media manager who can deal with the tweets, Facebook updates, and blog postings that you'll need to do on a regular basis to stay in touch with all those people you wouldn't want to meet in person.

All of these people can be hired as employees or retained on a freelance basis. Once you reach a certain level of fame, you simply won't have time to handle all of these details yourself, so pay other people to worry about these problems while you go off and get drunk.

Finally, you may need a business manager who handles the manufacturing and licensing of merchandise. This can be as simple as selling T-shirts and coffee mugs to marketing licensed products such as headphones, skin cream, or clothing that give people a false sense of belonging to a community of other people who worship the same celebrity for no good reason at all.

Everyone's support team will be different, depending on what you need, where you are in your career, and whether people like you or secretly throw darts at a picture of your face. If you're a musician, the first member of your support team might be a record producer, but if you're a fashion designer, then you might need a manufacturing partner first.

Even if you have no desire to enter the drug-filled opium dens of Hollywood, a support team can make your everyday life easier. Let your support team do the necessary but time-consuming work so you can focus on further promoting yourself and earning money to pay your support team before they mutiny and abandon you for someone else.

Pitfalls of Support Teams

Ah . . . little in life is the perfection we all seek. When you do everything yourself, you get all the credit but you have to do all the work. When you have a support team, you still get all the credit and don't have to do all of the work, but now you have to work with other people. It's a true rock-and-a-hard-place conundrum: If you thought managing yourself was difficult, try managing a handful of other reluctant egos that would rather be goofing off than doing anything productive to make you more famous.

The biggest problem is finding the right people. Once you find the right people, the next biggest problem is getting them to work for your benefit. Many agents will accept clients in the hopes that one of them will become a star. Until that magical moment happens, the agent will ignore these clients to make time for the ones who are actually making money. **Ultimately, success depends entirely on your own efforts, not on your support team.**

Besides getting the wrong people for your support team, a bigger danger is getting scammed by the numerous shady and dishonest people who prey on others. While many of them are legitimate lawyers, many more are simply con artists.

Here are some clues for when you might be dealing with a shady and dishonest con artist-and when you might be dealing with a shady and dishonest agent or manager who's actually legitimate on paper and well respected in the Hollywood community.

First, **never pay money up front**. Agents and managers only get paid when you get paid. That gives them an incentive to get as much money for you so they can get so that they do well for themselves as well. If anyone asks for money upfront, walk away. Even restaurants don't ask you to pay upfront, so if your local waiter can trust you, then any potential agent or manager should be able to trust you, too.

Second, **be wary of anyone who contacts you first.** Con artists prowl around social media networks like MySpace, YouTube, and Facebook looking for victims. While some legitimate agents and managers may spot talent on such social media networks (that's how Justin Bieber was discovered, which tells you the dangers of looking for talent on the Internet), it's more common for con artists to contact aspiring entertainers this way. You may be the next Justin Bieber, or you may be the next victim of a con artist who tries to trick you into think you'll be the next Justin Bieber.

Many agents and managers want to find new clients, but they know most potential clients will likely go nowhere. As a result, legitimate agents and managers will discourage people from contacting them because they're too busy making money with their existing clients.

On the other hand, con artists need a constant supply of suckers, so they'll place phony ads in newspapers or social media networks that say something like "new faces wanted" for commercials, movies or modeling and claim that "no experience is necessary." Generally the only show business jobs that don't require experience involve being naked for hire in one form or another. If you have spent your life dreaming about the privilege of being nude in front of strangers, you'll achieve that easily in Hollywood. Otherwise, look elsewhere to pursue your dream.

Third, **check how much an agent or manager wants from you.** Typically, agents and managers make 10 to 15 percent of whatever you make, so if a nightclub pays you off with a free prostitute, your agent or manager should get at least 10 percent of her, which means he can fondle her toes. **If someone asks for significantly more than 15 percent, ask questions.** That should be a warning flag that you're about to get screwed, and don't expect your agent or manager to fondle your toes in the process either.

Fourth, **make sure there's an escape clause in every contract.** When you sign up with an agent or manager, both of you can get out of the contract after a certain time period (such as one year) or by notifying the other party in advance. Screaming, "You suck and I hope you rot in hell!" over the phone may qualify as notifying the other party in advance, but it's not considered professional (although it can be emotionally satisfying).

Finally, look for "guarantees." Even the best agent or manager can't guarantee anything other than that they'll take 10 to 15 percent of your money. If somebody claims they can guarantee certain results, that's a big clue that they're probably lying. Think of politicians making campaign promises that they never keep. (Aha-you thought I was done with this! No such luck). *Never trust what anyone says.*

Be suspicious of any agent or manager who displays pictures of famous celebrities on the walls. Anyone can get pictures of celebrities to hang on the wall and make you believe they're represented by that agency. Remember, many celebrities are really scumbags so consider every celebrity's picture as one scumbag endorsing another and that will let you know how much you should trust a potential agent or manager.

Be wary of any agency or management firm that uses a name that sounds similar to a better-known agency such as the William Morris Agency. Con artists try to give the impression that they are connected to a legitimate entity. Likewise, be wary of any agent or manager who tries to go by the name of Jesus Christ, Mother Theresa, or George Lucas for the same reason. In other words, USE YOUR COMMON SENSE, don't let it fly out of the window when your feeling drunk on bright California sunshine, palm trees and dreams of stardom.

If an agent or manager pressures you into making a decision right now, make the decision to leave as soon as possible. Investigate and research any agent or manager to find out if they're legitimate or not. A legitimate agent or manager will understand your suspicions. They may still get annoyed, but at least they'll understand because they don't trust anyone in Hollywood either.

Finally, if an agent or manager promises you something that sounds too good to be true ("I can guarantee you a part in Steven Spielberg's next movie and you'll get to have sex with Jennifer Lawrence and Anne Hathaway at the same time!"), run far, far away. Nobody can guarantee anything, and anything that sounds too good to be true probably is (but it can still be nice to fantasize about it anyway).

Your Manufacturing Team

When it's time to manufacture and distribute products, hopefully you'll have enough money to hire someone else to do all the trivial work. Even if you do, you still need an actual product that you can deliver to customers so you can make more money off your fame. The chain of manufacturing typically consists of the following:

- ✦ Product Manufacturer—the sweat shop that actually makes a physical product to sell

- ✦ Sales Marketing—the people who annoy other people into buying the product

- ✦ Public Relations—the people who bombard the media with information to make the product look good, even if it might kill someone by accident

- ✦ Creative Advertising Agencies—the overpaid executives who dream up imaginative advertising campaigns that often cost a lot, yet still fail dramatically on a regular basis

- ✦ Media Buyout Agencies—the people who buy time on TV or the radio, or ad space in magazines and newspapers in hopes that it will reach the right people (but probably won't)

- ✦ Networks—the people who run and control television channels and radio stations, who will likely see most of their business evaporate in the face of the Internet

- ✦ Content Producers—the poor sap who does all the work creating something of value that all the leeches will try to latch on to for a cut of the profits

- ✦ Customer—the person who actually buys a product and indirectly pays for all the ineffective advertising most agencies charge companies to market their products to the consumer

In the old days, you had to manufacture physical items, ship them around the world in crates (after paying the longshoremen not to drop a few of your products off the back of a truck), deliver them to retail stores, and display them so customers could find and buy them. Such an antiquated method is extremely inefficient, which allowed many people to make a living doing relatively little.

With the Internet, content producers (you) have direct access to the customer, bypassing all the intermediaries. Now you can keep the bulk of the profits while getting your product in the hands of customers almost instantly.

Customers are happy because they get immediate gratification while sitting at home as their bodies degenerate due to obesity and lack of exercise by not shopping in an actual store. Content producers (you, again) are happy because you get immediate gratification by having money deposited into your account as your body degenerates due to obesity and lack of exercise by not walking into an actual bank.

Besides eliminating the middlemen, the Internet has also increased the amount of advertising people see every day. Going back in time again, you could put up a billboard and people would stare at it because there was nothing else to see. Nowadays, ordinary advertising doesn't sell as well, even if you give people a supermodel in a bikini to stare at. We just see too much, all the time. The billboard supermodel would have to be alive, flying around naked while shooting arrows at the sky that explode into giant balls of heroin for anyone to pay attention.

Today, advertising is all about entertainment. Watch Super Bowl commercials and you'll see how each commercial tries to outdo the others in humor, outrageousness, or creativity. Many people now watch the

Super Bowl as much for the commercials as they do for the game, which means they now have to time their bathroom breaks during timeouts on the field.

When promoting your own products, *entertain your audience.* Think of yourself as a snake oil salesman in the Old West, selling colored sugar-water to people. You're not just selling medicine; you're selling the scientifically proven, all-purpose medicine that can cure decapitation if you just drink enough of it.

Just as your personal fame depends on your own efforts, the success of your product sales depends entirely on your reputation to sell it. The more famous you are and the more your reputation supports your products, the more sales you're likely to make. Your team can help, but the final results are always up to you.

Go West or Go Global?

"It is clear our nation is reliant on big foreign oil. More and more of our imports come from overseas."—George W. Bush

Most of the world doesn't like America, but they do like American culture, which shows that most of the world isn't as smart as they think they are. In the old days, you could ignore the foreign market because most of them didn't have any money anyway. Now with the Internet and social media networks connecting the world (or at least the part of the world that can afford a computer and an Internet connection), what happens in America can be seen in Brazil, Israel, Japan, and Russia seconds later.

When developing your brand, think globally, even if you're just getting started in some obscure, desolate place, devoid of civilization like Detroit. (Ok am kidding, you Detroiters know you have a nice edge in music and depressed economies). If you don't think globally, like monster beings who never sleep other brands and celebrities will take your shelf space overseas and eventually wipe out the power of your brand locally as well.

Think of going global as a survival strategy. The more markets you can reach, the less likely all of your markets will fall apart at once. It's like taking out international insurance; many celebrities lose popularity rapidly in America where people are busy jumping on the bandwagon of a newer famous face because they forgot the older one three seconds earlier. Short of dousing our water supply with Ritalin, by appealing to people in Asia, Europe, South America, and other places that most Americans can't find on a map, you can insure your survival and marketability somewhere else.

Many singers and bands rocket to popularity in America and plummet just as quickly. Yet they remain popular overseas for years afterwards, while their American fanbase stares at them in dim recognition and tries to remember who they are and why they might have actually liked them sometime in the far past about three weeks ago.

To understand the longevity of American culture everywhere in the world but in America, just look at the popularity of Elvis Presley decades after he died. Approximately 22 percent of Graceland's monthly visitors come from Canada, England, Australia, Germany, the Netherlands, France, Norway, Italy, Japan and Switzerland.

There are even 428 official Elvis Presley fan clubs in 44 countries. Elvis Presley has sold more than one billion records worldwide, with approximately 40 percent sold outside the United States. Clearly, there's a huge market outside of our own national borders. By ignoring other countries, we risk putting artificial limitations on our own growth and potential income just because we might be afraid of people who don't act, speak and think like we do. Time to branch out and move beyond our American, well, *Amercanism*. In other words, get a life (and a fanbase) outside of your own backyard.

Just keep in mind that what works in one market may not work in another market and vice versa. When branching out to international markets, it's usually best to stick to the popular product categories that tend to sucker in people no matter what part of the world that they live in, such as:

+ Fashion

+ Beauty/Fragrance

+ Consumer electronics

+ Alcohol

Basically, people all over the world want to get laid, get drunk, and play with toys like video games and stereos. As long as you can appeal to the teenager mindset across different demographics, you'll never fail to sell products to people who can't find a better use for their money.

Social Media Networking in a Global Economy

Before Al Gore invented the Internet, news and information travelled as slowly as politicians investigating each other for corruption. Now with instantaneous communication through social media networks, news travels around the world within seconds. That means you could be reaching people in other countries, or doing nothing and letting your rivals reach those people instead of you *while you slowly rot into nothingness.* (Yes, I am a drama king—get over it and heed my message!! I like saying heed-it makes me feel powerful.)

Facebook alone has over six million users in countries such as the United Kingdom, Canada, Mexico, Chile, and Sweden. Among Facebook users, the most popular languages used include English (both American English and British English, which are nearly two different languages altogether), Spanish, French, and German.

As an English speaker, you can easily reach people all over the world. Yet if you give in to your xenophobic feelings, you're basically cutting yourself off from a huge potential market, so you have to decide if you like money more than you fear people who don't speak English. Don't fear other languages and cultures, fear getting beat out by your competition that doesn't fear other languages and cultures.

Even a relatively small social media network such as the music appreciation site, iLike, consists of roughly 695,000 fans globally with 40 percent of users in countries besides the United States. A major social media network like Twitter has plenty of users from Brazil, Mexico, the United Kingdom, France, Italy, Spain, Portugal, and Germany. Even though other countries may have fewer users, they all represent potential followers to add to your fanbase. The more people know about you in other countries, the greater your fame, even if you can't thank them personally in their native tongue.

With social media networking, you now have access to a global audience, whether you know it or not. With global communication as simple as sending an e-mail or a tweet, you have no excuse not to reach out to people in every country in the world, except for the people in countries who have publicly vowed to kill you.

Tackling an International Market

Here's the wrong way to sell something in another country: assume that whatever works in your country will also work everywhere else. For years, Detroit automakers were puzzled why American cars sold so poorly in Japan when those same models sold well in the United States. The answer finally came years later when Detroit automakers realized that the Japanese drive on the left side of the road (with the steering wheel on the right side of the car) while Americans drive on the right side of the road (with the steering wheel on the left side of the car).

By trying to sell cars to the Japanese with the steering wheel on the "wrong" side, American automakers ignored the needs of Japanese customers. This boneheaded revelation of the obvious highlights the importance of not assuming what works in your area should automatically work everywhere else on the planet.

Here's the correct way to tackle an international market: **find a local partner in that country who understands the needs of those particular consumers.** This keeps you from making major mistakes. A local partner can help with legal issues along with making sure you don't do something really foolish and insult your entire market without even knowing what you're doing.

Local partners can also customize your product and marketing with humor and cultural references that your target audience will understand and appreciate. This is why both math and pornography crosses national borders so easily, because numbers are a universal language and because pretty much everyone alive can understand the joy of watching good-looking naked people.

Ideally, a local partner will help you maximize your success in that particular market. If your local partner can't do that, then they'll probably just try to fleece you out of your advertising money while wasting your time on ineffective marketing campaigns, just as if you were a gullible client of an incompetent advertising agency in your own country.

Cracking an international market can be especially easy if you already have a presence, such as through movies, TV shows, or some other way that people in that area might have bootlegged your content and viewed it illegally.

Even though he's dead (or at least living in hiding all these years), Elvis Presley's brand currently has 175 licensees worldwide selling products in 122 countries with over 7,000 active products in the market-place. If a dead guy can make so much money overseas, there's certainly room for you too. Inspiration at its finest.

In the United States, you can see examples of foreign brands and celebrities succeeding in the American market. At one time, "Made in Japan" implied something flimsy and cheap. But as time lurched forward and things took their natural course, Japanese carmakers Toyota and Honda kept making gradual improvements while American carmakers focused on cutting costs to maximize profits. Eventually, the Japanese carmakers developed a reputation of quality and reliability, a reputation that American carmakers are still trying to reach today as they battle the reputation that "Made in America" now represents something flimsy and cheap.

The lesson is clear. It's possible for foreign brands to succeed against even local brands, and if you're going to fight a World War against the United States, it's in your best long-term, economic interest to lose. Perhaps in retaliation for Hiroshima and Nagasaki, the Japanese unleashed their Pokémon franchise on the United States. Pokémon convinced children to spend all their money on cards depicting cartoon monsters that didn't look at all like real monsters, who were all busy running for political office.

Other examples of foreign brands succeeding in the United States include Italian fashion designers, Australian actors, British TV hosts and personalities, and Latin actresses and singers, because looking at the breasts of attractive women will always cross cultural boundaries. Identify foreign brands in your own country and then study how they may conduct business differently in their home countries. You shouldn't be surprised to find multiple differences.

Basically, every marketing campaign in a foreign region begins with a media campaign to attract awareness. This can involve tours, interviews, and stunts with local celebrities on inane talk shows that are just as ridiculous as our own. (But I for one feel better knowing that their programming can suck too. Go America!!)

While you're promoting your product to the unwashed masses, you need to be signing deals with local business partners who can help you navigate the tricky cultural barriers so you can sell something successfully in that region (this usually boils down to knowing which local officials to bribe).

You'll need a local partner who has invested in your product so they'll have an incentive to make money too. Then you may need to recruit retailers, sales people, and licensees, depending on your product. Even if you're selling something over the Internet, you may still need a local partner to help you customize your website and marketing message.

In Germany, knapsacks are often referred to as "body bags," but in America, that term is more closely related to a bag for holding dead bodies. While serial killers and psychopaths might be interested in buying such items for their victims, it's probably not the market the German company wanted to reach when they marketed body bags to Americans. I am just going to throw out an even larger "oy" here and move on.

In India, Pepsi once ran an ad showing cricket players being served Pepsi by a boy. While seemingly harmless, the local people felt that the ad glorified child labor.

In the United States, Gerber is well known for making baby food. Yet in France, "Gerber" is the French word for vomit. Although babies are known to convert food into vomit with surprising ease and regularity, it's hardly an appealing image for mothers.

In Germany, latte is a well-known word for an erection. So when companies like Starbucks tried to promote a "morning latte," they inadvertently promoted waking up in the morning with an erection. The word "break" means "destroy," so taking a "morning latte break" implies destroying that erection created in the morning. How do we say "not good" in German?

If the United States just took over the world and made every country behave and act like America, then we wouldn't need to worry about cultural issues. Since that's never going to happen, despite the desire of hardheaded extremists, the best alternative is to find a local partner who can help you sidestep cultural mishaps.

The International Social Media Networks

Everyone knows that by using Google, Facebook, and Twitter, you can reach a worldwide audience, especially if you show compromising pictures of yourself over the Internet. (Except for me. My compromising pictures are just eliciting some random mockery and derision, along with a few bribes to take the pictures down.) However, there are many other ways to reach people through local social media networks. For example, Google dominates worldwide search, yet if you were trying to expand your presence in China, you wouldn't worry about your Google ranking as much as your Baidu ranking.

Baidu is the number one search engine in China. If you only focused your web page rankings on Google but ignored Baidu, you'd miss out on a large percent of the Chinese market that would love nothing more than to buy your products, violate copyrights, and pirate counterfeit versions all over Asia (and on eBay for American consumers to buy back at a much lower cost).

While Baidu dominates China, Russian Internet users prefer the Yandex search engine while South Koreans use the Naver search engine. You can find plenty of Russians, Chinese, and South Koreans on Twitter and Facebook, but every country tends to have their own popular social media networks where the locals can gather and make fun of Americans. (We sure give them plenty of material.)

Bebo is popular in the United Kingdom, Orkut dominates in India, while Badoo has proven especially popular with users in Russia and Brazil, who likely send messages to each other, wondering how Russians and Brazilians could find a common area of interest. With so many thriving social media networks all over the world, you'll need to learn the cultural differences of a market and discover which social media networks are popular in that region. Or you can just outsource the whole project to somebody in a Third World country who can do the whole thing for you at near-starvation wages.

With the Internet, even individuals now have the power to sell products to gullible people all over the planet. With the barrier to entry so low and the profit potential so high, it only makes sense to look into expanding in foreign markets as soon as possible. There's a whole world out there just waiting to hand you money. All you have to do is give them a reason to give it to you. And it doesn't even have to be a good one—it just has to work.

CHAPTER 6

What's Next?

"Change your life today. Don't gamble on the future,
act now, without delay."—Simone de Beauvoir

You Have a Crystal Ball, Now What?

Well, my friends, we come to the end of our journey. Now that you clearly see that the future involves branding yourself in the media that plays on TV, cell phones, computer screens, and in the real world where you can walk into oncoming traffic if you're texting without looking where you're going, consider yourself forewarned. If you decide to play the Fame Game, play by the rules and it can be lots of fun. Remain ignorant of the rules and you'll only experience frustration and confusion while remaining powerless to achieve your dreams.

You are a product, so you need to sharply define the following:

+ What is your product?

+ Who are you?

+ What do you want to be?

+ Who is your target audience and what do they resonate with?

When you can define who you are, what you have to offer the world, and who your target audience is, you can start focusing on defining your personal brand:

+ What is your name? (If your real name sounds awful, make up a catchy stage name.)

+ What is your visual brand? (Think of a logo or graphics that identifies you in the way a company like IBM or McDonald's displays their name.)

+ What is your personal style? (Picture your wardrobe, hair, and makeup that defines how your fans will see you.)
+ What do you want to do in your life. Include real life examples/ applications, even if you are not striving for Hollywood limelight?

Your personal brand defines how people see you. Are you an expert in a particular topic like cooking (Wolfgang Puck) or as someone full of advice (Dr. Phil McGraw)? Maybe you're better known as a funny person with a lot of energy and facial expressions (Jim Carey), as someone with a great voice (Jewel), or as someone who has a way with words (J. K. Rowling)? Everyone has a special talent, even if it involves making farting noises with your armpit, although that type of talent will only take you so far in show business.

Once you know your personal brand, wake up every day and remind yourself of your brand. This will help you behave in ways, consciously or unconsciously, that will serve it best..

It's not enough to define and promote your brand wherever you go and with everyone you meet, even if you don't like the people you see. You also need to define and promote your brand over the Internet through your blog, Facebook pages, Twitter account, and any other social media network you may use to make friends with people you would never want to meet in person. Your brand's presence extends beyond your physical appearance and into your virtual existence in the digital world of the Internet.

Whether you're going to school, going to work, meeting with friends, or pursuing a show business dream, your life is about to change once you start promoting your brand. Imagine people excited to see you, willing to offer their help and resources, and giving you opportunities, job offers, and promotions of all kind.

As you move towards success effortlessly and easily by moving with the stream instead of swimming against the current, you'll beat the competition and enjoy your life as you reach the major milestones on your way to your big goal. The difference will simply depend on knowing your brand, promoting your brand, and making every day another step towards your eventual goal of world domination, or at least fame in your local neighborhood.

By seeing yourself as a positive brand you can use to help others, your quality of life and efficiency in achieving your goals can improve dramatically. It's a known fact that attractive people get things in life easier than others. What people don't realize is that attractiveness is more than physical appearance.

Attractiveness is the perception of you that you've planted in the minds of others. It's in your hands to create, shape, and hone your image to turn strangers into adoring fans who will strive to help you succeed in all areas of life.

Pursuing fame can be scary and it won't always be easy, but the alternative is to settle for mediocrity, and that's a far more dangerous fate. You have to decide where you want to live: in the twilight of mediocrity and obscurity or in the exciting Twilight saga full of vampires, hot epic love, red carpets, and big money. Is there really a choice here?

You have met the Fame Game, and now you are up to bat. Make me a proud papa as I retire to my porch to watch the grass grow and wait for you to come tell me how well you are playing.

The power is in your hands. Now go out and use it.

Index

About the Author

Sergey Knazev is a business development, digital media, and PR and marketing specialist with a proven success record in startup and mid-market brand management and development. Sergey has formal training in both marketing and finance as well as Internet and technology, which makes him uniquely qualified for projects involving transition of legacy businesses into digital sales and distribution models. Sergey's core expertise lies in the areas of Internet strategy development, content production, management, marketing and licensing; entertainment and pop-culture PR & marketing; and brand and product development, sales, and marketing.

In May 2010 Sergey Knazev founded 360 EMA, an entertainment and brand management company, specialized in brand management and development, licensing, product development, marketing, sales, and distribution. 360 EMA represents leading talent and lifestyle brands for business development, brand management, product development and manufacturing, licensing, PR and marketing, Internet strategy, and social media management. Brands under 360 EMA management currently exceed $180 mln a year in sales and deliver up to 125% in annual growth and enjoy some of the highest profit margins in their respective product categories.

Prior to establishing 360 EMA, Sergey Knazev launched and sold a number of major projects, including VOIP wholesaler Concent Telecom and it's retail B2B and B2C division IT Headquarters, specialized e-commerce, and Internet marketing and telecom services, which he founded and ran from 2001–2006. The company was sold after reaching revenue of over 1.42 mln per month.

After selling Concent Telecom and IT Headquarters Sergey co-founded and held positions in real estate and private equity investment companies, Ocean Properties and Longwood Investment Partners, as well as a media company, StarzLife Media. Starzlife specialized in celebrity news content production and licensing to magazines, newspapers, and TV channels that operated in 24 countries and had over 240 major TV channels and magazines as customers, including CNN, ABC, NBC, Time Warner, Wenner Media, Hearst Publishing, Bauer Publishing, ACP Publishing, and many others.